CW01649704

J31
£2-00

All the Photo-Tricks

This book is sold subject to the Standard Conditions of Sale of Net Books
and may not be re-sold in the UK below the net price

All the Photo-Tricks

Ways and Ideas off the Beaten Track

Edwin Smith

Edwin Smith—The Photographer
A Preface by Olive Cook

Focal Press, London and New York

© Copyright 1973 by Focal Press Ltd

All rights reserved. No part of this publication may be reproduced, stored in a retrieval system, or transmitted, in any form or by any means, electronic, mechanical, photo-copying, recording or otherwise, without the prior permission of the copyright owner

ISBN 240 50837 8

First Edition December, 1940
Second Edition December, 1942
Third Edition June, 1947
Fourth Impression May, 1952
Fifth Impression June, 1954
Sixth Impression March 1957
Seventh Impression November, 1959
Eight Impression November 1961
Ninth Impression July 1965
Fourth Edition September 1973
Eleventh Impression September 1975

Printed in Great Britain by Biddles of Guildford

EDWIN SMITH—
THE PHOTOGRAPHER

A Preface by Olive Cook

At the time when this light-hearted book was written Edwin had not yet made his name as a photographer. Although his choice of words and knowledge of technique reveal something of the character of his extraordinary gifts there is little in these pages to suggest the course he was to follow later. This preface attempts to sketch the story of his development and so to place *All The Photo Tricks* in the perspective of his life's achievement.

In fact he came to photography almost accidentally and never intended to make it his profession. Painting was his first love and he was trained as an architect. Edwin was born in St. Paul's Road, Camden Town, in 1912 and spent most of his early life in that part of London in St. Pancras Way, until he moved to Hampstead when he was twenty three. During the four years of World War 1 when his father was fighting in France, Edwin and his mother stayed with his grandmother and aunt at Ponder's End, then fringed by cornfields. He always recalled these years with pleasure, and despite conditions which would be intolerable to the tender social conscience of today, he thoroughly enjoyed his childhood in Camden Town. His father, who in his letters shows a lively intelligence and gaiety, was a bus conductor who spent all his time and money on political activities, so there was never a hope of any home other than the two small first floor rooms where Edwin grew up without running water or any conveniences. But opposite, occupying two houses, lived his paternal grandparents, to whom he was very attached and an uncle and aunt with several children. The cousins explored all north London on roller skates and played boisterous street games encouraged and applauded by Grandfather Smith, who watched from his open window wearing a skull cap.

He attended the local elementary school, as it was then called, a typical Edwardian LCC building in Great College Street.

Although later in life he studied with complete concentration all the subjects that interested him, he disliked school from the first, as he disliked every discipline to which he had not chosen to subject himself. Shortsightedness, which was not discovered until he was ten years old, added to his sense of alienation. It is to the credit of his teachers that they recognised his unusual talents. Even at that time he drew with facility and excelled in making little paper constructions. When Edwin was twelve his headmaster arranged for him to be transferred to a trade school attached to the northern Polytechnic in Holloway and here he was taught all the practical building crafts - bricklaying, plumbing, carpentry and decorating. He excelled in them all and found them much more to his taste than academic subjects. He again attracted the notice of his teachers who entered him for a scholarship which he easily won, to study architecture at the Polytechnic.

At home these years were fraught with difficulties. His parents had separated soon after he left the trade school and Edwin was painfully aware of all that led to it. His resolute, courageous mother was now the breadwinner and Edwin suffered acutely from his dependence on her and from his cramped quarters in St. Pancras Way. But he had by then developed his life-long philosophy of 'co-operating with the inevitable', as he called it. He made one of the two rooms into the prototype of his later workrooms, began to paint seriously with the support of one of his teachers at the Polytechnic, Cecil Stevenson, and enjoyed his widening circle of friends.

In 1930 Edwin won a scholarship to the RIBA. But even with a scholarship the strain on his mother's resources was eventually too great and Edwin had to abandon the course before fully qualifying. He accepted the situation without wasting time on useless regrets and without the slightest bitterness. And probably this interruption of his studies was of slight importance, for Edwin's growing attitude to modern architectural practice would have made it impossible for him to follow a conventional career as an architect.

Although he had not completed his degree, Edwin was given a job in Marshall Sisson's office in 1932. He found office life utterly uncongenial and the work that went on there disillusioning. Architecture, it seemed to him, was no longer an art, or scarcely a profession even. It was just a business.

During a long summer without definite plans, Edwin amused himself with a camera when he was not drawing or painting. He had become interested in photography a few years earlier when he saw some reproductions of the work of Atget who died in 1927. It was then that he acquired a simple Box Brownie with coupons given away with packets of cornflakes. But now a friend gave him a quarter-plate camera and he began to explore the possibilities of the medium with the thoroughness with which he did everything. Its attraction for him is revealed by a passage in this book:

> "The man who lives in his eyes is continually confronted with scenes and spectacles that compel his attention or admiration and demand an adequate reaction. To pass on without pause is impossible and to contine after purely mental applause is unsatisfying; some real tribute must be paid. Photography, to many of its addicts, is a convenient and simple means of discharging these ever recurring debts to the visual world."

More than anyone I have known, Edwin lived by looking, and the camera provided an exquisitely accurate means of recording the visual experiences which so delighted him. And although in these pages he writes so ably about photography as an art of deception, his real concern as soon as he became involved with the medium was to reproduce as closely as possible what had stimulated his eye. He never thought of photography as an art, but as a miraculous recording device.

The first photographs to show the impress of his inimitable style were close-ups of ferns, dog daisies and hedgerow plants taken while Edwin was working on an agreeable job that had most opportunely come his way—the conversion of a Kentish oast house for his friends Dorothy and Trevor Tennant.

Another friend, struck by the freshness of these images, mentioned Edwin's name to the editress of *Vogue* and it was in this periodical, most unsuitably, that Edwin's work was first reproduced. He maintained that it was all due to an error, the editress having mistaken his name for that of the eminently voguish Chetwynd-Smith. As soon as Edwin made it clear that he was plain Smith the commissions came to an abrupt end. It was just as well, he thought, for at that time he had no knowledge of developing and printing and suffered agonies waiting for the local chemist to produce the pictures on time. But his photographs had been noticed and from that time the demand for them never stopped. Without ever having intended it Edwin eventually became an almost full time photographer.

The process was gradual, much slowed down by the outbreak of war. It was just then that Edwin was asked to write this and other books for the *Focal Press*. It was then too that he began his long association with the *Saturday Book* whose first editor, Leonard Russell, had admired Edwin's photographs of street scenes, pubs, the circus and fairground and above all of cats which were for a time the subjects of his choice. It seemed then that chance in the form of photography had provided an ideal solution to the problem of earning a living while leaving ample time for painting.

When Edwin and I first met, photography took up no more of Edwin's time than one or two days a week and he was devoting himself to painting, engraving and every form of print-making. His knowledge of techniques was astonishing—later he edited two important works on the subject—and his knowledge of the history of painting was as impressive. He loved all the materials and appurtenances of the art, always ground his own colours and throughout his life kept a collection of canvases, boards, paper, powder colours, inks, pastels, brushes and pencils big enough to stock a shop. For a short time during the war Edwin worked as a camouflage artist. It meant going daily to an office in Park Lane and although from the first day he was *Edwin* and never *Mr. Smith* to his employers and though they turned a blind eye to his frequent absences and to his invariably late arrival in the morning, Edwin could not tolerate the monotony of office routine and after a few months resigned.

For a few years after the war, Edwin went on taking photographs of subjects which moved him and disposing of them to publishers while spending the greater part of his week painting. His photographs now were nearly all of architecture or landscapes. He was not and never had been attracted by portraits. He used to say that to turn the lens on a person seemed to him an invasion of privacy. On the rare occasions when a friend persuaded him to take a portrait photograph the result was so alarmingly naturalistic, so revealing of every blemish that the sitter fervently wished he had never made his request.

In 1950, Thames and Hudson commissioned him to take the photographs for a big book on English parish churches. The subject enthralled him more than any other on which he was asked to work. He said in 1970 that the village church had given him some of the most poignant visual experiences of his life. It was a perpetual source of wonder and gratitude to him that it was possible to walk alone and unquestioned without the irritation of words into the innumerable, exquisitely articulated structures of our countryside and browse there at leisure.

All the photographs for this church book were taken with a mahogany and brass half-plate veteran called the Ruby, a truly massive affair with a huge solid stand. It was wonderfully precise and remained Edwin's favourite camera though he had to replace it by more easily portable instruments as the pressure of work increased. His cameras were always, however, at least twenty years behind the times and he heartily despised all miniatures. It was not until 1970 that he acquired a relatively modern camera, a second-hand Linhof.

When Edwin arrived at a church he would dump his equipment behind a pier, under a bench or perhaps under the collecting box table until he was ready to begin work. He was never to be seen, as so many photographers are, with his camera draped about his person. It was always discreetly satchelled or, if it was the Ruby, carried in a suitcase. Edwin would spend some time strolling round the exterior of the building, then savour the interior, enjoying not only the immediate pleasures of the eye but thinking also of the peculiar needs of the camera. Usually he became excited by a number of possibilities and always worked in the lighting conditions that existed at the moment when he decided to start. Interiors usually necessitated the use of a black cloth over the head and exposures that varied in length from 10 seconds to as many minutes. He never used photographic lamps except for individual works of art, and did not possess them until the late sixties. Edwin would adjust the lens with his spectacles pushed up on his forehead, for his near sight was abnormally sharp. Then, when he was ready he would measure the passage of the seconds by a whispered incantation: "Cat one, cat two, cat three, cat four . . . which did not alter even when he had long outgrown his early obsession with cats. He would stand by his camera smiling encouragingly at his subject and peering at it intently with his short-sighted gaze.

This book of Parish Churches was a huge success and Edwin was from that time deluged with commissions for similar books. Between 1950 and 1971 he completed more than 25 and contributed to many other volumes. With all his modesty, Edwin was pleased by the reception of his work and this as well as his completely realistic assessment of his meagre chances of making a livelihood from his painting prompted him to accept all his commissions.

He travelled extensively throughout Europe and this in itself was extraordinary, for when we met he had not left London for several years and disliked and avoided travel. He suffered greatly from the noise of modern cities and never left home without earplugs. He invariably set out with the greatest reluctance and delayed his departure until the last possible moment. But once away he gave himself up entirely to the visual experiences of the journey. Edwin always lived absolutely in the present and used it to the utmost. One of the delights of being with him was to feel his intense awareness of the divine, magical, ecstatic reality of the moment.

Once embarked on a project, Edwin would work with absolute dedication, often starting before breakfast and going on until the light faded. He made hundreds of exposures, of which he knew that perhaps no more than a dozen might be used; and he would walk miles to find the vantage point which best disclosed the character of the subject. Just as he used the given light in an interior so he would accept the given state of the weather outside. In the log books in which he always noted the time of day and the light conditions for every picture he took the most frequently occurring word is 'grey'. Edwin never tried to impose his will on the theme: it was again a question of 'co-operating with the inevitable'. It was no doubt this attitude which so often brought chance to his aid.

He arrived for instance in a Sussex village on a chilly spring evening with time to work before dinner. The light was marvellously expressive, a dream-like twilight which revealed every tile and plant and enhanced the strange reality of an incredibly romantic crucked and crooked manor house juxtaposed to trim Georgian cottages and shallow gardens enclosed by fat, closely cut hedges or white railings. This chance of light, moment and mood produced some magical photographs. In the bold sunshine of the next morning the essence of the place was obscured by an unwelcome element of caricature, the result of the ineluctable smartening and refurbishing of many of the old houses. Again, Edwin had just set up his camera at Arbor Low when the disc of a ghostly sun loomed through a blanket of pallid cloud to illumine the bleached ritual stones; and at Vaux-le Vicomte a gardener in a straw hat and loose tunic pushed a wheelbarrow along one of the formal walks at the exact moment when Edwin had focused on the subject, giving the scene scale and a mysterious, almost medieval aspect.

Photographing abroad was usually accompanied by difficulties, not the least of which was bureaucratic obstruction. Edwin was never perturbed. His charm, unfailing good humour and gentleness disguised a steely resolve and tenacity which overcame every obstacle and were as much the secret of his success as the knowledge and affection with which he approached his subjects. Once in Naples when we both wanted to work at the Palazzo Reale we were told by the director that permission must first be obtained from the Ministry of Finance. A whole frustrating morning was wasted in an ugly building like a giant radiator lying on its side while we waited for an interview which lasted barely five minutes. "You may work for three days only," announced a severe, humourless official, "And the fee will be £100 sterling a day." I was too dumbfounded to speak, but Edwin immediately and calmly replied, "That seems most reasonable. I'm sure our publisher will agree. I will telephone him from our hotel and bring you the payment tomorrow." The official was as speechless as myself. We returned to the Palace where Edwin soon had the director exclaiming at the Ministry's outrageous demands. "Can you work without a tripod?" he asked, "If so, I will tell the attendants to look the other way and you can work for as many days as you like." In fact by the end of the first day the attendants were carrying Edwin's equipment and helping him to change the arrangement of Palagio Pelagi's barbaric furniture and to remove objects from cases.

Authors and publishers often furnished Edwin with lists of subjects. They sometimes turned out to be ludicrously unpictorial and then Edwin wasted no time on them. He photographed only what stimulated him. And although his knowledge usually equalled or exceeded that of his authors his vision was never clouded by historical associations. The revered connections of Aachen and Charlemagne and the 8th century, for example, did not prevent Edwin from perceiving at once that the Cathedral was scarcely as good as St. Bartholomew the Great. "And", he wrote, "it is as far below a good English parish church as a starling is below a curlew." The Corinthian capitals, lauded in the guide book, were wholly unconvincing: "They seem to have been cut yesterday and I strongly suspect they were." He almost passed by the tawdry 1350 bust of Charlemagne without another glance, but he was on the other hand much excited by the figures on an ivory book cover, smooth as "blanched almonds" and by some bronze balustrades showing taut, oddly grouped lozenges, loops and wiry foliage. And these are the subjects of memorable photographs. A meeting with the Dom Provost, Monsignor Stephany, redeemed the whole visit to Aachen, however. He and Edwin spent a day together and became friends. "He is charming and so evidently recognises me as a fellow-devil mis-routed in life."

For Edwin did feel he was mis-routed. Despite the fact that his name as a photographer was now internationally known he would never allow that he was fully committed to the camera. It was not until 1971 when he was lecturing in Bristol that he ever referred to himself as a professional photographer and then it was with a very wry smile. It is true that his joy in the medium was such that he never took the shortest walk unaccompanied by a camera, but he liked to think of photography as a side-line. For this reason he refused until the late sixties to install running water in his dark room, disdained all the latest gadgets and made do with an antiquated enlarger. At the same time he was taking more and more photographs for a serious purpose of his own. They were of landscapes in all seasons and weathers and Edwin saw them as a means of conveying his sense of infinity. They are the counterparts of the remarkable Blakelike gouaches and drawings of his last years. For he never stopped painting.

Photography by itself could not absorb his amazing energy and creative imagination; and he has left a larger body of work than most full-time painters who live to an old age.

1973 Olive Cook

BOOKS BY EDWIN SMITH

1938 PHOTO TIPS ON CATS AND DOGS by Edwin Smith *Focal Press*

1939 BETTER SNAPSHOTS by Edwin Smith *Focal Press*

1940 ALL ABOUT THE LIGHT by Edwin Smith *Focal Press*

1940 ALL ABOUT WINTER PHOTOGRAPHY by Edwin Smith *Focal Press*

1940 ALL THE PHOTO TRICKS by Edwin Smith *Focal Press*

1952 ENGLISH PARISH CHURCHES, with text by Graham Hutton *Thames and Hudson*

1954 ENGLISH COTTAGES AND FARMHOUSES, with text by Olive Cook *Thames and Hudson*

1955 SCOTLAND, with text by George Fraser *Thames and Hudson*

1957 ENGLAND, with text by Geoffrey Grigson *Thames and Hudson*

1957 THE BRITISH MUSEUM, with text by Geoffrey Grigson *Thames and Hudson*

1960 ENGLISH ABBEYS AND PRIORIES, with text by Olive Cook *Thames and Hudson*

1960 POMPEII, with text by Marcel Brion *Paul Elek*

1961 GREAT HOUSES OF EUROPE, ed. Sacheverell Sitwell *Weidenfeld and Nicolson*

1962 VENICE, with text by Marcel Brion *Paul Elek*

1963 GREAT GARDENS, ed. Peter Coats *Weidenfeld and Nicholson*

1964 THE ENGLISH GARDEN, with text by Edward Hyams *Thames and Hudson*

1964 BRITISH CHURCHES, with text by Olive Cook *Studio Vista*

1964 ATHENS, with text by Angelo Procopiou *Paul Elek*

1965 PROSPECT OF CAMBRIDGE, with text by Olive Cook *Batsford*

1965 THE WONDERS OF ITALY, with text by Olive Cook *Thames and Hudson*

1965 THE AGE OF CHARLEMAGNE, with text by Donald Bullough *Paul Elek*

1966 THE MAKING OF CLASSICAL EDINBURGH, with text by A.J. Youngson *Edinburgh University Press*

1966 IRELAND, with text by Michel Macliamor and Olive Cook *Thames and Hudson*

1967 GREAT INTERIORS, ed. Ian Grant *Weidenfeld and Nicolson*

1968 SCOTLAND, with text by Eric Linklater and Olive Cook *Thames and Hudson*

1968 THE ENGLISH HOUSE THROUGH SEVEN CENTURIES, with text by Olive Cook *Nelson*

1969 THE GRAPHIC REPRODUCTION AND PHOTOGRAPHY OF WORKS OF ART, WITH TEXT BY Edwin Smith and John Lewis *Cowell*

1970 ENGLISH COTTAGE GARDENS, with text by Edward Hyams *Nelson*

1971 ENGLAND, with text by Angus Wilson and Olive Cook *Thames and Hudson*

1971 ROME, with text by Stewart Perrowne *Elek Books*

1971 LONDON, with text by David Piper *Thames and Hudson*

To be published in 1973, HATFIELD HOUSE, with text by David Cecil *Rainbird*

There will be an exhibition of Edwin Smith's photographs at the 1973 Aldeburgh Festival and comprehensive exhibition of his photographs, paintings and drawings at the Minories, Colchester early in 1974.

CONTENTS

THE ART OF DECEIVING

An ostentatious avowal of honesty is the commonest prelude to an act of deception, and it cannot be reasonably doubted that he who first had need to claim that the camera could not lie concealed a well-worn retouching pencil behind his ear or beneath the folds of his generous tie.

Successful deception is best practised by those of honest repute, and since false coins only find credit if enough true ones have preceded them, the creation, or exploitation, of confidence is the trickster's major task.

For better or worse, it seems that photography, more than any other pictorial medium, enjoys the confidence of the practically-minded majority of to-day. The painter and sculptor had limits set only by their powers of invention and execution, and no obligation to believe that their creations have ever endured the yoke of concrete existence.

Such belief, however, is imperative for the spectator of a photograph; he knows that photographic records cannot yet be made of the imagination or an imaginary series of events, and is consciously aware that every scene and object must have had its origin in material reality.

It is the dim, but definite, awareness of its natural origin that gives the common spectator his faith in the photograph, a faith which even flagrant abuse finds difficult to shake. Few still believe that the camera cannot lie, yet so accurately does the photograph approximate to what we are pleased to call reality, that any interference with its integrity, whilst it does not entirely deceive, upsets our sense of logic and order far more than would a similar dislocation in any other medium.

Few, for instance, are seriously disturbed or deceived by a painting that depicts a horse as big as a house; such an image, though successfully simulating reality, is of obvious mental and manual origin and has no weight of real existence nor any outrageous implication.

This same phenomenon in a photograph, however, despite our consciousness of trickery, has an authority and an air of reality that is more difficult to dismiss; both images, we realise, are those of actuality—a real horse and a real house, the relation is unreal, but nevertheless convincing, and if not deceived we are at least disturbed.

This basis of belief and common confidence in the camera's vision makes photography the deceptive medium *par excellence*, and it is the principal purpose of this book to catalogue the means whereby the photograph may be made to mislead. Other matters have crept in that would properly have no place in a Directory of Deceit, but it was thus hoped to offer a more complete collection of photographic effects.

The purposes of camera trickery are few and simple, and though we may observe that the tendentious press and cinema are not above its use to mislead, amusement rather than malicious deception is the usual intention.

The power to set the visible world upside down, to decapitate our friends, haunt their houses, and distort their wives, is one that may appeal to the anarchist in us all; it is the only justification for many of the tricks to be described.

But, for the imaginative photographer, and others who resent the camera's too slavish dependence on commonplace reality, who envy the painter his freedom of creation and covet his powers to mould the world closer to his heart's desire, the fomulas that follow will more than amuse.

Their imaginative use will remove the camera one step further from the tyranny of everyday appearance, and one nearer the world of ideas, granting power to suppress prosaic fact in favour of creative imagination.

Photography at every stage is rich in opportunity for experiment and adjustment. Of all mediums, indeed, with none is it so miraculous that what goes in at one end comes out intact at the other; possibilities of odd goings on are endless—in the camera, the developing tanks, the printer and enlarger, and even the photo work-table.

The "straight" photograph is surely the greatest triumph! At each and every stage, as most have learnt from unfortunate experience, "something can happen," and in themselves these seeming misfortunes frequently constitute an improvement upon reality and form the basis of many intentional photographic effects.

Our present purpose is to encourage things to go wrong, in orderly fashion, at all the critical stages of photo technique in the camera, in the darkroom and everywhere that opportunity offers. To you that are a darkroom as well as a daylight photographer, every step is under control and this whole book is written for you; the man who halves the fun with his dealer, halves also his opportunities, but his half is a rich one nevertheless.

★

Any camera can be used, from the simplest to the most elaborate, but the most universally suitable, as will soon become apparent, is *the camera equipped with a focusing screen the same size as the picture,* in one form or another. The reflex, in any size, is ideal, as is the view camera with a back focusing screen taking cut film or plates.

Since time exposures are often an obligation of the process, the speed of a lens is relatively unimportant, but a good firm, *adjustable tripod is quite indispensable.*

Lighting, generally, need be no more than that provided by normal household fittings; the use of photofloods and other over-run electric bulbs will brighten the subject and shorten the exposure, but they are by no means a necessity.

Film material unless otherwise stated for specific reasons, is assumed to be the normal *panchromatic* type. The speed is relatively unimportant unless short exposures prove a necessity, when film should naturally be of a faster rated speed.

Most of the methods are described as "within-four-wall" affairs, it being assumed that they will occupy dark winter evenings and other confining circumstances, but, it will be obvious, few need be so confined if it is not your wish and if you do not feel that bright sunlight makes your magic look a little insipid.

★

In all the recipes, *idea* will be the operative word, and the least dispensable part of your equipment; no gadget is an adequate substitute for imagination, and without it every technique can produce results as trite as any snapshot.

Each method is the door to a vista which is in most cases, and at the present time, endless; and, since many of the means are interconnected, you are ever likely to enter one familiar door and emerge at another.

But, only go far enough, and with enough persistence, and new doors are there to be found, new vistas, and, perhaps, a room full of mad photographers anticipating your entry. No lingering on the threshold!

LAZY SHUTTER

One of the rare and happy opportunities for the camera to transcend its function of common recording, and show us images that the eye could not observe without its aid, is provided by the object that moves more quickly than the camera shutter.

We are all, by now, familiar with the manner in which the fast shutter isolates, and freezes for our concentrated attention, fragments of movement which are only observed by the eye as fleeting parts of a unified whole. The separate movements that go to make up the flight of birds, the rapid motion of running and jumping humans and animals, and scores of similar swift actions, that, before the advent of the ultra-fast lens and film, were matters of rough conjecture, are now the commonplace visual experience of every newspaper reader, and not the proper study of the trick photographer.

But the opposite effect, in which, by the too slow action of a lazy shutter, or by leaving the shutter entirely open, the total track rather than the isolated fragment of the movement is allowed to record itself within the camera, though no more a trick is at least uncommon enough, both in repute and effect, to justify mention here.

The technique of making such pictures is simplicity itself—literally the subject takes its own photograph. Any primitive camera will serve for this; indeed a fast lens and film are a positive drawback, and, if it proves impossible to stop the lens down far enough to prevent serious over-exposure on the slowest film material obtainable, a deep filter of appropriate colour, or what is known as a neutral density filter, must be used to decrease the amount of light entering the camera.

The camera is set up before the subject on a very solid tripod, or other firm support, so that though the subject is encouraged to move, the camera stays rigidly put. Whether the exposure is made with a very slow shutter speed or whether the shutter is left open and things just left to work themselves, depends very much on the nature of the subject and the degree of distortion required. Subjects must be treated on their own merits.

A great diversity of moving subject matter may be treated by the lazy shutter, but all will have one quality in common: they must be either white, or at least lighter in tone than the objects or background against which they are pictured.

The emulsion of any film material, you will remember, is light sensitive, and will record an impression of any source, or reflection, of light, retaining its latent image even if it should be extinguished during exposure—having once made its mark it can go, the film will remember it.

But, conversely, any dark or shadowed object that is replaced during exposure by a light or light-reflecting source, will be cancelled out and rendered invisible, the film just forgets it—preferring the light.

Thus, a white bird, travelling across a dark sky before a lazy shutter camera, leaves a record of its flight as a dense streak across the film—the bird reflects light, the sky reflects little. But a black bird, travelling across a light sky, leaves almost no evidence of its flight across the film, since its successive movements are continually revealing white light—the exposing agent.

This too, is rare magic. But, since there is no proof that the black bird was there in the first place, satisfaction is fleeting too. Many subjects are suitable for lazy shutter treatment.

▷ *Stars will require only a normal aperture, anything between f4 and f8, though more will not necessarily be amiss, together with a film of moderate speed. So long as the morning light is not allowed to cancel the evening's effort, the longer the camera is left open to the night sky the longer will be the tracks of stellar movement, and the minimum period for any effect worthy of the name is something like an hour.*

The heavens revolve around the Pole star, which remains more or less in a fixed position. It, therefore, will leave no track, and if the camera is pointed so that the Pole star forms roughly the centre of the plate, the star tracks will form arcs of a true circle whose centre is in the middle of the picture—quite satisfying as those things go.

Clearly, the stars nearest the Pole will make the shortest tracks, those nearest the horizon the longest, for any given

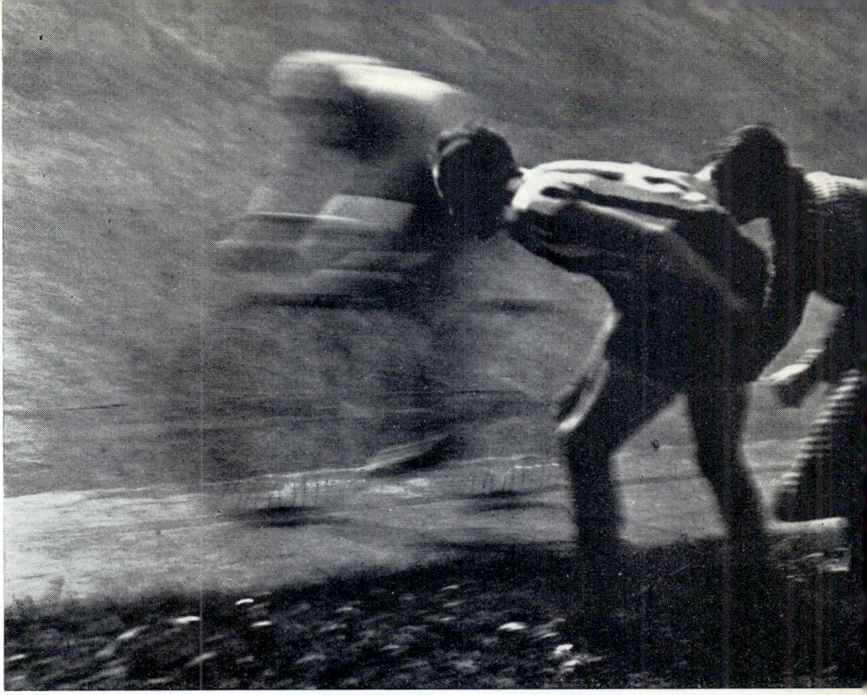

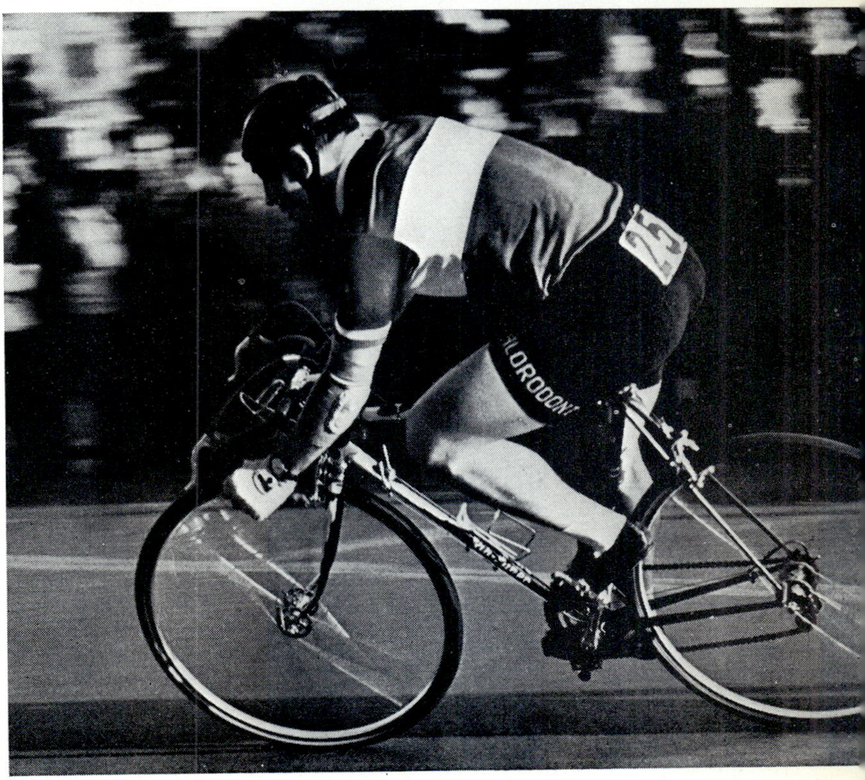

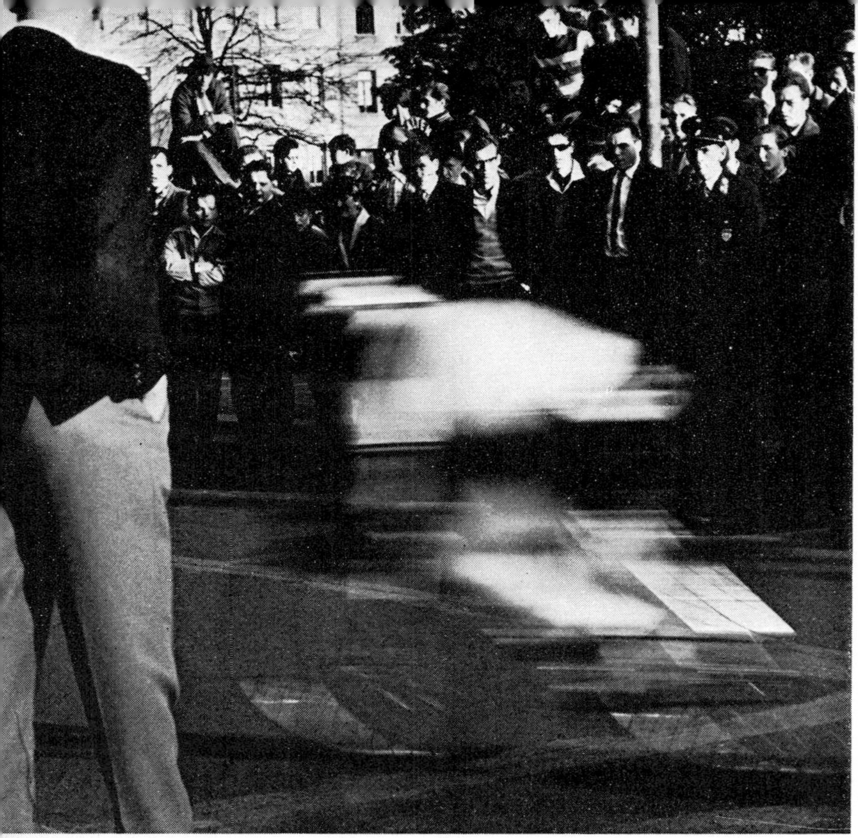

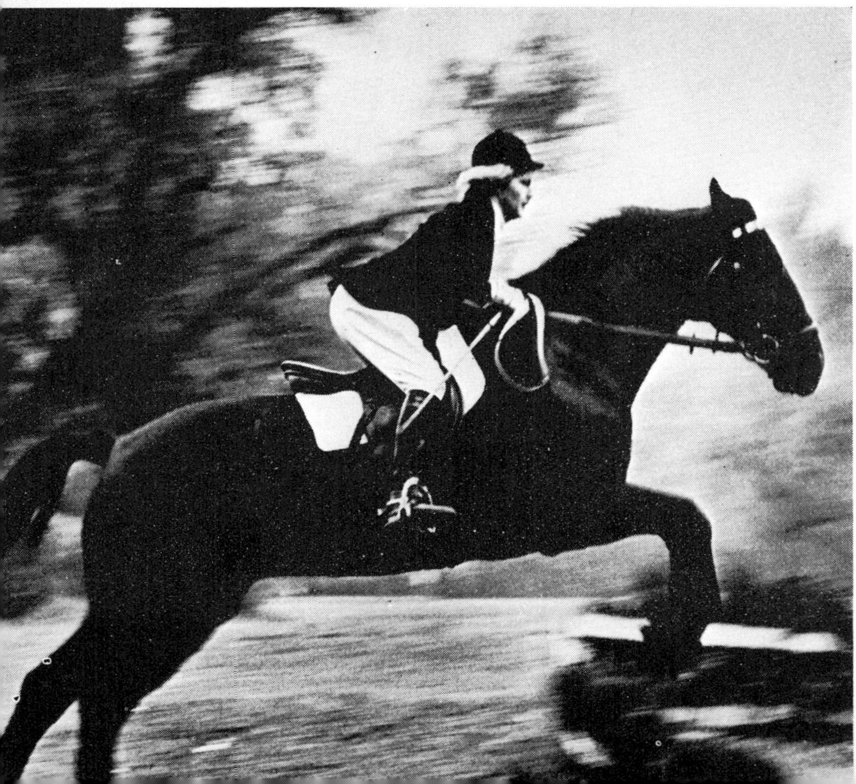

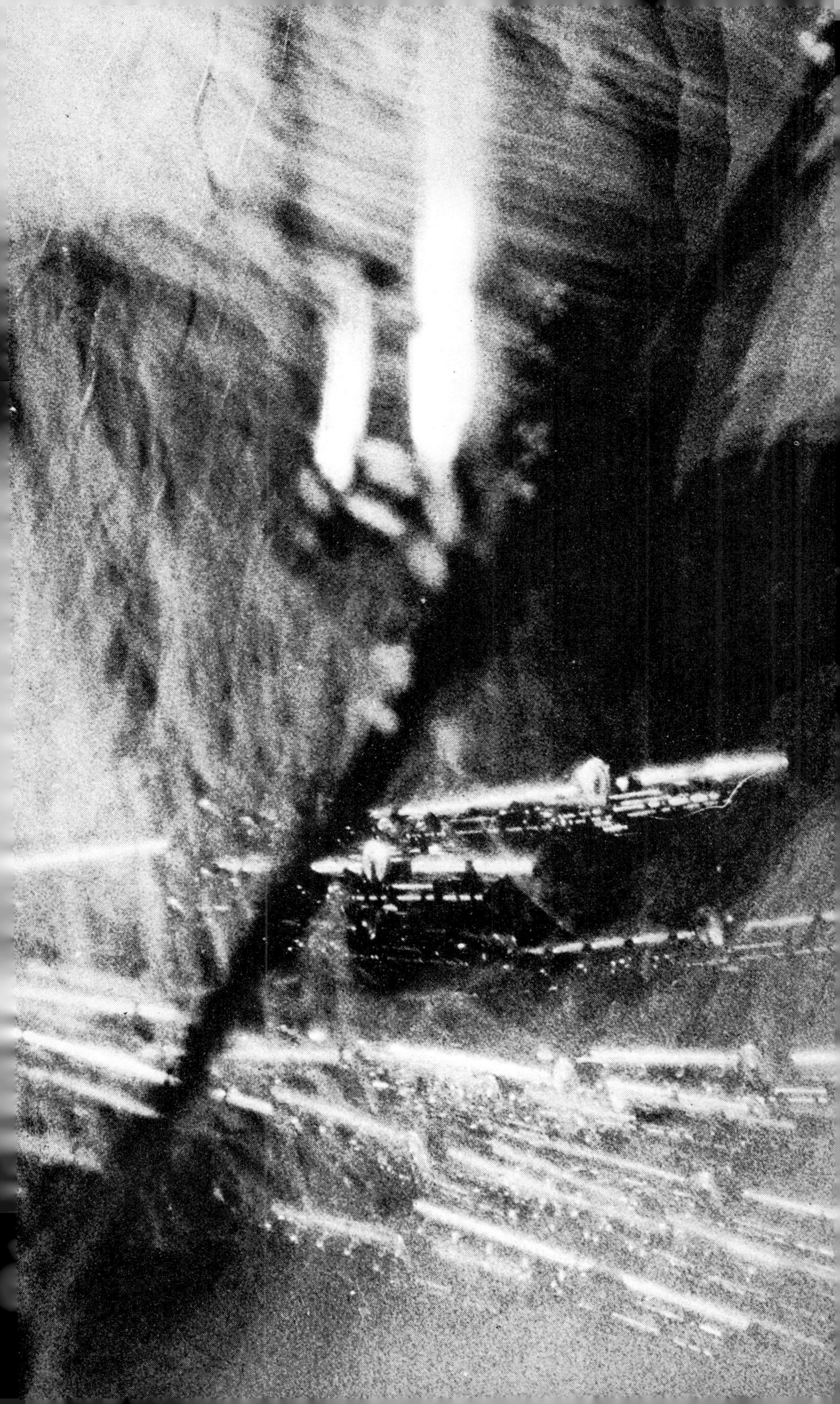

SHUTTER TRICKS

Page 25 Top. A split-second exposure, combined with a sympathetic camera swing, failed to capture a sharp image of this racing cyclist. Slight horizontal elongation of assistants and grass in foreground is due to camera "panoramming." Ghost-like appearance of cyclist due to his own movement during the period of exposure: notice how his white tones have streaked and how the darker ones have been in some places totally overlaid by the lighter background. A symbol of speed!—*G. Schuh.*

Bottom. Panning the camera to match the speed of the cyclist renders him sharp but blurs the spectators in the background.—*Kudolf Kulda.*

Page 26. Variations on a theme of speed. The cyclist and horsewoman present an identical situation. And here are two quite different solutions. *Top,* stationary camera. *Bottom,* panned with the subject.—*Rudolf Kulda.*

Page 27: Multiple exposure on a moving subject. The flautist was shot repeatedly within a short space of time giving a mixture of blur and sharp outline.—*Neil Hughes, Harrow School of Photography*

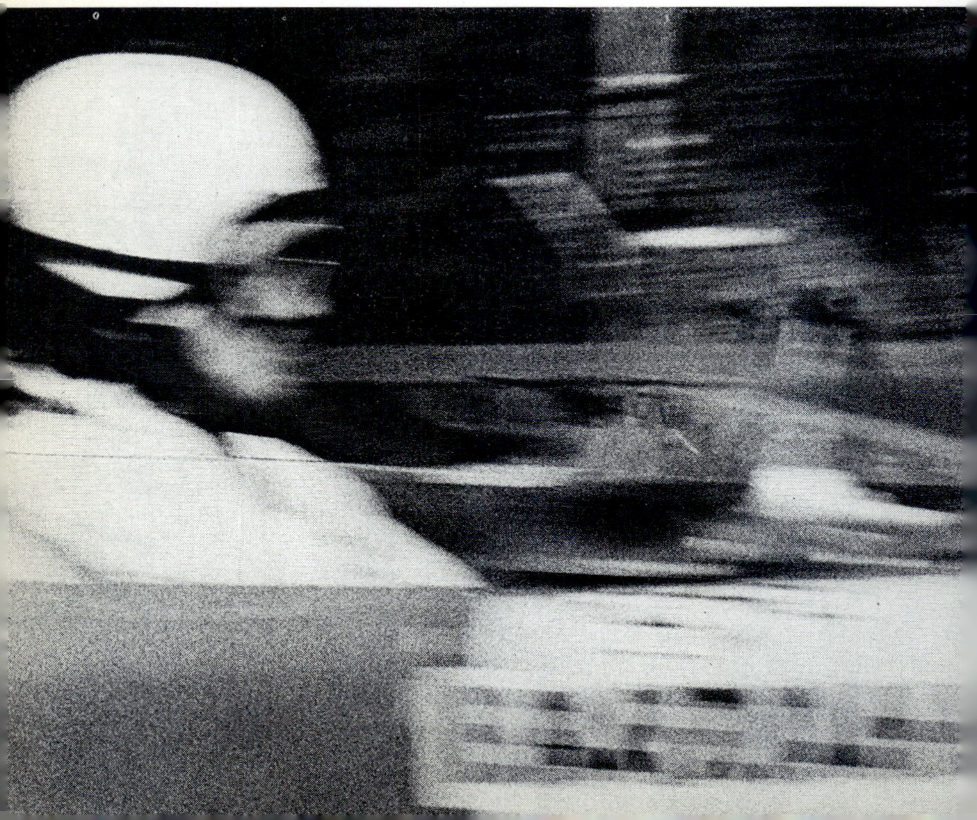

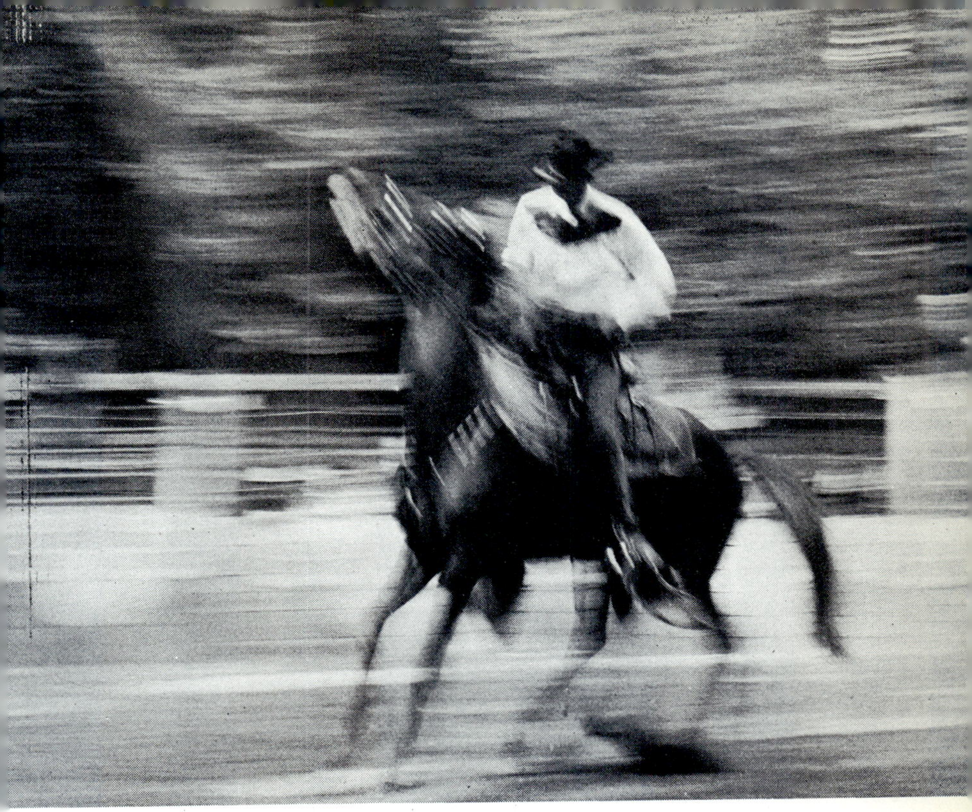

Above. A feeling of movement in the subject itself as well as in relationship to the background is possible by choice of a relatively slow shutter speed.—*Francisco Hidalgo.*

Left: "Blur in detail." When looking through a long focus lens a faster shutter speed is needed to gain a blur equivalent to that from a lens of normal focal length. This is because a long focus lens magnifies not only the subject but also its movement. For this picture of a racing driver even the 1/30 sec. exposure time gives a broad blurred effect at this focal length. The same effect is, of course, obtained by enlarging a smaller section of a picture taken with a lens of shorter focus.—*Rudolf Bieri.*

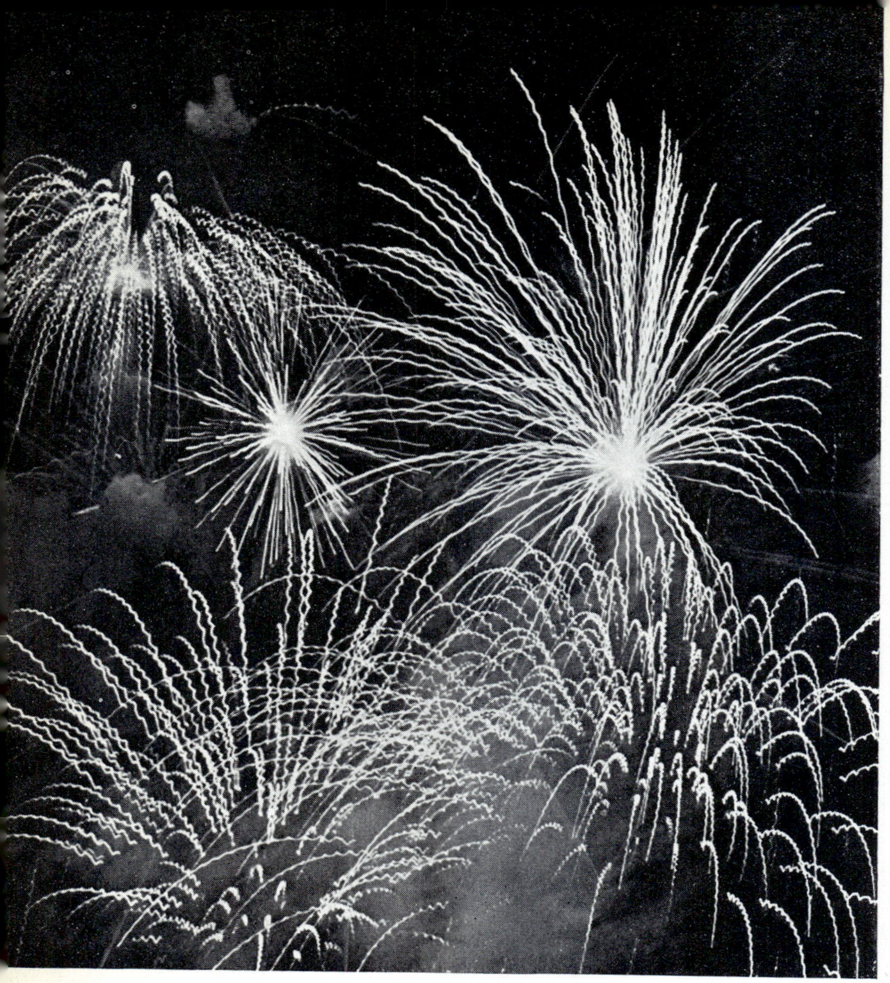

Above: Five separate rocket bursts brought on to a single picture plane by the lazy shutter, through an aperture of *f*4.5 on a fast panchromatic emulsion. The shutter remains open while the bursts record themselves, but, if the intervals are long, it is simple to give five separate brief time exposures at the five critical moments.—*H. Gorny.*

Opposite: A lazy shutter yawns at the night sky for two hours, the camera rotating with the earth and recording every star in view as an arc-like track. Camera points towards Pole Star which forms the approximate centre of the circle, each star recording on the film one-twelth of its apparent daily movement round it—those near the pole moving least, those further moving most. The diagonal streak is pure good fortune—a convenient falling star.—*P. Popper.*

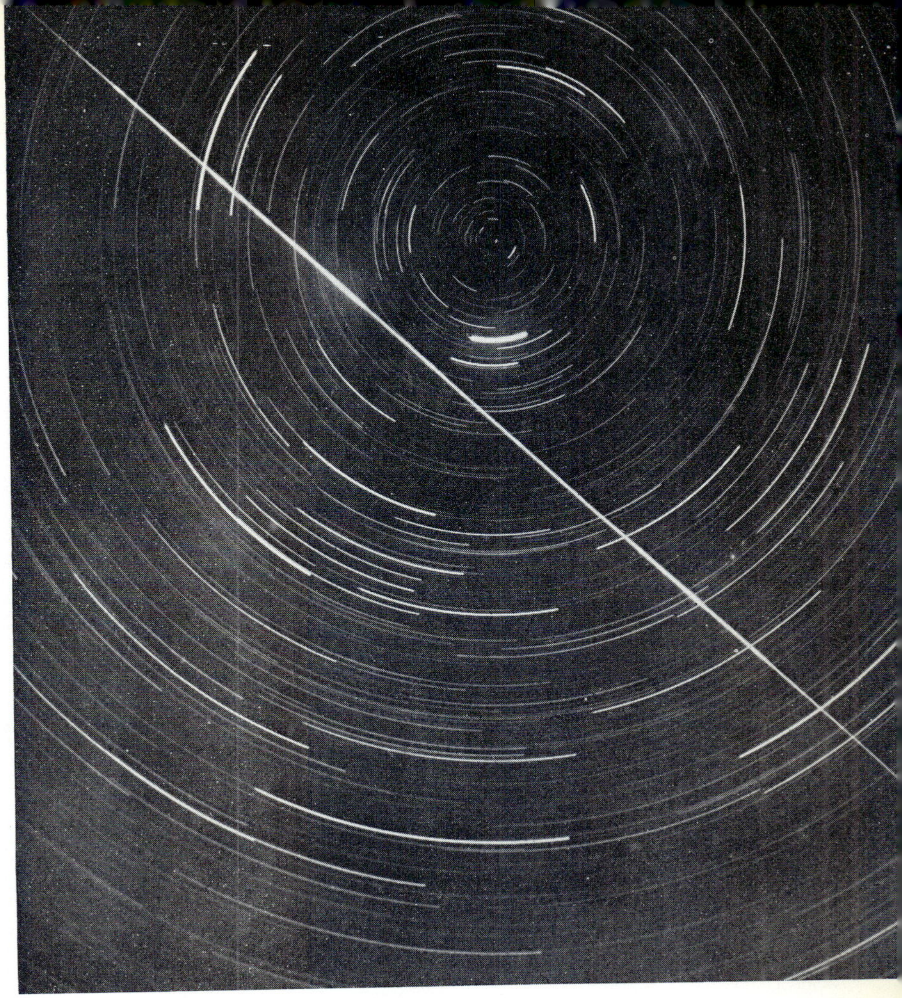

Page 32: Top: A flash of lightning, recorded by the lazy shutter on a dark or night sky, is combined with a suitable stormy picture by double printing of the two negatives. When of sufficient area the lightning negative may be printed in combination—face to face—but in this case the large black cloud provides a simple masking line for dividing the printing exposure into two separate compartments.—*H. Gorny*

Bottom: This tree trunk is an immobile subject, but a blur was induced by changing focus during the long exposure. Taken to its limits a blur becomes just an abstract shape.—*K. W. M. Stegers.*

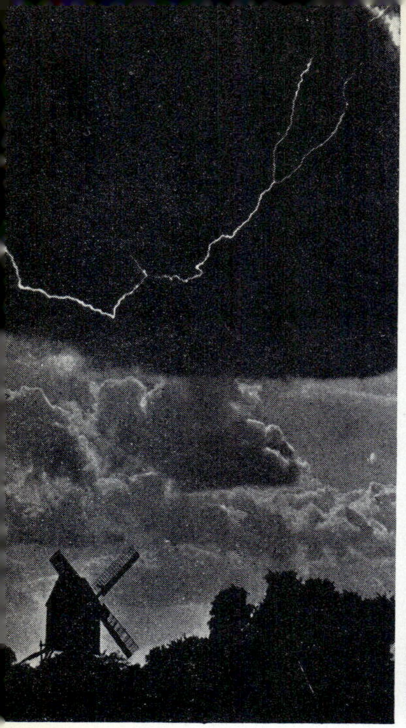

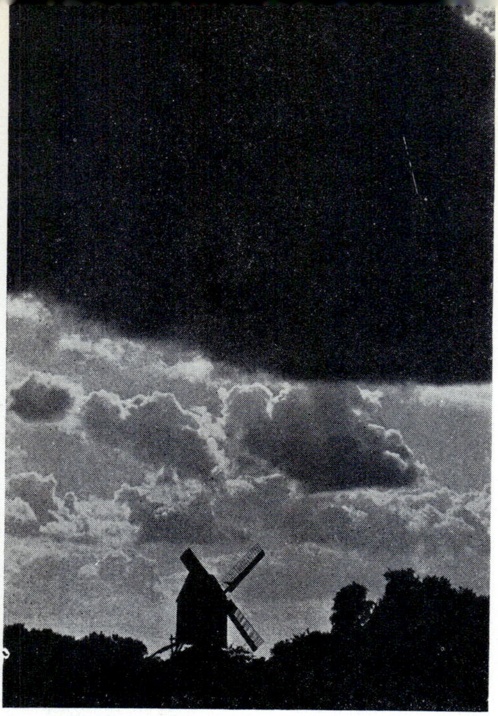

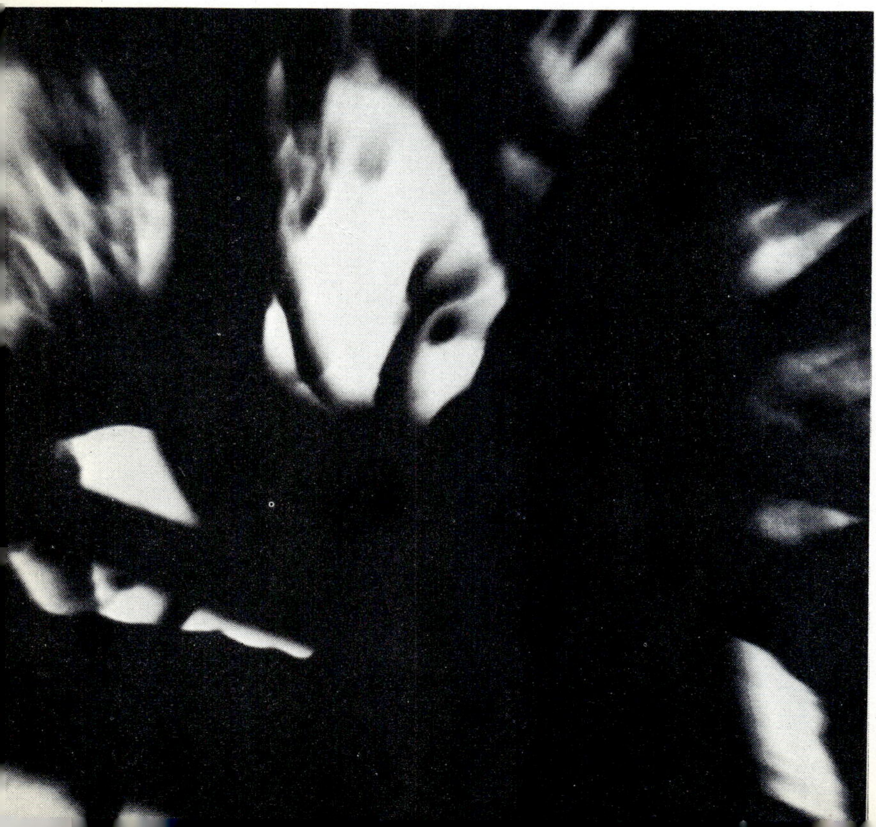

period, so that a viewpoint towards the horizon will be more rewarding, for the same expenditure of effort, than one straight up in the air.

To relieve the slight monotony, and add a fatter line to the thin pencil tracks of stars, the camera can be arranged, in suitable seasons, to include the moon, which will leave a track of its movements in a similar manner.

▷ *Falling snow at night, or when seen against a shadowy building or other background of dark tone, will leave white tracks over the surface of the film. Their length will depend both on the speed of the fall and on the duration of the exposure—right down from top to bottom if the shutter is left open, and the snowfall is rapid and shorter if recorded with a slow shutter-speed.*

These lines, made by the light reflected from each individual flake of snow, are much more expressive of the pictorial effect of a snowstorm than each tiny flake frozen in mid-air by a split-second exposure, so that if this effect is desired rather than an odd photographic curiosity, a lazy shutter-speed between 1/8 and 1/4 of a second for a moderately soft fall will be just right.

▷ *Lightning, whether by day or by night, can always be relied upon to record itself through an open shutter, and the over-eager photographer who tries feverishly to synchronise his shutter with every crackling flash is just being likeably foolish.*

Night is really the only lightning opportunity, since the camera can just be pointed out of the window, in the vague direction of the storm, and the pair of them left to get on with it, several flashes, if you are very lucky, being recorded on the same plate.

Use, for preference but not necessity, a wide-angle lens—to cover a wider space of sky and so increase your chances, and try to mark out a good clear patch of sky that is not intercepted by odd pieces of tree, chimney, or ubiquitous television aerial, which may only cut up your best flashes in a tiresome and often inexplicable manner.

▷ *Fireworks are but another kind of lightning to the camera, and no other treatment beyond opening the shutter and leaving the effect to work itself will be necessary.*

A reasonably distant viewpoint is recommended so that the long, stem-like tracks, as well as the flower-like bursts of the rockets are recorded. There is no limit to the number of separate burst, and other firework effects, that can be recorded on a single film, but the camera should not be left openly staring at a whole evening's display. It is a good plan to use a lens cap between bursts, for even the minimal glow of a night sky will give a slight fogging if the exposure is protracted.

The effect of too many tracks and bursts can be a little confusing and uncharacteristic of the origin. It will be more satisfactory (usually) to wind on the film after every three or four bangs.

▷ Lights of vehicles make intriguing snaky patterns through the dark streets at night, and are seen to maximum advantage from the high vantage point of an upper window.

For variety it is best to choose a point where two roads cross, or where one branches off, or makes some sudden change in direction. The lines of light will then twist and interlace, or take sudden swerves to one side or the other as the vehicles dash on, up the wrong turnings, and back again.

Within reason, and bearing in mind the danger of fogging, the longer the camera is left, and the busier and better lit the street, the more the tracks and the stronger will any surrounding buildings record, until the road assumes the appearance of a flowing river of light.

▷ Fair roundabouts (Gallopers to the initiated), and any so-called pleasure rides of that kind, that are well illuminated at many points on their diameter and go accurately round in a circle, provide really fine material for lazy shutter treatment. Open the shutter and let a turn or two of the machine record itself on the plate. The points of light, with their precisely circular movement, trace out intriguing volumes of a semicylindrical and conical nature that are one of the most satisfying results of this particular technique.

▷ Tapers or burning matches, if carried about a darkened room, or moved about in twisting convolutions before an open-shuttered camera will also leave a record of their every movement. With a good memory for the preceding movements, it is possible to draw simple line pictures, or write short words, in mid-air before the camera, in the plane of focus.

Daylight opportunities for lazy shutter tricks must make use of natural dark backgrounds.

▷ Flowing water, like falling snow-flakes, looks least natural when frozen into immobility with an excessively high shutter-speed. The pictorial effect is not in the least suggestive of the flowing element, but of mere glassy stillness.

Depending on the speed of flow, and the direction in relation to the camera, shutter speeds of 1/4 or 1/8 of a second will allow a little of the current's movement to register on the film, and thus suggest the direction and nature of the flow. If the current is fast and at right angles to the viewpoint 1/30 would achieve the same result.

▷ *Smoke, from a neglected cigarette, or blown before the camera with an open shutter and approximately in the plane of focus, will, if lit in a manner that strongly contrasts it with a dark background, create shapes of a ghostly and thoroughly unforeseeable nature as the film records its wreathing movements.*

Such images have rarely much suggestion of their narcotic origin, consisting mostly of vague misty shapes. But these can be well combined, by double printing in the enlarger, with certain portrait and landscape negatives.

▷ *Ghosts can be conjured up in any room or street by encouraging acquaintances, in light-coloured clothing, to walk smartly across the camera field during a prolonged shutter exposure. A 1/8 to 1/4 second should do, depending on the speed of movement and the degree of ghost definition required.*

The figures are rendered partially transparent and register in a series of white streaks of vaguely human volume—evidence of their movement before the open shutter.

▷ *Backgrounds for static objects, that are being recorded normally by time exposure, can be ingeniously contrived by the movement of fabrics and surfaces of various kinds, during the time that the shutter is open.*

Thus, a plain atmospheric background of a near white nature can be obtained, without the bother of stretching sheets and smoothing folds, if an assistant (you could even leave the camera and do it yourself) gently shakes, or otherwise moves, the sheet from side to side during the time of exposure.

Neutral grey backgrounds can be made from any old fabric or large sheet of paper that happens to be conveniently lying around, providing it is kept constantly moving so that textural and other detail is not recorded.

Printed materials, particularly those consisting of small white dots on a background of darker colour, produce very attractive backgrounds in this shifting manner, the spots elongating into whirls and lines according to the direction of the movement. The result defies easy explanation of its production.

▷ *Light movement. To ring a slight change. If, instead of moving the subject, the artificial light source of any scene is moved, during exposure, to another position in the room, the condition mentioned earlier—in which the light cancels what was once shade—is fulfilled, and the shadows are lightened without the use of a second lamp.*

It is possible, by such means, to light subjects and rooms of considerable area with a single lamp of normal power, not of course with all the finesse of careful arrangement but with a success and brilliance that is surprising considering the simple means used.

The shutter is opened and the light directed in turn, with a slight waving motion, to all parts of the subject, only taking care that no polished surfaces, mirrors, or glass, reflect it back into the camera lens.

If the lamp is kept constantly moving, and its position in relation to the camera always slightly changed, the final picture will be evenly lit, with few shadows. Should this be unsuitable to the subject matter, the light should be directed for a longer period towards one side of the subject than the other, giving a better modelling.

▷ *Emptying a street. To ring another change. If the exposure time required is divided into many small and separate units, moving vehicles and pedestrians, provided the street is not too busy, can be prevented from recording on the film, and an effect of utter and complete desertion obtained.*

By so dividing the exposure, only those absolutely stationary parts of the scene that appear consistently in the same position in every unit of the exposure, will record as an image on the negative. Unfortunately, under modern conditions of permanently parked cars this artifice can be impossible to work. But all moving objects, appearing in a different position each time, and for but a minute fraction of the required exposure, will build up no image.

The important point is to arrange a total exposure time long enough to divide into a large number of small units, and a small aperture, together with a very slow film or a heavy filter are steps in this direction.

Thus, if the total required exposure is adjusted to, say, two seconds, this can be divided up into 60 exposures of 1/30 of a second, or 120 and 1/60, according to the amount of patience at your disposal, and business of the street. However, it is sometimes advisable to slightly increase the number of units, since the total amount of light, with such intermittent exposure, may be rather less than with a normally continuous one.

In waiting for parked cars, and other temporarily stationary objects to move, remember that too long delay, on a day of brilliant sunshine, involves a movement of all the picture shadows. If too long, this will result in a shadowless and unnatural light which can, of course, be pleasing.

Continual re-setting of the camera shutter, without disturbing its settled position, is a very ticklish job unless the tripod or other support is really rock steady. Make sure of this before beginning.

Besides revenging oneself on an over-curious populace, who always seem to turn up in swarms whenever a photographer appears, this technique can hopefully be tried to obtain uninterrupted pictures of architecture, in streets that are never completely empty at that hour of the day when the light is just as required.

▷ *It need not be stressed, of course, that any moving object, recorded with a slow shutter-speed, will leave a record of its movements on the film. The swifter the movement, and the longer the exposure, the more blurred and distorted the effect. The variety of subject that can be so treated is almost without number, and need not be separately dealt with here.*

Attention is drawn, however, to objects whose action is divided into two independent halves—the legs and body of a running man or animal, for instance. If such subjects are recorded, with a comparatively slow shutter speed for the nature of the action, by swinging the camera in the same direction as the runner, his body will be registered in a more or less normal manner, whilst his legs appear like strange, fantastic wisps of smoke.

This "panning" action, in which the camera, though held otherwise with absolute steadiness, is moved in direct relation to any moving subject by swinging the body from the hips—keeping the object sighted in the viewfinder and exposing during the swing, can be used to successfully capture many movements that would otherwise be too rapid for a shutter speed of 1/60 to 1/125 of a second.

With a normal still-camera technique the moving subject would be recorded as a drawn-out streak against a perfectly sharp background. In the swinging method the tables are turned—streaking and blurring the background, but recording the moving subject with a maximum sharpness compatible with a restricted shutter speed. The blurred background elongated in the direction of the camera movement, is not a disadvantage merely to be tolerated; it has a quality far more suggestive of high speed than one whose every detail is plain.

▷ *Taking advantage of conditions mentioned earlier in this chapter—where dark-moving objects render themselves almost invisible against light backgrounds, any chosen part of a moving subject, if darkly clad, can be made obscure by waving it before the sky or other light background. A shutter-speed of something like 1/30 to 1/60 of a second should be employed, so that, though the moving member is not registered sharply, any slight but inevitable movement of the main subject itself is stopped.*

▷ *A further lazy-shutter dodge, producing swishy streaked-out high-lights suggestive of speed and beloved of the magazine illustrator, depends upon partly reversing the subject before an open-shutter camera after the main exposure has been made.*

A normal, straightforward, and full exposure of the subject—a standing motor-car, for example—is made. The shutter is closed and the lens aperture reduced as far as possible. The car is then set into a gentle reverse—just releasing the brake on a slight backward incline would be sufficient—and the camera shutter opened during its backward movement of, say, two or three feet, or even right out of the picture.

The effect of this manoeuvre is to produce a streak, in a backward direction, of all the subject's highlights, and a normally sharp image of the half-tones and shadowed areas.

DISTORTIONS

In its infancy the camera offered so many distortions and original conceptions of the visual world that photography was almost an artistic medium.

Years of earnest industry on the part of many otherwise worthy gentlemen, however, have changed all that. Distortions and aberrations of the lens have been reduced to a final minimum and photographic chemists have all but succeeded in producing an emulsion that renders colour in tones acceptable to the eye as true.

It must be realised, though with certain regrets that the days of the black daffodil and the white bluebell, the curved vertical and the blurred edge, are already part of a more exotic past.

But, despite the persistent desire to reduce a camera to the status of a mere recording instrument, and make it conform to the standards of prosaic vision, the photographer of spirit and imagination still has several vantage points from which the dull-witted may be outraged and confounded.

It will be sad when the camera can no longer bring before us images that are not a commonplace of everyday observation and when its powers are finally reduced to the mere technical task of recording what any clear-sighted dullard can witness.

The following collection of distorting methods are seeds that may grow in fertile minds. Some, perhaps, will not seem solid enough to justify these claims of liberation. But, in all, the intention is rich suggestion rather than a rigid rule of thumb.

Reflection

The alternately shrunken and swollen images in the distorting mirrors that could once be found at the end of every seaside pier, being obviously so grotesque, could provide consolation in the feeling that one's multiple imperfections stopped short of such monstrosity. Confidence in one's fundamental superiority to these ribald reflections was so great that the image of reality might at that moment, have been greeted with the loudest laugh of all. I can never really rid myself of the furtive feeling that one of those mirrors was perfect, and never suspected.

Comfortable or not, the laughter was real and will be sustained if the phenomena is photographed, or produced by one of many photographic methods.

The obvious means, and one which is recorded only for the sake of completeness, is to photograph the actual reflection in a large distorting mirror. But, as such mirrors are now to be found only in rare fun fairs and places where photography is inconvenient, time would be wasted in discussing it.

Any curved surface, if it is sufficiently highly polished, will reflect a distorted image. The convex variety that recedes the chin and brow and gives to the nose an embarrassing air of inquisitiveness, is to be found in comparative abundance.

The effect can be observed, and recorded by the camera, in the decorative silver spheres known as witch balls, in crystals, and in the smaller edition of the same thing that is used to decorate a Christmas tree. The hub caps of car wheels, particularly if large and chromium plated, the backs of large and highly-polished silver spoons, and the convex mirrors that are framed for wall decoration will all reflect a centrally bulging image.

All the reflectors mentioned are of spherical convex shape and therefore exhibit distortion in every direction—large in the middle but falling away top, bottom and on both sides. The reverse effect, in which the nose recedes and the brow and chin project; and reflections which are distorted in one direction only, are most successfully obtained on a polished chromium plate such as those sold for glazing prints.

These plates are pliable in every direction and produce distortions of all kinds. They are obtained in several sizes, but one measuring 30 cm. x 25 cm. (12 in. x 10 in.) is suitable and economical. Stainless steel glazing plates are unsuitable. Ferrotype glazing plates are much cheaper and produce similar effects, but, being black, the image is very dark and needs a much longer exposure.

A similar observation applies to any other reflector of coloured surface—the *silver surface reflects the most light, the darker the colour, the greater the loss of light and contrast, and the longer the consequent exposure.*

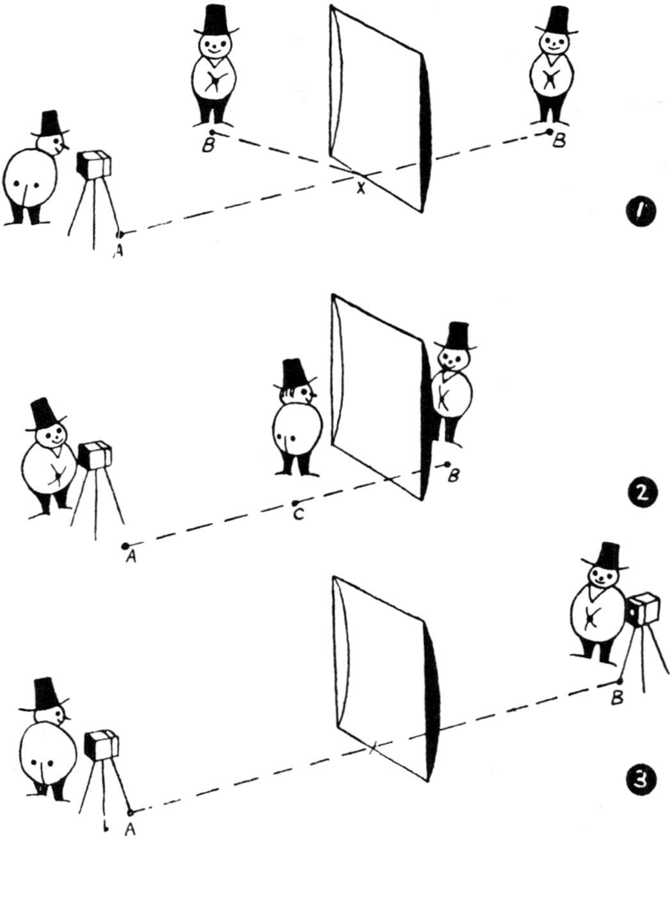

DISTORTING MIRROR FOCUSING

In all three drawings a photograph is being made of the reflection in a distorting mirror, and in all three instances the focusing distance is represented by the dotted distance *A* to *B*.

In drawing *1* the reflection only is being recorded, in drawing *2* the camera includes the real as well as the reflected, therefore, though the extreme focusing distance for the reflection is still *A* to *B*, a depth of field must be provided that covers the distance *C* to *B* to get all equally sharp. In drawing *3* the vain photographer makes his own, and his camera's, self-portrait. No depth of field required.

A substitute for the chromium plate, and one without the drawback of dark colour, is a large sheet of silver-foil paper. It gives a surprisingly clear reflection, can be curved and twisted in endless ways, and is, indeed, the most pliable reflector of all.

Detailed instruction on the use and possibilities of any distorting surface is quite superfluous, a few moment's reflection before any of them will show you all there is to see. But, there is just one technial trap that you may pitch into—it concerns focusing.

When using a camera with a focusing screen you will discover that the reflected image does not lie in the same plane as the surface of the reflector, for when this is sharply focused the reflections are seen to be hazy. This is because the reflection of any object lies a similar distance behind the reflecting surface as the object does before it—like a glimpse into another world.

Thus the face that is three feet in front of the mirror, or reflector, is, in effect, three feet behind it and this point must be focused on for the image to be sharp.

Any focusing screen will visually demonstrate this fact, but in its absence the focusing scale must be adjusted to a *distance equalling the distance of the camera, plus the distance of the subject,* from the reflecting surface.

In other words, if you are photographing yourself reflected in a silver ball, and standing egotistically beside your camera three feet away, the focusing distance is six feet; or if the camera, kept at this same distance, is directed at the reflection of an object six feet from the ball, the distance for focusing will be nine feet.

In those cases where the intended effect implies an equal sharpness of reflection and reflecting object, as would almost certainly be the case with a witch ball or tree decoration, a car hub cap or any complete and interesting shape, the *lens must be considerably stopped down* to get all planes in sharp focus.

The surface and bounding lines of the chromium or other polished plate or of the silver-foil paper, can be of no interest whatever and stopping down the lens to get it sharp is a waste of time. Focus on the reflection and forget about the surface. Be content in the knowledge that any of its small blemishes or imperfections will be out of focus, and therefore imperceptible in the final print.

A complete catalogue of distorting reflectors must include water. Long, long before the mirror, its rippling surface played strange and fascinating havoc with reflected objects. Its effects, as you can observe, are at a maximum when the ripples are deep and near together, and at a more pictorial minimum when they are shallow and widely distributed.

Such reflections, of course, are seen and recorded upside down, but they should be offered to view, when printed, so that the objects are shown right way up. This has the effect of temporarily concealing their liquid origin and creating a disturbing illusion.

When estimating distance, as before, forget the surface. Subjects in front of the camera,touching the water's edge will be in the same plane as their reflection. The reflections of more distant objects, that lie beyond the pool or pond, will be the same distance away as the objects themselves.

Looking down into pools or puddles is like looking up to the object itself—the image projecting downwards a similar distance as the actual object upwards. A tower forty feet high will thus appear to descend forty feet into the water, and, if its top must be sharp, this will be the focusing distance.

▷ *The uses of reflected distortion are mostly humorous, and since nothing amuses humanity more than its own image, this is the usual raw material. No other objects are barred, however, and possible combinations are endless.*

Large distorted faces loathe competition, and are best seen against plain neutral backgrounds. A dark cloth, arranged immediately behind the sitter's head, will localise the reflection in the desired manner.

▷ *Alternately, very fine pictures have been made of complete rooms and their occupants, including the camera, without any special background or other preparation. Windows give troublesome contrasts and the mirror will best be arranged so that these are not completely included.*

▷ *The clearest and brightest images are obtained when the light falls directly on the subject rather than upon the reflecting surface. To this end the reflector is arranged so that it comes between the sitter, or scene, and the source of light, whether this is a window or an artificial light source. The chromium plate, witch ball or what-not, can be used in this manner so that it screens the light from the camera itself—the camera looks at the shaded side of the reflector—but not from the subject.*

▷ *Self-portraits with the camera are effective, but the camera is not a necessary accompaniment to all distorted reflections. With close portraiture it is only necessary to place the camera adjacent to the sitter and point it towards his reflection, and with the all-embracing view it is a reasonably simple matter to conceal the camera behind a book, flowers, or a card with a small hole cut away for the lens.*

▷ *Water is, perhaps, an out-door affair, but specially arranged trays of water, large cups of coffee, and other liquid opportunities of the household should not be altogether neglected.*

Tall, slender objects are best for water distortion: trees, towers, isolated columns and statuary will waver alarmingly when the print is turned wrong way round.

The Wide-Angle Lens

Perspective is a distortion that all have grown accustomed to, the convergence of lines that we know to be parallel causes no confusion, nor do we convulse with amusement—as properly we should—when a far-off man and a near-to fly seem identical in size. Such fundamentally comic phenomena we explain away by the ratio of size and distance, and we are not amused.

However, if the effect is portrayed pictorially, and with sharp enough exaggeration, our eyes get suspicious and a sense of distortion and humour return simultaneously.

A homely example, and one with which most are familiar, are the gigantic boots in the foreground of some amateur snapshots when the sitters have been arranged with legs outstretched towards the camera. Every amateur textbook warns one against such effects—this one tells you how to get them.

Distorted perspective can be produced with any normal camera to a degree that might, perhaps, cause comment. But the use of a lens with an extremely wide angle of view will so emphasise near objects at the expense of far, that the results can often be ludicrous.

The angle of view embraced by the lens on the average camera is approximately 45°, and its pictures correspond, nearly enough, to the field of view that the human eye can clearly encompass.

The angle of vision of the combined eyes is almost a full 180° as you can easily verify by moving a hand round from behind the head while keeping your eyes fixed on a point directly in front of them, but this extreme range cannot receive simultaneous attention; we are only dimly aware of its periphery and must re-direct our gaze if we wish to examine the hand in detail.

Because of this, and because our vision is also binocular, effects of extreme distortion are not a natural condition of

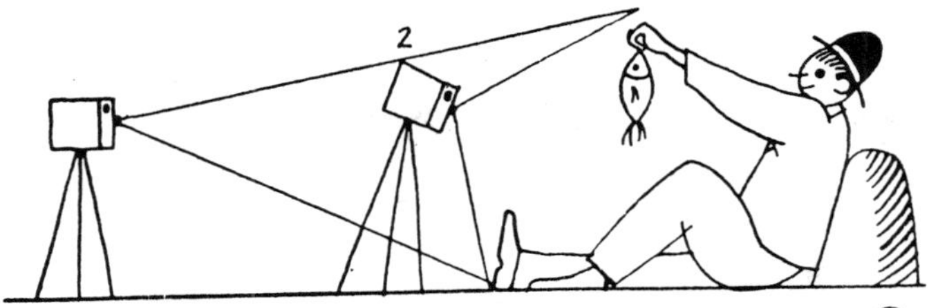

1

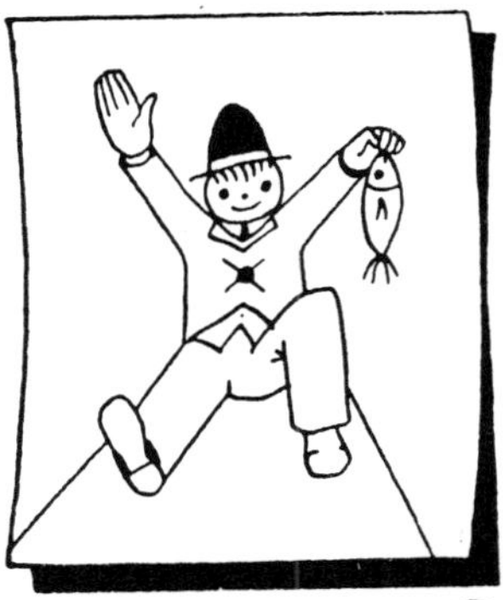

2

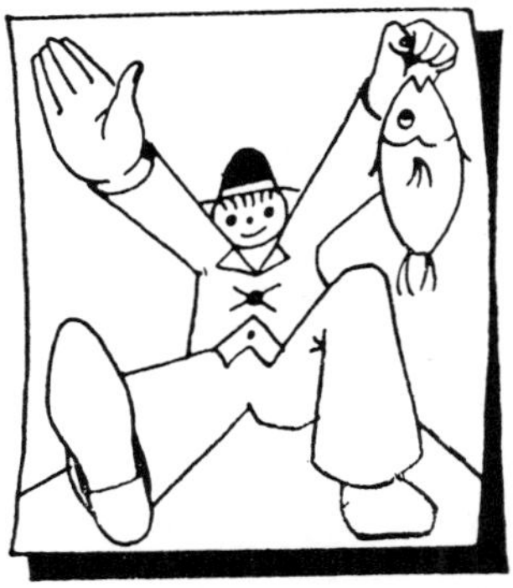

3

WIDE-ANGLE LENS

A lazy fisherman displays his diminutive catch, and a cunning camera does its tricks.

In drawing *1*, two camera positions are shown—the first adopted by a camera with lens of normal focal length and angle of view, the second by a camera with lens of short focal length and consequent wide angle.

The perspective effect of the first is shown in drawing *2*—a result of normal proportion; the effect of the wide-angle lens is shown in drawing *3*—an extreme exaggeration of the nearer parts at the expense of the far, produced by excessive nearness of view.

The effect of a wide-angle lens used from the further camera position would be a fisherman of normal proportions as on drawing *2*, but on a very much smaller scale.

normal sight. The use of one eye can induce effects of exaggerated perspective that are common even to the lens of normal angle, and which are often quite disturbing, but a wide-angle lens, bringing on to the flat plane of a photograph, for examination by clear and concentrated vision, an angle of view embracing some 75° to 100° produces effects far outside the range of human optical powers.

Such lenses are commonly adopted for work in restricted conditions, which leave no room for choice, and where precautions can be taken to reduce the inevitable distortion to a minimum, but the intention to exploit their powers to the full produces effects of fantastic distortion.

The camera whose lens is interchangeable—the 35 mm. and larger technical cameras among others—can substitute a *lens of short focal length* for the normal objective. A few whose lens is technically a fixture can sometimes be doctored to include a wider angle if the lens and shutter component is unscrewed and another, of shorter focal length, substituted from a smaller camera.

Failing these, it is cheap and simple to obtain a *supplementary lens* or extension tubes that will increase the range of the lens some several degrees, without interfering in any way with exposure times.

Equipped with any of these the camera is set up—usually on a tripod or firm support—before a subject, or series of objects, that offer scope for effects of exaggeration. The principle is one of *concentrating in the immediate foreground objects which are small,* or relatively smaller than those further from the camera.

The subject is distributed in several planes, the nearest not more then twelve or eighteen inches from the camera, and the furthest as far as the depth of field will permit—usually some five or six feet. If your subject is on a larger scale, say out of doors, where the furthest plane is infinity, the nearest can be put off as far as three or four feet, or to the limit of the focal depth. On technical cameras the back and lens panel may be adjusted to tilt the plane of focus and, in effect, greatly extend the depth of field.

Such wide distribution of planes necessitates extreme depth of field, and the lens aperture must often be reduced to an absolute minimum. A good principle in this connection is to *focus on a point a little nearer the camera then the mid-point between the extreme plane and stop down* as far as the diaphragm will go.

▷ *Uses of this technique will suggest themselves if you keep in mind that the maximum effects are made by contrasting the extreme enlargement of near objects, or parts of an object, with the extreme diminution of those further away—dwarf the large and enlarge the minute in the same picture.*

Ideas already worked, some of them to the point of imminent expiration, include the recumbent figure with enormous feet, empty hands outstretched and fully spread, or clenched in the form of an enormous punch, hands holding glasses, tennis rackets, a variety of lethal weapons or any other object intended to loom large or have emphasis.

Opportunity can be taken to ingratiate yourself with fisher friends if the outstretched hand holds the latest proud catch, or, even grosser distortion, if the fish is held on the rod with the angler at the extreme end. Unless the light is brilliant it may be difficult to keep exposure short enough to stop probable movement, and a solution is to suspend the small fry from some point outside the camera's range. The string or cotton can be made to coincide, in the camera, with the fishing rod or even with the outstretched hand of the angler—as far in the background as his conscience will allow.

▷ *Any number of distortions can be made in the foreground of an otherwise normal portrait by placing bottles, small glasses, spectacles, musical instruments, flowers and any object that suitably suggests itself.*

Copying

Perspective is basically responsible for yet another photographic distortion. We are tolerably familiar with the optical illustion whereby a flat plane will appear thin and compressed if viewed from the extreme side, or dwarfed and stumpy if seen from below at an acute angle.

You will remember, perhaps, the old-fashioned autograph album trick of fantastically elongated letters that made no sense until the page was held almost level with the eyes; or the practice whereby the warning words to motorists, painted on the road, are stretched out to compensate for the acute angle and speed at which they are viewed.

This phenomena of compression is observable, to some degree, in the solid, and is part of the power of the wide-angle lens, but extreme effects can only be seen when the image is in one flat plane.

If a flat image—a painting, drawing or photographic print—is viewed with one eye from either side, from top or bottom, the image will appear compressed in that direction, the nearer the eye, and the more acute the angle of vision, the greater the compression. Replace the eye with the single lens of the camera and the effect can be recorded photographically in the normal manner.

Though any pictorial image can be distorted by copying, the maximum disturbance is obtained by so recording another straight photograph. The print to be used should be made with *as much detail and contrast as possible,* be black and white, and preferably glazed. These conditions, though not vital, will give most success.

The size of such a print will depend upon the lens extension of your camera, whether it can copy size for size, or is limited to a certain maximum distance. With careful technique it will be possible to get a very small image so sharp, and of so fine a grain, that greater enlargement will be possible, but, whatever your equipment, a print no *smaller than 10 in. x 8 in. (18 cm. x 24 cm.) is to be preferred.*

The top and bottom of any frame or bounding lines will be shown in steep perspective and, unless they are subsequently trimmed, will destroy the intended illusion by giving a clue to its production. When making a print for such copying, therefore, it is advisable to *leave as much space above and below the object as possible*, any trimming will then leave the central image untouched.

The effects cannot be made clearer by wordy description, the range will be apparent once you have begun, but mention of extra subtleties and refinements will not be out of place.

By bending the print vertically down the middle and folding the sides back away from the camera a swelling effect on one axis is produced. To lessen the risk of cracking the print with an actual crease, it will be best to *bend it round a block of wood,* or a similar right-angled substitute, that has a slightly rounded corner, pinning the ends temporarily in position.

This procedure gives a thin effect, a fat one can be obtained by bending the print horizontally across the middle. Once begin bending and a whole range of new effects come into being, one corner bent towards or away from the camera has as effect all its own, hills and valleys contrived by buckling and pinning has another, the possibilities are manifold.

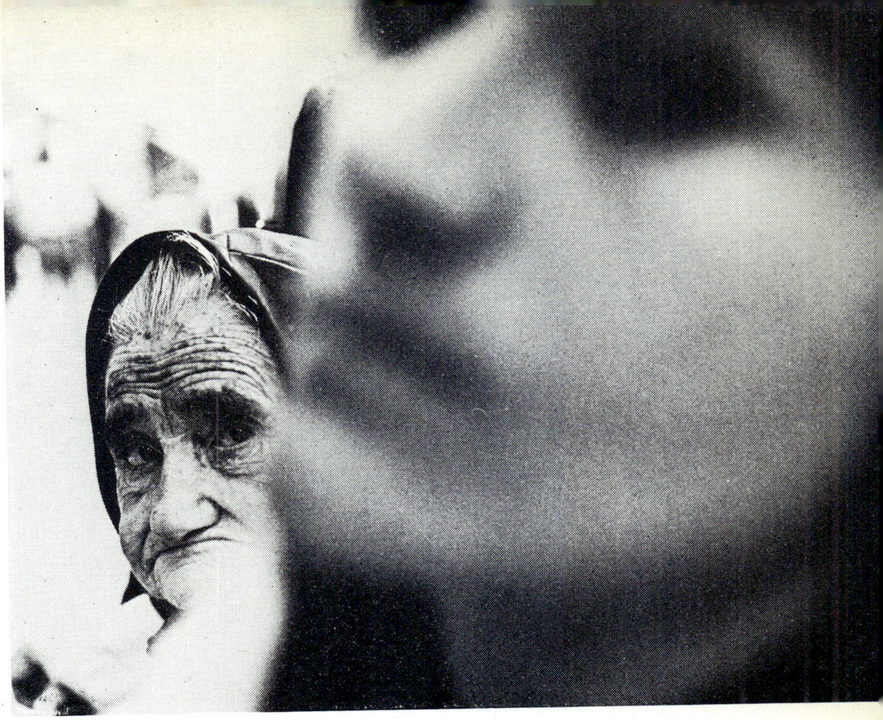

DISTORTION TRICKS

Above: Relative sizes can be played about with by placing subjects at different distances, where selective focus can give sharpness differentials that we do not consciously see in real life.—*Ilan Rosenburg, Harrow School of Photography.*

Below: Wide angle pictures grossly exaggerating near parts at the expense of far when used very close to the subject.—*Edwin Smith, Kodak.*

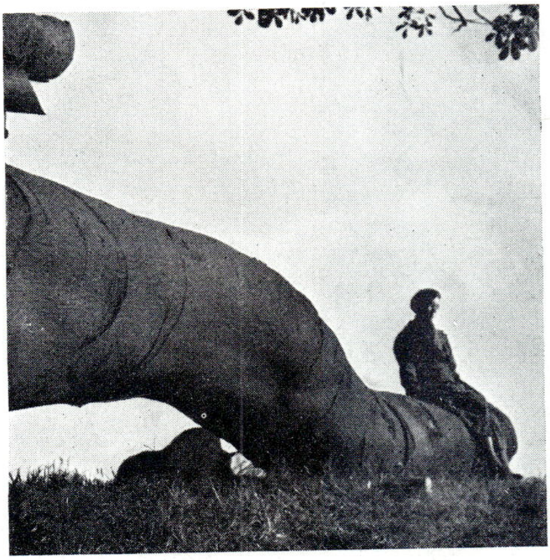

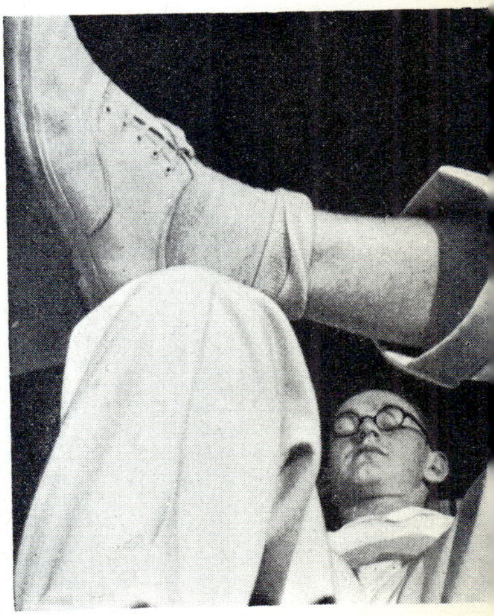

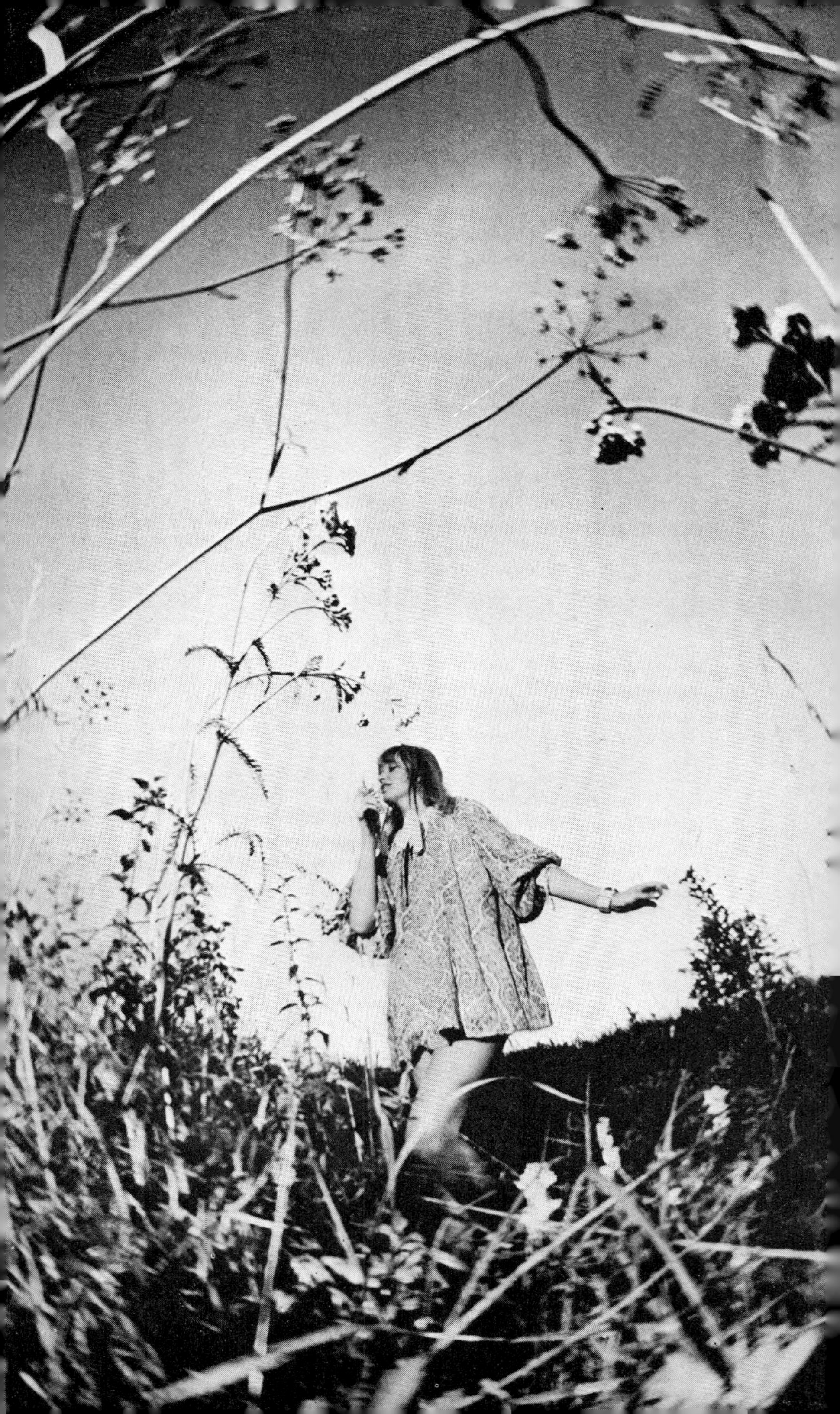

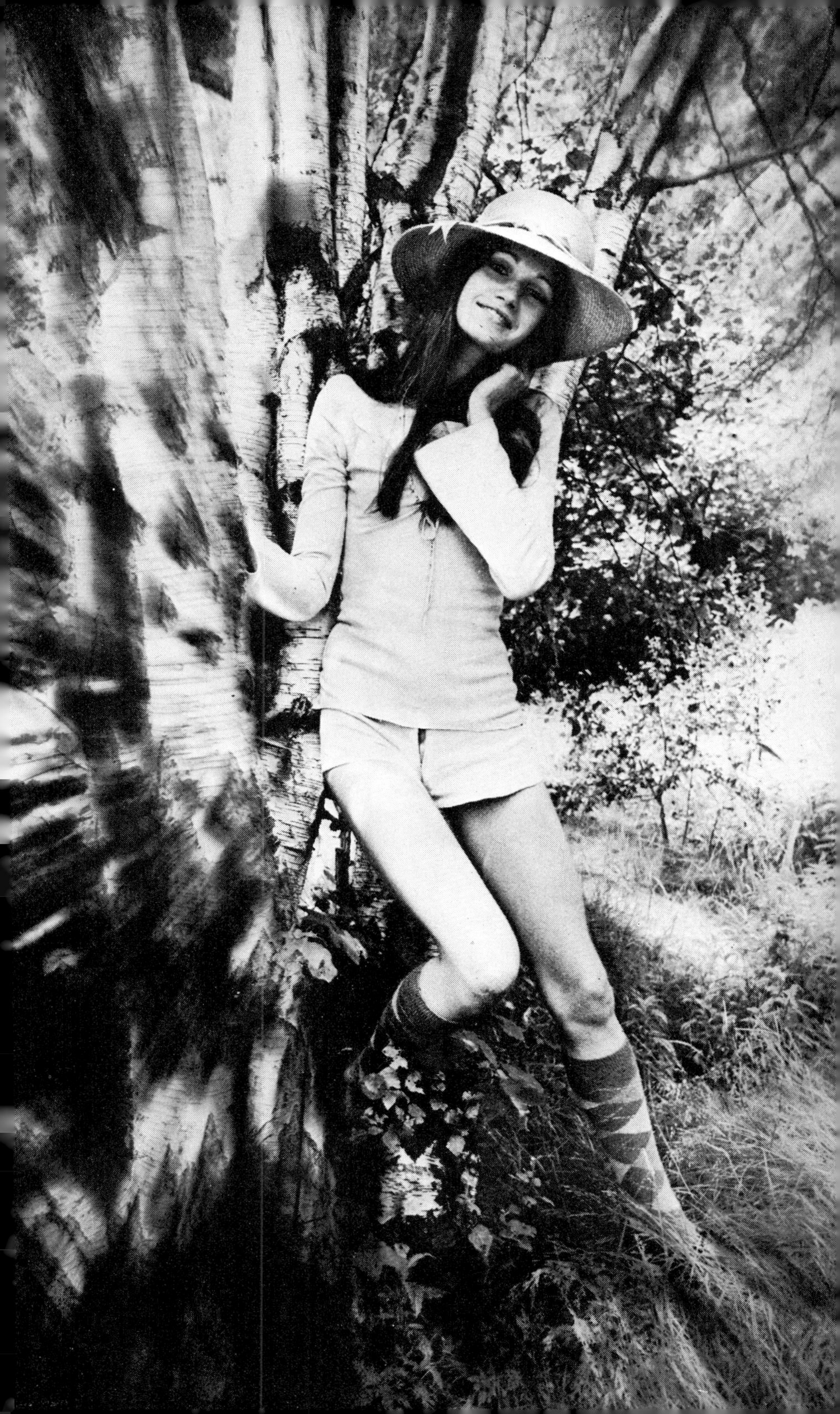

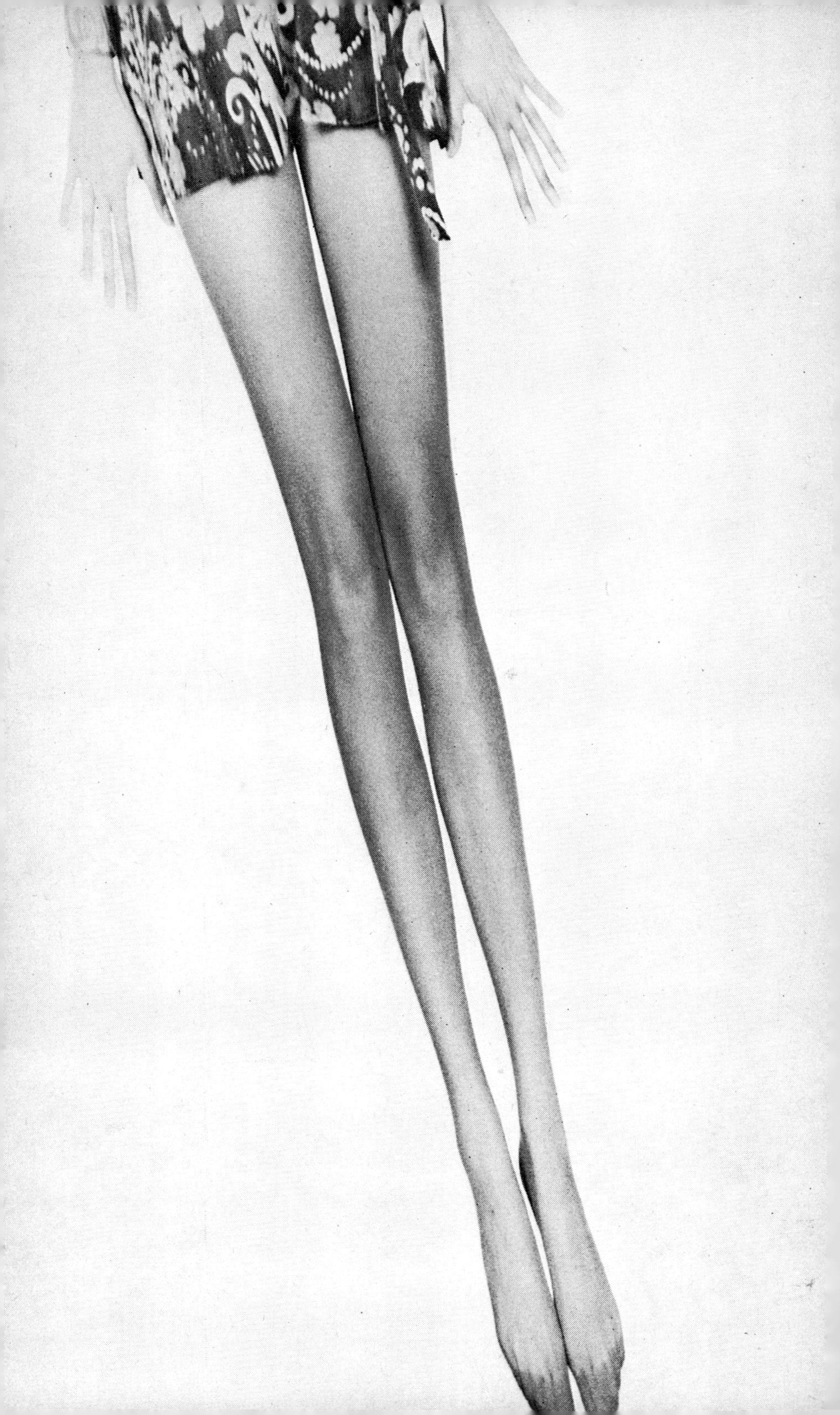

Page 50: Special distorting mirrors and lenses offer their own distinctive effects which are only worthwhile however, if the actual subject matter selected takes advantage of those properties.—*Michael Barrington-Martin.*

Page 51: This convergent blur can be achieved at the shooting or printing stages but usually the distortion is most effective if the central subject retains a "straight" treatment which, in enlarging, can be done by masking.—*H. Witts.*

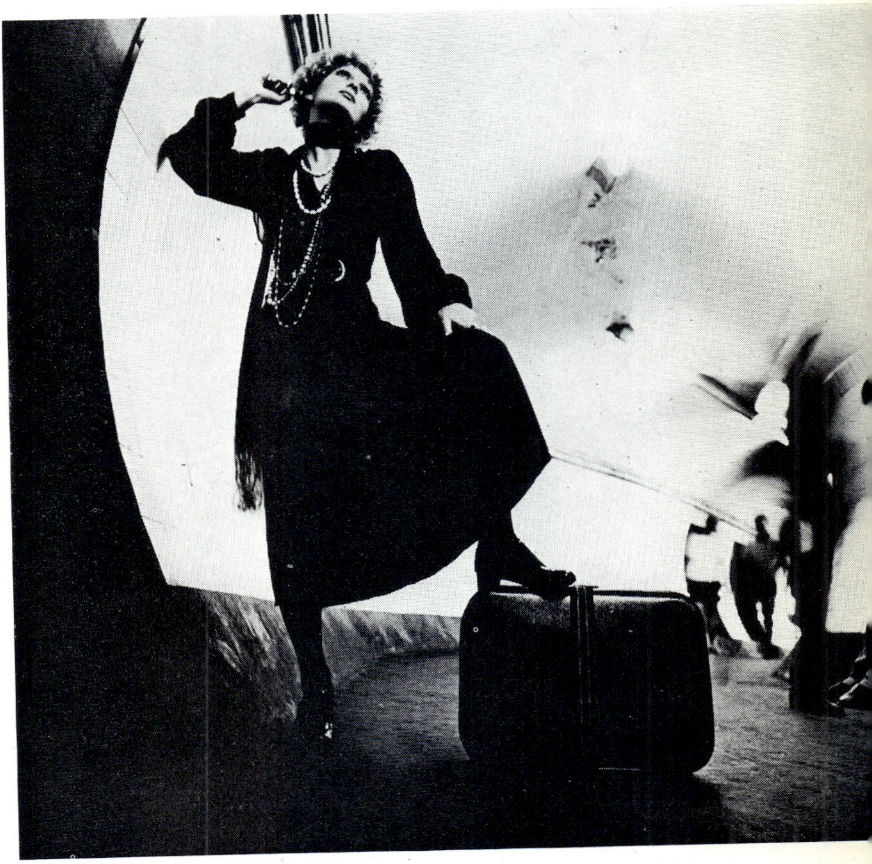

Left: Elongation is possible by shooting a subject through a distorting glass or by lining up a reflected image seen in a distorting mirror such as a bent metallic glazing sheet with a highly polished surface.—*Michael Barrington-Martin.*

Above: Apparent distortion by using a wide angle lens in an unusual environment. The curvature is of course in the subject not the camera.—*John Thornton.*

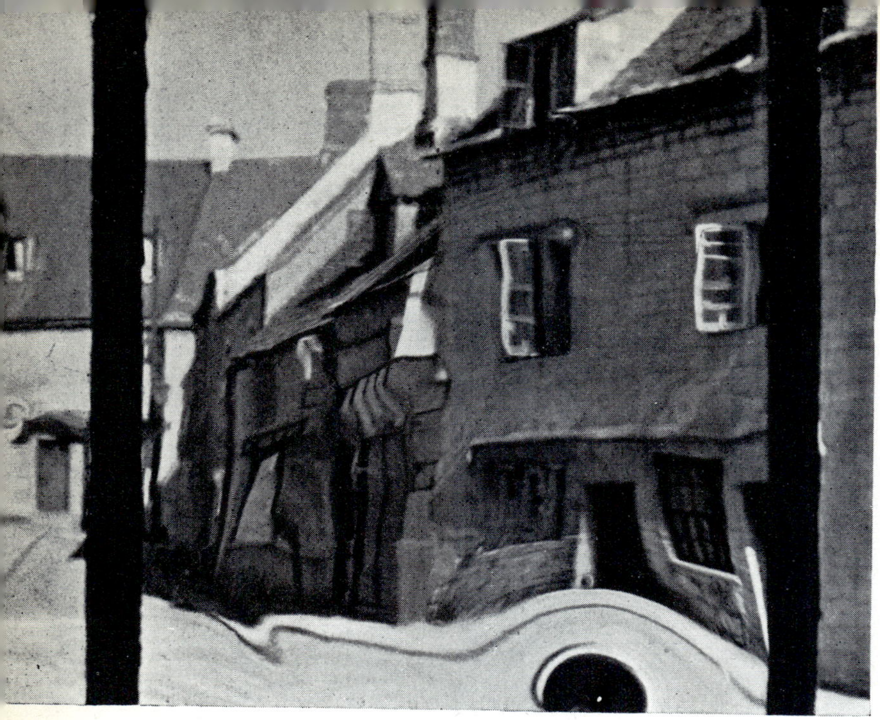

Above: This naturally-produced distortion was seen through an old casement, probably the village inn, whose glass was twisted in the familiar antique bull's-eye fashion. It was only necessary to direct the camera gaze—the glass did all the rest.—*Hugo van Wadenoyen.*

Opposite: Top left shows how a backlit subject becomes a textured silhouette when seen through a reinforced glass door. *Top right* shows the intriguing diminishing effect of a large negative lens held before the face. *Bottom left* can be obtained by copying a straight print with base curled up near to camera, or enlarging on to printing paper with bottom edge bent down away from enlarger. *Bottom right* shows the reflection in a chromium glazing plate dented in the middle.—*Jonathan Holtom, Kerstrin Bernhard, Kollar, Edwin Smith.*

Page 56: Top: Beneath the enlarger a flat printing paper gives a normal print. By humping the paper across the middle so that the middle of the beast occurs upon a hill, the head and tail in a valley either side, the printing paper yields the stretched distortion seen below.—*H. Gorny.*
Bottom left and right: Other distortions are possible by bending the paper irregularly or horizontally.—*Unknown photographer, Weegee.*

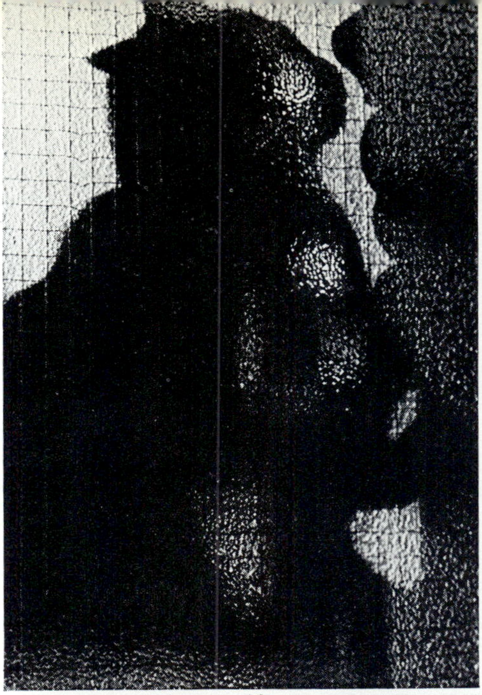
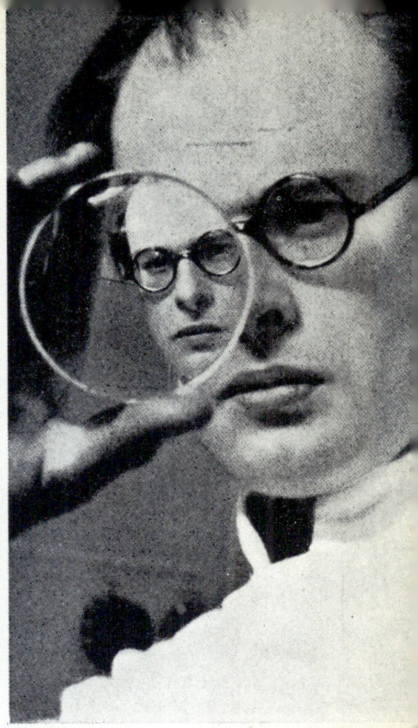
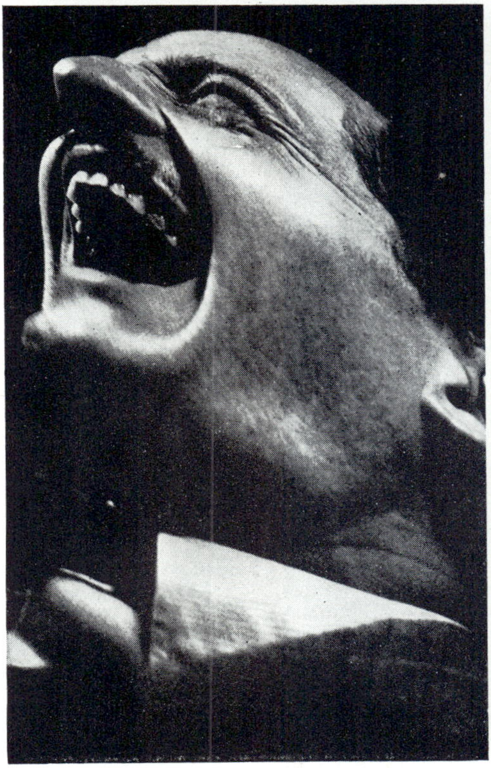
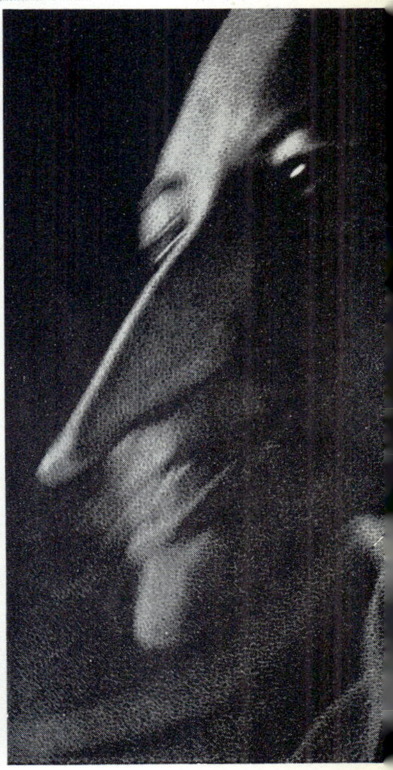

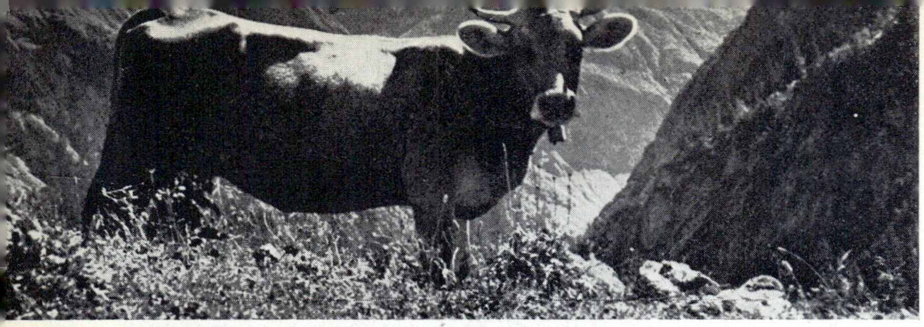

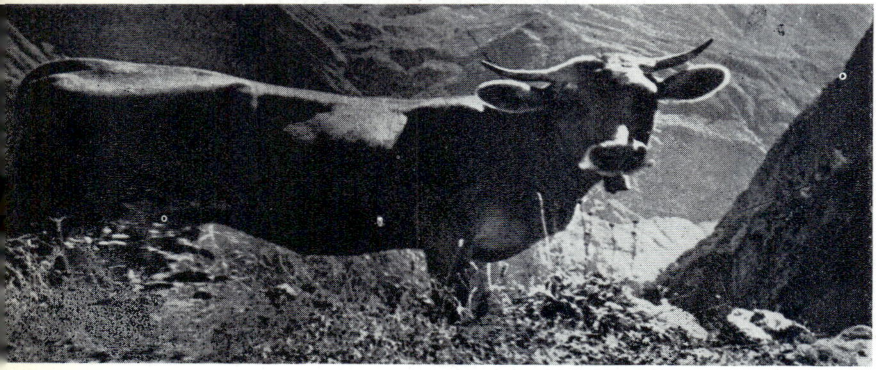

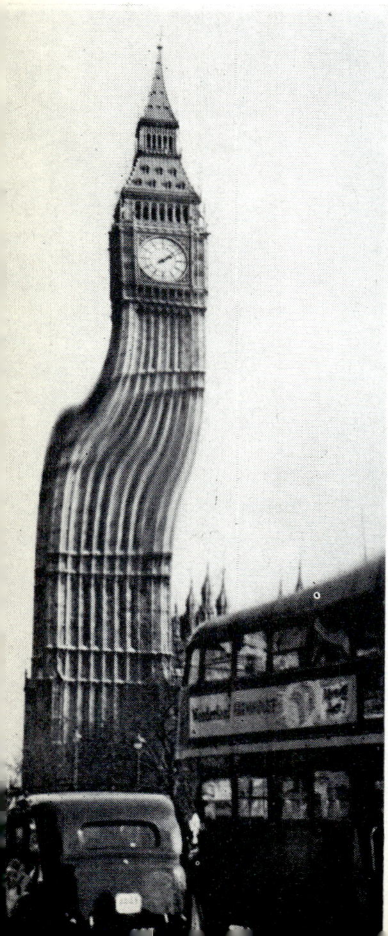

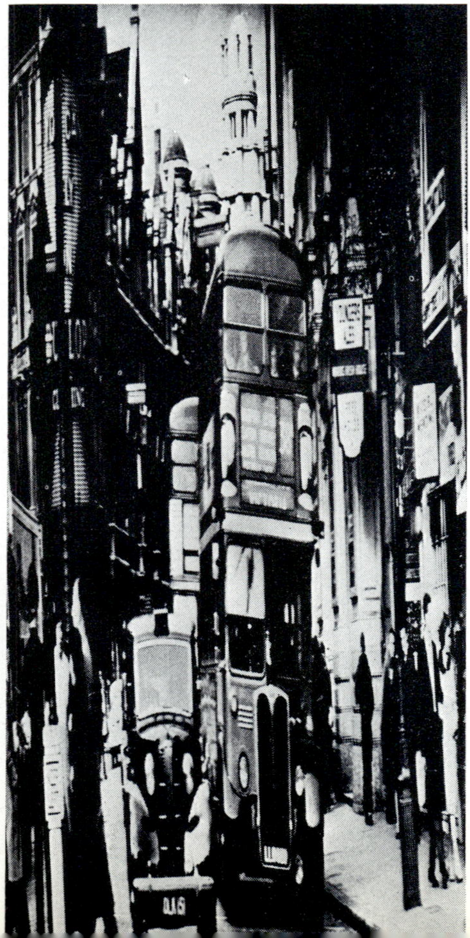

It must be remembered that as any form of tilting, bending, buckling or what-not, implies a *depth of field* to cover the *two extreme planes, the lens must therefore be stopped down.*

▷ *Uses made of this technique, as can be well imagined, have fastened on the portrait—full length and close-up. All subjects are suitable, however, if you are in the distorting mood, except, perhaps, those that show a great number of parallel lines in the direction of the proposed distortion. These, by diminishing in obedience to the laws of perspective, will often reveal the nature of the trick and spoil the intended illusion.*

▷ *The technique is comic in its results and implications, but has practical uses. Emphasising certain natural characteristics at the expense of others it can be used in fashion photography to exaggerate an effect of elongated elegance, or again to correct the excessively converging vertical lines of a building where, owing to restricting conditions, the camera had to be tilted at the time of original exposure.*

Shadows

On the same principal by which a distorted image is produced from an inclined plane, an elongated and distorted shadow is obtained if the surface on which it is cast is not trully parallel to the casting object. Thus the long shadows thrown by the morning or evening sun, and the swollen variety cast upon side walls by the headlights of passing cars, are two examples commonly observed.

Since they show no detail, fantastic shadows are perhaps the least effective of all distorting methods, but, given the lingering popularity of the silhouette it seems at least worthwhile to record a means by which its rather staid effects may be distorted.

The actual production of the shadows is very simple and need not be described; a few moments' practice with a portable lamp and a plain wall will reveal the utmost possibility, and it is immediately obvious how to place the model in relation to the surface to create a desired effect.

For maximum success the shadows must be sharply defined with no double edges, or penumbra, to diffuse the contrast. The sun casts such concentrated shadows but is rarely available at the moment, and in the position, you require indoors.

Electrically speaking, a pearl or opal bulb or any bulb in an obscured glass fitting will give a diffused light without strong contrast between light and shade; for the present purpose, therefore, such lighting is unsuitable.

If you do not have a spotlight, domestic or photographic—which gives a fine sharp shadow, a normal domestic bulb of the "clear" variety is the best you can do, and will give a reasonably hard shadow on a light surface.

If your subject is quite immobile, and the room free from draughts, a *candle is the ideal light source for the fantastic shadow*; it gives absolutely no penumbra and is a reward for your patience.

The shadows cast by a low sun on the road, or any horizontal surface, are excellent materials, particularly if they are observed from a high viewpoint. Seen from above, so that the ground and the camera back are almost parallel, low sun shadows are the best of their kind, and one has only to observe the exaggerated shadows of passers-by, a horse and cart, or better still a bicycle, to see the pictorial possibility.

Whichever way round it may have been taken, a shadow photograph should, of course, always be presented to view as if it was the object itself, or a straight silhouetted view of it.

Backgrounds need not always be plain. The street surface for example, will offer a variety of texture that should not be neglected. Indoors there is no objection whatever to a patterned or textured ground, so long as the effect is light in tone and does not obscure the contrasty boldness of your shadow.

If necessary, contrast can be improved by the use of a slower film than normal, or by *slight under-exposure and prolonged development* of a normal material but these refinements need only be employed if the original contrasts were particularly poor.

Except focusing, technical skill is unnecessary. It is only desirable to create a *depth of field*, if the shadows are taken at an angle, and not with the camera back parallel to the shadowed surface.

▷ *The uses of shadow distortions are simple and few, and such pictures must be their own justification. Faces, figures and any object of exotic or interesting shape are good material and may be themselves included in the picture or used solely to create the effect.*

▷ *Combinations of actual and artificial features give opportunities for strange effects, disembodied heads and the like being made from bowler-hatted footballs or more simply cut from*

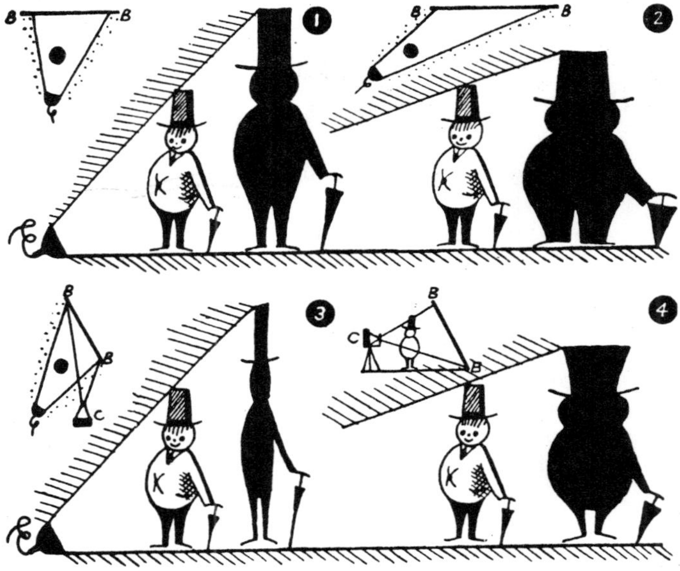

DISTORTED SHADOWS

The position of the lamp, and the angle of the camera to the surface, conditions the shape of the shadow.

In *1*, a low light gives a tall shadow. In *2*, shining obliquely at an acute angle, the low light gives a fat shadow.

On to a surface tilted at an angle away from the camera, the low light gives a very thin result, as *3*. By tilting the background towards the camera, the low oblique light gives a fat shadow in which the head is larger than the feet, as *4*.

cardboard. Small scenes may be cut from stiff paper, or small objects erected on the table top, and their shadows can be cast on an inclined backcloth, or on the table itself so that the camera sees them from above.

Enlarging

The method of distorting by copying an inclined plane—be it another photograph or a shadow, or a bent and buckled surface, can be often simply carried out in the darkroom when making the original print, and without an intermediate copying process.

Enlarging is a process that is rich in strange effects and tricks, of which distortion is not the least effective.

The enlarger, like a back to front camera, instead of recording an image projects one, so that if a loaded enlarger is substituted for the camera, and a sheet of printing paper for the copied photograph or shadowed surface in methods described on pages 48 and 57, the effect will be a direct distortion of a very similar kind.

That is, instead of copying a bent and buckled image with the camera, one projects a normal image on to a buckled or bent sheet of printing paper with the enlarger.

Starting simply, we tilt the frame that holds the paper, or the board on which it is pinned, at an angle; this has the effect of elongating the image in the direction of the tilt—the steeper the angle the longer the stretch.

Thus, if the tilt is made along the length of a vertical negative the image is lengthened, and if across the breadth of a horizontal one the image is widened. These are points to remember, since it is a reversal of the condition obtaining in the method described on page 48. Where, when copying a print the paper was tilted sideways to elongate and longways to compress a vertical image.

Another reversal worth noting is that the enlarged image is larger at the bottom of the incline that at the top; that is, the nearer the enlarger the smaller the image, whereas the nearer the camera the larger in the copying method.

Again, it will be noticed that a *convex effect is obtained on a concave sheet of paper* (large nose, small chin and brow) beneath the enlarger, and a *concave image on a paper that is bent to a convex shape.*

This point, and many others, will be a matter of common observation in the darkroom, but it will help to remember that the *enlarger is literally an inside-out camera* and reverses its effects.

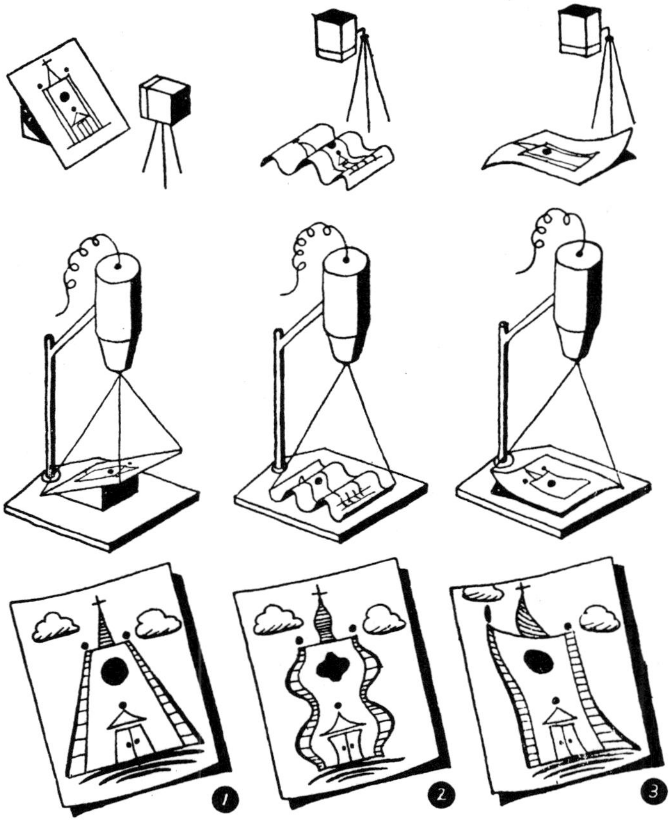

DISTORTION: COPYING AND PROJECTING

Two opposite means of obtaining a similar result.

In column *1* the normal image of a tower is distorted, by copying and projection through the enlarger, so that the base is larger than the top. Before the camera the print must be arranged so that the base is nearest the camera, but through the enlarger the base must be at the bottom of the incline—or furthest from the enlarger.

Similarly, results *2* and *3* are obtained by opposing tactics—print *2* being produced by copying a print buckled into three hills and two valleys, or projecting on to two hills and three valleys. The reversed curves of *3* are obvious.

By bending and curving the printing paper in the manners described in the method on page 48, the effects of the distorting mirror are easily equalled and often excelled. Bending in the middle, or curving either way, raising or depressing one corner, or alternate corners, are all means of obtaining results that are easier to see than describe.

The rippling distortions of the comic mirrors, in which the image is alternately thick and thin, are obtained by *buckling the paper into hills and valleys* and pinning it into place. The image will be thin on the hill top and fat in the valley; the higher the hills the greater the effect.

As soon as the printing paper is moved out of a flat plane focusing becomes a problem. The solution is achieved by *focusing on a point a little nearer to the enlarger than midway down the incline* and *stopping down the lens* to its limit.

With curved paper, and hills and valleys, it is best to focus on a flat plane at the point mentioned above, which can be done by placing a piece of paper like a bridge between the curves, and focusing with the aid of an orange cap on the enlarger lens to prevent fogging the paper. The lens is then stopped down to obtain a depth of focus sufficient to cover the extreme planes.

Since the *paper nearest the enlarger receives a more intense light than the paper further away*, means must be adopted to equalise matters by exposing the further parts longer than the nearer.

This is best achieved by *shading and spot printing*, two dodges with which most will be familiar. Both are means of intercepting the light between lens and printing paper so as to hold back light from the nearer, and prolong the exposure for the further, parts of the image.

Shading can be done with the hand bent to various shapes to fit the image on the paper—the nearer the hand to the paper the smaller and sharper its shadow. It is, properly speaking, a device for keeping light off.

'Spot printing' or 'burning in' however, is a method of letting through small enclosed spots of light to the portions of the picture that require a much longer exposure than the rest of the image; it can be done through appropriately cut holes in black sheets of paper, or by the cupped hands arranged to let a particularly shaped spot of light through them.

Shading with the hands is the best possible way to even out the light intensities on an inclined sheet of paper, moving the

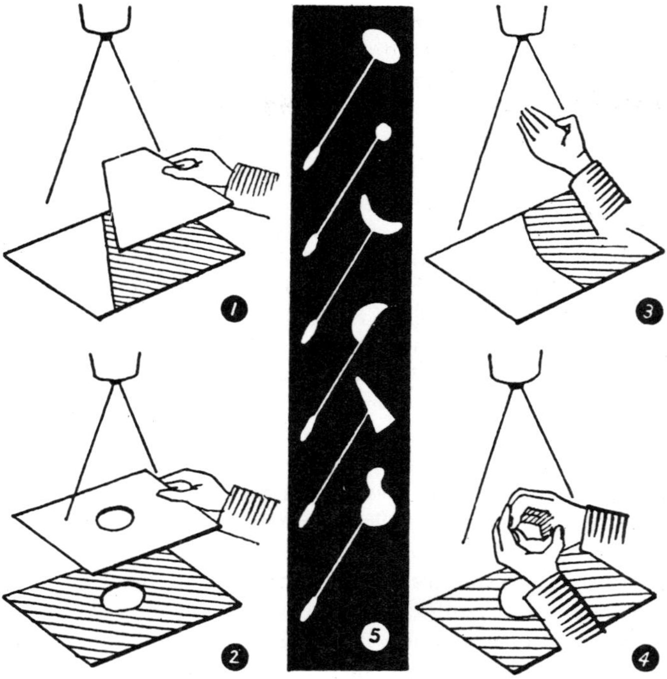

SHADING AND SPOT PRINTING

Drawings *1* and *3* show alternative methods of shading during enlargement—by a cut mask or with the hand. Drawings *2* and *4* are alternative means of spot printing—through a hole cut in a mask or made by the cupped hands.

The black panel *5* shows a number of small useful masking shapes arranged on the ends of pieces of thin wire. These can be used to shade, or hold back light from, any small isolated patches that could not otherwise be easily screened.

hand to and fro beneath the light beam, starting above the top of the slope and gradually obscuring more and more of the paper until the bottom is reached. The total time taken is a matter that depends on several things: the density of the image, the steepness of the slope, the amount of enlargement and the aperture of the lens; it will therefore be a matter for experiment and experience.

Shading will also help to even exposure for some types of curving and bending, but hills and valleys need very careful spot printing. Here it is not so much a question of difference between the highest hill and deepest valley, which is often negligible, but the very low intensity of light received by the sides of the slopes, the steeper they are the less light they will receive.

Unless these hillsides are given prolonged exposure the effect on the finished print will be a series of light streaks occuring wherever the paper was buckled.

A long slit can be formed by the two hands, or cut in a mask of black paper, and kept slightly rotating—about a quarter of an inch in each direction—above each hillside in turn, after the general image has received its full exposure.

Because of this difficulty of absolutely blending the tones of the various slopes, hill and valley distortions and any very exotic curves and bends, are best made on a *matt surface paper.* This makes it possible to adjust inevitable differences of tone by treating them with graphite from a very soft carbon pencil, or retouching crayon, rubbing the pigment in until it blends.

A copy negative is then made of the final result. Indeed, it will be found generally advisable to *recopy* on a new negative any masterpiece that you may achieve by the more complicated bending and buckling methods, it being next to impossible to repeat these effects twice running.

▷ *The uses of enlarging distortion include the more or less serious as well as the customary comic. We can, for instance, undistort a negative that shows distortions of an unintentional kind, and that could not be avoided at the time of exposure.*

High towers and buildings, for which the camera had to be tilted when shooting, will often show converging vertical lines which are not stressed enough to seem intentional but look plainly unpleasant.

If the printing paper is tilted in the opposite direction to this convergence—so that the top widens out at the bottom of the

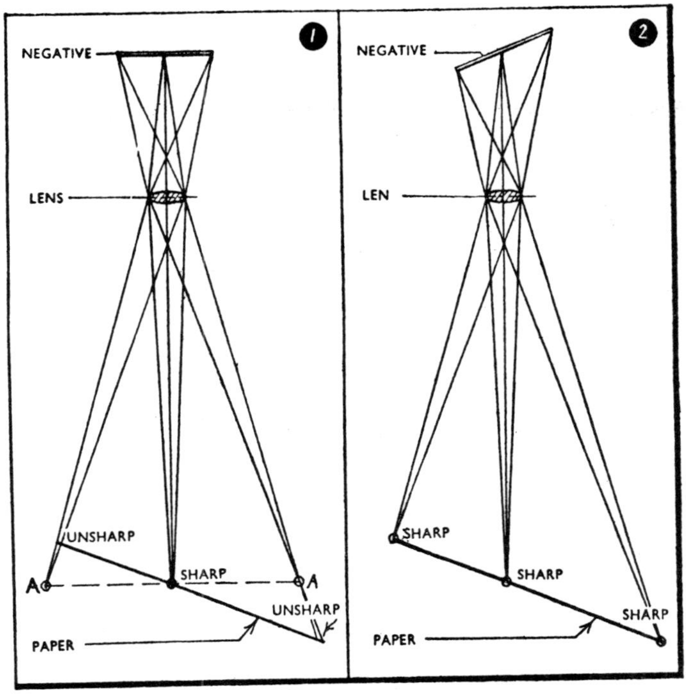

TILTING PAPER AND NEGATIVE CARRIER

The image of a negative in drawing *1* is projected on to a plane of sharp focus *A–A*. If the paper easel is tilted, to produce any effect of distortion, only the centre of its image in the plane of focus will be sharp. To produce an evenly-sharp result the lens must be considerably stopped down and the exposure consequently increased.

By giving a sympathetic tilt to the negative carrier–in the opposite direction–the plane of focus is conveniently adjusted to that of the paper, and less stopping down or increase of exposure will be necessary.

incline, and the bottom narrows down at the top, the effect will be cancelled out and the verticals become parallel.

▷ *It will be found an additional help to tilt the negative carrier in the opposite direction to the paper. This helps to reduce the tilt of the paper and defeats the inevitable elongation that tilting involves, and which can, indeed, be a grosser distortion than the original faulty verticals.*

▷ *Paper tilting can be most effective, and almost impossible to detect, if it is kept within reasonable bounds. By such means elongations of the figure and other strange distended effects with many other subjects are obtained. With the human form it is advisable to keep the head at the top, or small end, of the slope—it appears definitely top-heavy when occurring at the other.*

▷ *In a similar manner, natural characteristics of the face can be emphasised in the cause of flattery. If the paper is slightly tilted up towards the chin, the brow becomes bloated in the intellectual manner, whereas the reverse gives to the jaw an effect definitely pleasing to the pugnacious. Most convenient, you must admit, to possess such powers by mere tilting; restraint, however, is an essential part of success.*

▷ *The comic uses of enlarging distortion differ in no wise from those of the other method, and most all can be duplicated by twisting and turning the paper in one direction or the other.*

The enlarger can be used to further distort an already odd negative, and so carry the joke to its utmost limit. It is possible, thus, to make the original photograph with a wide-angle lens, or with a normal lens in such a way that the near planes are unduly emphasised, to make a distorted copy of a print from this negative in the appropriate direction, and finally to enlarge this distorted distortion on to an inclined or bent sheet of printing paper.

Masking and Moving

The enlarger can be responsible for yet another variety of distortion based, not upon the possibilities of bending and tilting the printing paper, but upon masking and moving the paper during the exposure of a single negative.

By masking parts of the printing paper during an exposure and subsequently shifting the negative or the paper holder before completing the exposure, a series of distortions can be produced in which an image is compressed or elongated to any desired extent.

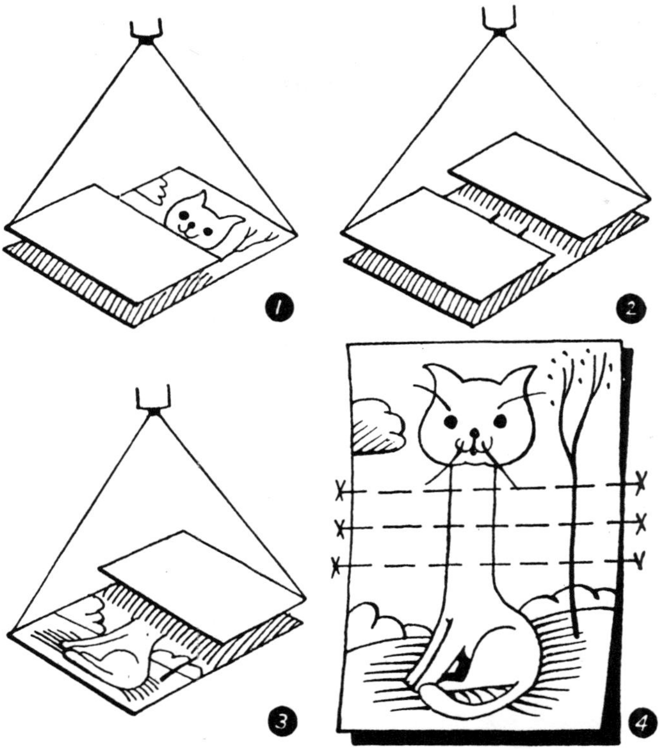

MASKING AND MOVING

1. The printing paper beneath the enlarger is masked so that only head and neck record. *2.* The paper is moved and a second mask employed so that only the neck unit records, this process being repeated as often as desired—moving the paper each time. *3.* For the last exposure one mask is used to obscure all parts of the paper previously exposed, revealing only the last unit of neck and body attached. *4.* shows the result with the neck unit repeated twice.

An essential for the success of this method is a master sheet of paper on which can be marked the principal outlines of the projected image. A spoilt but undeveloped sheet of printing paper of identical size and thickness to the paper intended for actual exposure is ideal.

The chosen negative is placed in the enlarger and projected, in the customary manner, on to the sheet of paper used as the key or register. On this paper is accurately *marked the outline or other distinct features of the projected image* . . . suppose that the negative shows a close portrait, of which we wish to elongate the neck, the key will be marked with the outlines of the head and shoulders, and a very accurate indication—by two lines—of the neck's position.

The effect of extension is achieved by repeating that portion of the negative which shows the neck, the paper holder or the negative carrier being moved after each exposure so that one neck begins where the other left off—accurate joining being made possible by the use of the key to register each successive image.

It is obvious that unless parts of the image are masked in some way, not only the neck, but all other features of the face will be repeated after each movement. This is avoided by the use of *masks of black card or stiff paper arranged so that they lie about a quarter of an inch above the paper's surface*, and supported on two rulers laid across two thin books or some similar device.

These masks are so adjusted that one only is used to obscure the shoulders—below the neck—for the first exposure, and thereafter the two are used to make a slit allowing passage only to the image of the neck, and its background, across the width of the negative.

For each extra exposure of the neck, the paper holder or the negative carrier and the two masks are adjusted, with the aid of the key, so that the bottom of the last neck fits exactly on to the top of the next.

For the last exposure, when it is considered that the extension is sufficient, the end mask is removed so that the shoulders can print with the last exposure of neck.

The *successive positions of the slit formed by the masks must be marked* on the key, or on the margin of the actual print. Their accurate alignment is essential for the complete success of the method, and a *red or orange cap to place over the enlarger lens* is invaluable in this connection, since it will enable one to adjust the actual sensitive paper beneath the masks without the risk of fogging.

The method will certainly be less complex in practice than it sounds, perhaps, in theory. Think of it as a means whereby a chosen strip of the negative can be repeated indefinitely—without fogging the portion already, or the portion to be subsequently, printed and the purpose of each operation will be apparent.

The same technique can be used to produce an effect of distorted compression if a portion of the negative, instead of being repeated, is omitted altogether and the two cut ends made to join.

To prolong our previous example. An exposure is made of the top half of the portrait by masking the neck and shoulders, and an exposure joined to it of the bottom half by masking the neck and head, by this means the neck is omitted and the head made to sit directly on the shoulders.

The images are correctly aligned in the same manner as before, by marking the vital points on a key sheet of paper and shifting the negative or the paper into the required position.

In both methods accuracy of masking and marking are most necessary for successful results, *exposures also must be accurately timed*, and repeated for each extra exposure, or the printing tone of some of the strips will inevitably vary.

▷ *The example of the elongated or omitted neck suggests the uses of this particular method; many negatives can be so treated with great success. The effects are mostly humorous, yet some have, an air of fantasy, and even rightness, that is very satisfying to the imagination.*

Thus repetitions are on record in which the eyes of a portrait have been repeated two or three times, one above the other, and a particularly fine moustache has been triplicated in the same manner. The effect can be both comic and completely convincing—more real than reality.

▷ *Animals offer splendid opportunities for elongation in a horizontal direction, particularly if the negative shows an extreme side-on view. The distance between fore-legs and hind-legs can be of your own choosing and limited only by the amount of printing paper at your disposal.*

This last point, incidentally, must be kept well in mind when extending any photograph. Decide how much you intend to elongate and make sure that the paper provides ample room to include the end of the subject after the last repeat.

Animals are also ideal material for compression, and the

proximity of tail to nose is only dictated by finding a part of the body of identical depth at each end. It being clear that to make a successful, and more or less invisible, join of any kind the parts must be of similar dimensions or the illusion is a failure.

▷ *A pronounced pattern in background will often join awkwardly when a part is missed out, or stutter obtrusively if the part is repeated: backgrounds should therefore be as neutral and non-committal as possible in negatives that are to be elongated or compressed. An exception is made of backgrounds containing strongly repeating and self-contained units—such as the palings of a fence—where one missed out or a few more repeated would never be noticed.*

Beyond tentative experiments with animal and human forms, little has been accomplished with either of these distorting methods, and both are consequently rich fields for experiment by anyone of resource and imagination.

Melting the Emulsion

If you have ever yielded to the temptation to dry your negatives rapidly over a radiator, or before a fire, your negative album might already contain some excellent distortions. One problem with the melting trick these days however, is that film manufacturers have made modern emulsions so resistant to any nasty happenings that they do not respond so easily to such maltreatment.

Of all distorting methods this is certainly the most drastic, the least under control, and the least predictable. Negatives that are valued or impossible to replace should be duplicated before being submitted to the irrevocable, for, once distorted—or destroyed—in this manner they can never resume their previous shape.

The accidental technique, by which negatives are left to dry over excessively hot radiators, leaves much to be desired. If the heat is intense the swollen emulsion tends to fall off the gelatine in small lumps, and distortion becomes so exaggerated that the image loses all resemblance to reality.

Absolute control is, of course, quite out of the question, but the melting image can be encouraged and guided in certain directions if precautions are taken.

All the *surplus water must be removed* from the chosen negative, with a *viscous sponge or wet chamois leather*, or left to drain in the drying rack until the surface is quite even.

When the emulsion shows a smooth damp surface, unbroken

by any "pimples" of unevaporated water, it is held over a *gentle current of warm air*. This will best be supplied by a *small spirit lamp or a minute gas jet*, or any moderate source of heat.

On melting, the emulsion begins to assume an appearance of liquid glass, and when this is noted the negative is twisted, turned and tilted so that the image begins to flow in more or less the desired direction. It will be noted that the emulsion has a tendency to continue, for a moment, its movement in one direction after the negative has been turned the opposite way. Allowance must therefore be made by *stopping just short of the actual requirement.*

Cooling is rapid, but should not be accelerated by open windows as the danger from dust and grit is extreme. Leave in a horizontal position and when the emulsion is set, replace the negative or plate in the drying rack.

Hard-hearted emulsions, that are obdurate and will not be melted, should be given a *preliminary bath in a solution of dilute ammonia.* This will soften all but the positively flinty and those will always yield to a *bath of caustic potash*. After both treatments the negative should be *washed for fifteen minutes before melting.*

The most successful meltings are achieved with *glass plates* rather than with film, since glass provides a constantly flat and solid surface for the liquid emulsion. Gelatine film tends to curve and buckle under the influence of heat, and if near a naked flame will often literally smoulder with anger. Should there be no choice but to use it, space should be left at each end of the film for attaching wide *film clips*, these give you something to hold and prevent the worst effects of buckling.

Effective distortions, but even less predictable than those obtained by direct melting, can be contrived by *fixing your film in very warm hypo*—say, 90° to 100°F. (32° to 38°C.) instead of the customary 68°F. (20°C.).

This not only melts the emulsion, but frequently creates small pits and craters in odd successions all over its surface. Sudden immersion in cold water heightens this reticulation effect, but, as will be readily imagined, the whole business is an absolute gamble and you stand to lose everything in the hope of getting the truly remarkable.

▷ *Distortions obtained by melting are unique but unforeseeable, the powers that order such things may produce many masterpieces, but they have many "off" moments and accept no responsibility for their many utter failures.*

Because of this, it is only occasionally that the process produces anything superior to the comic, and this is its most common use.

Any negative will serve, but the changes of success are probably highest if the image shows a number of rigidly straight lines in any direction. The distortion of these will be more telling than those in which the shapes are already amorphous.

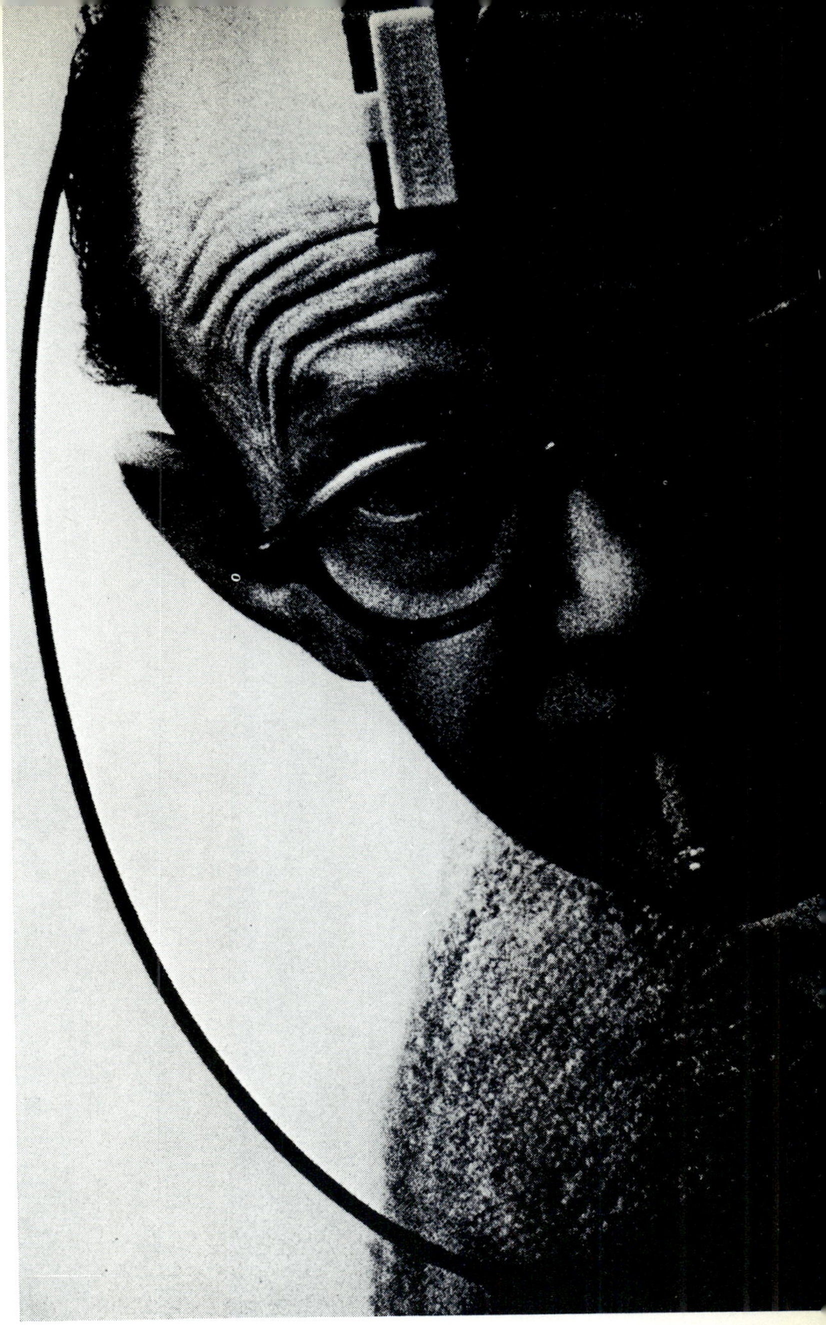

MIRROR TRICKS
Self portrait in a mirror, which, far from trying to hide the camera, even makes a positive virtue of it by including it as an essential part of the composition. The circular line is the cable release.—*Rolf Winqvist.*

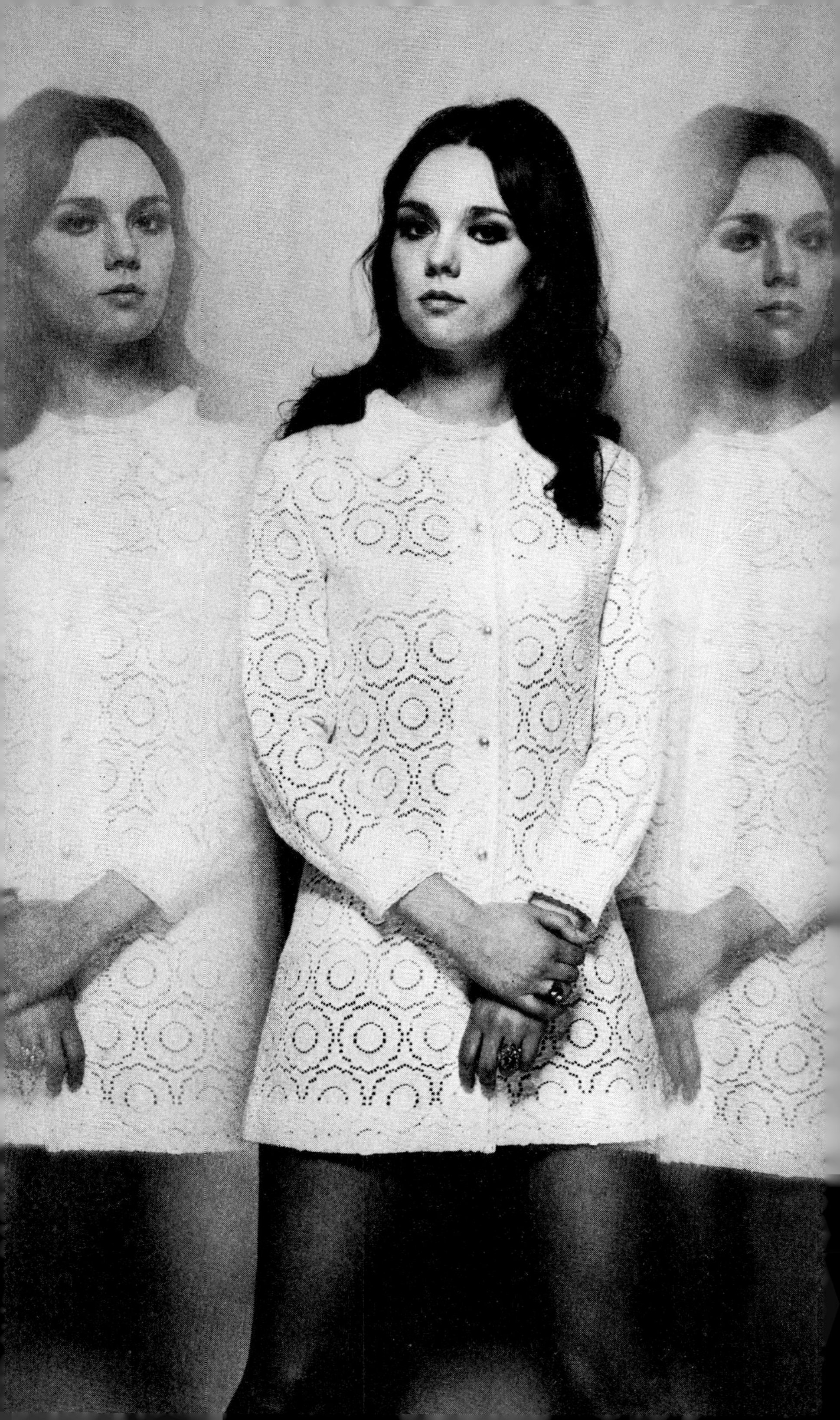

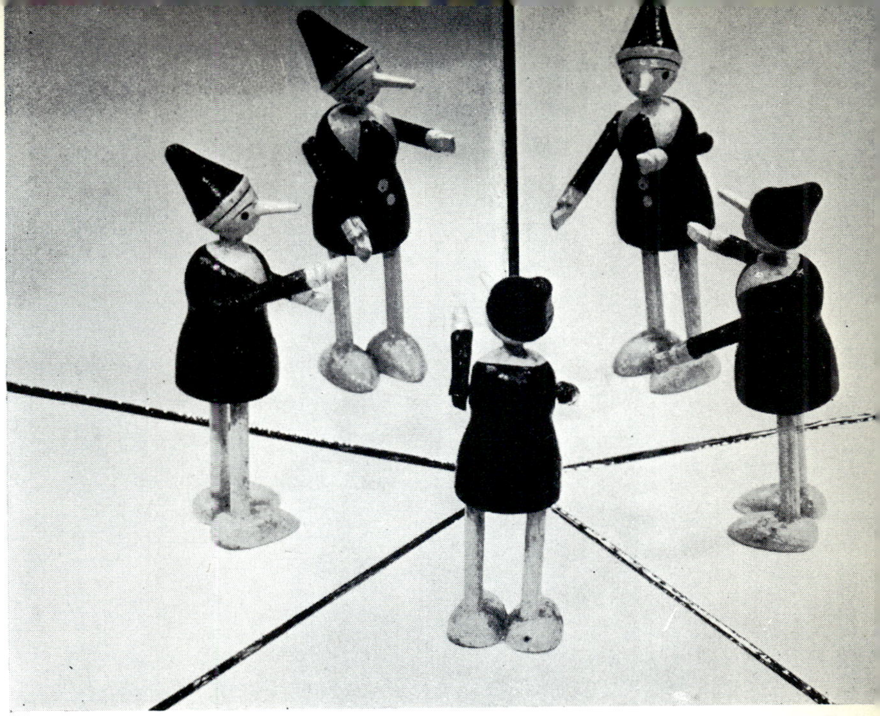

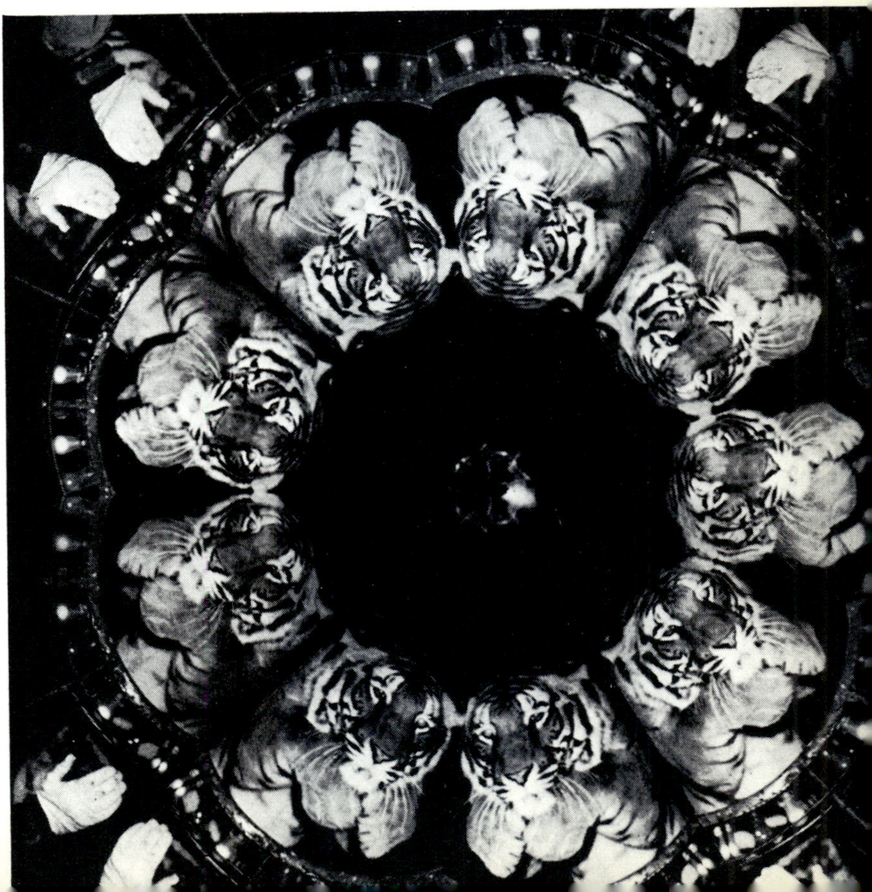

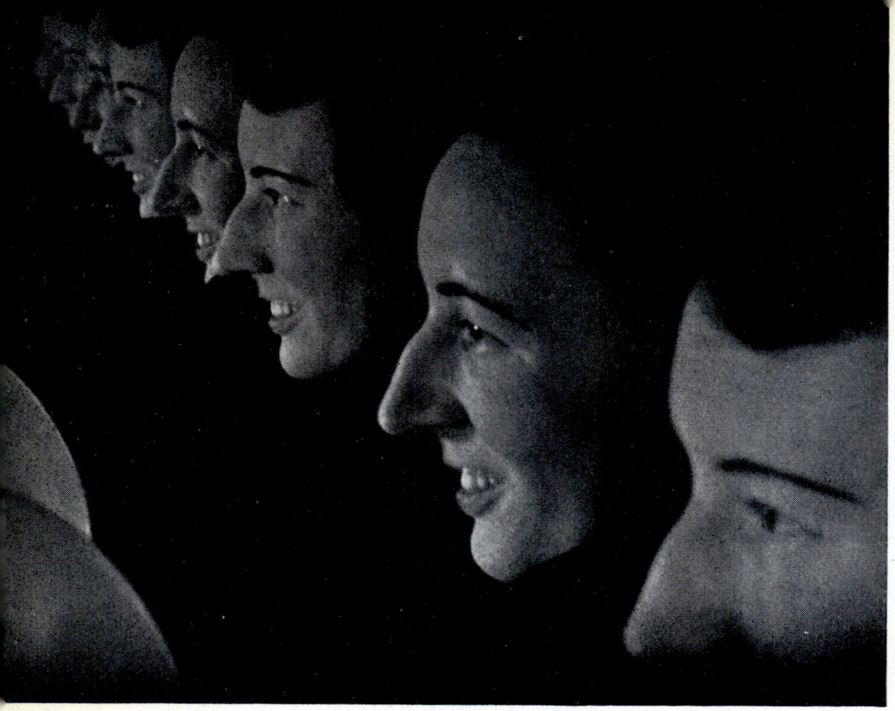

Page 74: Multiple printing with negative placed once the right way round and twice reversed left to right with the reversed images printed diffused.—*Michael Barrington-Martin.*

Page 75: Multiple images, *top* from mirrors placed at right angles behind the subject, and *bottom* from small mirrors in front of the lens.—*W. G. Briggs* and *Weegee.*

Above: A pair of mirrors set parallel; the model sits between, holding an air balloon, the camera peers over the top of one mirror from the side nearest the balloon. The lighting is from the side, between the mirrors. The mirrors are not strictly parallel since the images disappear around a very slow curve. Good depth of focus is needed to get a long range of sharp images—in this case *f*22 on a quarter-plate.—*Edwin Smith.*

MIRRORS

Though few can boast that they have never been deceived by a mirror, or confused its reflections with reality, custom and sophistication have staled our vision and made us generally immune from the illusions of the looking-glass.

But, in common with the young of all species, the camera retains an enviable innocence of vision; like a bird it is blind to the mirror's surface, seeing only a reversed reality lacking no part of colour or substance.

The camera is deceived by a reflection and records it with the same impartiality that it records the world we walk in. Photographs made with the aid of a mirror differ in no wise from those achieved without, and, except for a left to right reversal, offer almost no clue to their reflected origin.

For the common every-day purpose plate-glass mirrors are adequate, but they provoke problems without solution in a few isolated instances. These principally occur when any object of unusual brightness is included in the reflection.

Normal mirrors are, of course, silvered on the back, and thus, any brilliant object such as a window, a bright high-light, or any highly-illuminated surface, is *reflected with a double image*—the anticipated one from the silver surface, and a dimmer, but less desirable one from the front surface of the glass.

This effect is rarely noticed when looking straight into the glass since the two images almost overlap each other, but seen obliquely, which is the normal camera view, they are distinctly revealed and impossible to avoid.

A reflector which comprises a single surface is the only solution to a double reflection. Such are provided by the *metal mirror, or the glass mirror which is silvered on the front surface.* Both alternatives are excellent, and though both are rather expensive, they are worth procuring if it is intended to make much photographic use of the mirror's powers.

Otherwise, the normal mirror is adequate for most occasions and its use is assumed in all the following methods.

The Single Mirror

With the aid of a single mirror it is possible to make a photograph at any angle without moving the camera out of its customary vertical plane.

Thus, with the camera set upright, as normal and a mirror set at an angle in front of it, accurate straight pictures can be made of the ceiling, the floor, or objects at right-angles to the camera either side, according to the direction in which the mirror is turned.

The angle, or tilt, of the mirror nearer to or further from the camera is obviously responsible for the angle at which the surface or object is seen. Thus, a completely right-angled view—to the ceiling, floor, or wall on either side, when the camera is positioned level—is only obtained if the mirror is placed at a true angle of 45°, with its reflecting surface turned up, or down, or towards either side.

Steepening the tilt of the mirror by inclining it towards the camera gives an increasingly oblique view of objects *behind* it in any plane—the ceiling, floor, or either side wall.

Flattening the tilt of the mirror by inclining it away from the camera gives an increasingly oblique view of objects *before* it, though here a limit is set by the fact that as the incline gets too shallow the actual world before the camera can be glimpsed over the mirror's edge.

If you can tolerate an occasional glimpse of yourself, all these points will be immediately grasped by visual demonstration in front of a small portable mirror, noting how the reflected view changes—and the nature of the change—when the mirror is tilted in various directions. The camera sees what the eye sees and can simply record it.

If, in fact, you are familiar with the precept—*the angle of incidence equals the angle of reflection*—this will not be news to you, and you need take no risk of actual practice to realise the full implications of photography with the aid of a mirror.

Some means of supporting the mirror at the desired angle must be contrived. If the camera is supported on the table and the mirror directed upwards or to either side, adequate support can be provided simply by books, or similar solid objects.

When the mirror must be directed downwards, or the camera

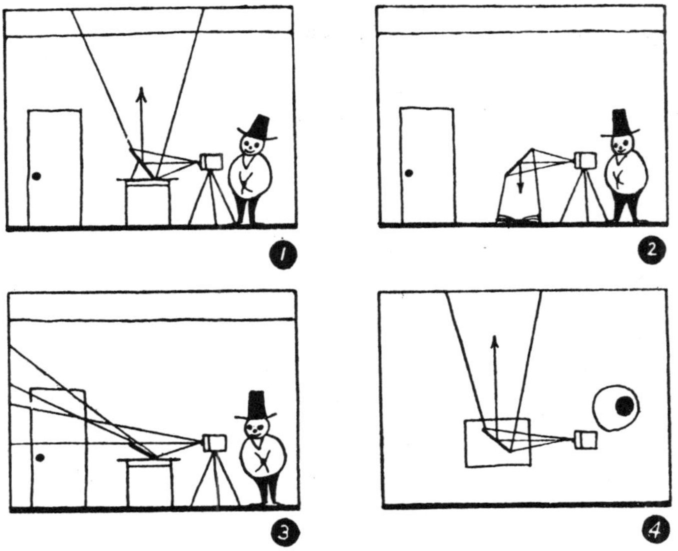

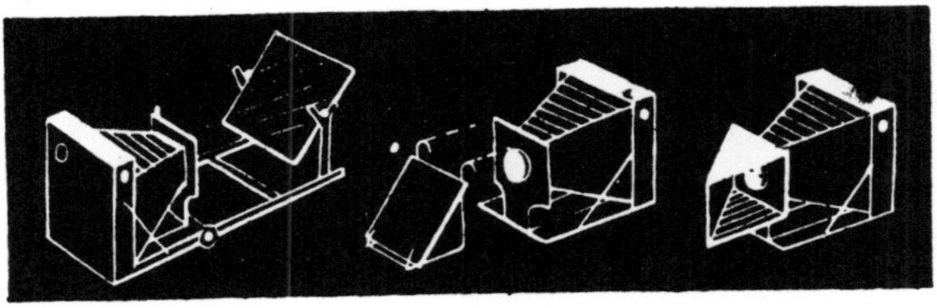

MIRRORS

In drawing *1* a mirror at an upward angle of 45 degrees turns the camera's gaze at right angles towards the ceiling. In *2* a similar mirror-angle, but in a downward direction, turns it at right angles towards the floor. In *3* a shallow mirror-angle permits the camera to see the actual world over its top, mixed with a reflection of objects above it. In plan, *4* shows the camera's gaze turned at right angles to one side, by a mirror-angle of 45 degrees.

The black panel shows three gadgets for attaching mirrors to the camera—the first in a revolving manner, the second on a wire support, the third on a triangular box.

stands freely in the centre of the room on its tripod, however, it becomes difficult to make do with such improvisations and some *supporting gadget* must be made.

If the mirror is small and light, an angular frame of stiff wire can be made to support it that will clip on to a part of the camera, or a more solid affair can be constructed similar to that shown in the diagram on page 79.

Reflections are responsible for absurd mistakes in focusing, and many first attempts at mirror photography fail because the mirror has been regarded as a framed picture, in one plane, rather than a window to a scene in three dimensions.

A camera with a focusing screen will make quite clear the relative distances of objects seen in reflection, and remarks relevant to the present occasion may be consulted on page 40, where they were made on reflected distortions. To sum up the situation, *the focusing distance will be accurately found if the distance of the lens from the mirror is added to the distance of the reflected object from the mirror*, and ignoring the reflection for all purposes of distance calculation.

Reflections will always show the image reversed from left to right, and are so recorded by the camera. In portraits, and more or less abstract pictures, this reversal can be ignored. Indeed a wrong way round image is often more acceptable and seemingly truthful to the subject of a portrait since this is the view they get of themselves when standing before a mirror.

But, for accurate photographs of interiors, subjects showing lettering, or anything that makes good sense only one way round, when printing or enlarging the *negative must be reversed* in the carrier, so that the emulsion is uppermost. This corrects the original reversal.

▷ *The photo possibilities of mirrors are limited only by your own imaginative powers, and their use will open many strange doors. The acrobatic contortions always associated with the odd camera angle are rendered quite unnecessary by the tilted mirror, which permits the camera to look over its shoulder, round the corner, or up in the air, without ever losing an even keel, or the camera man his air of infinite respectability.*

A mirror tilted at 45° in front of the camera, reflecting side uppermost, gives a worm's-eye view of any subject or surface immediately above, and in this manner may be accurately recorded painted and decorative ceilings or any object in that plane.

▷ *If the tilt is diminished, so that the mirror falls away from the camera, the view is no longer a direct right-angle upwards but an angular view of objects and surfaces above and in front of the camera.*

At a certain point the camera sees over the top of the shallow incline and records a part of the actual world immediately in front, as well as the reflection of things above and in front. As the edge of the reflecting surface is not in focus. The two appear blended, without a hard join across the plate, and very interesting combinations of reflection and reality can be so obtained.

For simplicity of focus, it is well to keep the two objects to be blended in the same plane—one above the other, the top object will be reflected upside down, like a mirage, below the other and can be easily observed in the focusing screen of the camera.

▷ *The mirror tilted at 45°, but with the reflecting side looking downwards, gives a completely right-angled view of the floor or any object below the camera in that plane. This is most convenient for copying from other photographs, pages from books, old prints or any small object laid flat upon the table, or larger objects and people spread out on the floor. Any horizontal subject, where it would be inconvenient or hazardous to tilt the camera over it, and still place oneself high enough to arrange the view and focus accurately can also be handled in this way.*

As before, tilting the mirror further from the camera changes the view to objects further away and in front of the camera, and a similar blending of reflection and reality is eventually obtained in which the reflection is now on top and the actual view below.

▷ *A mirror stood in front of the camera, so that it makes an angle of 45° when looking down on both, will deflect the camera's vision accurately to either side, and if the mirror is attached in this position pictures can be made at right-angles to the subject, or round corners without revealing the photographer.*

By turning the mirror away from the camera in this position, objects to the side, but further in front, come into view. As before, reality is eventually glimpsed beyond the mirror and the familiar blending mentioned above can again be observed—this time with a horizontal instead of a vertical division.

▷ *It has probably become apparent that the mirror, in accurately changing the direction of the image at right-angles, can be used to increase the distance between camera and subject more than the dimensions of the room would otherwise permit.*

Thus, in copying a large picture where the distance before it is not sufficient for the camera to work, a mirror at an angle of ***45°****, between picture and camera, will enable the camera to be placed at right-angles to the picture along the side wall. The distance gained is the distance from camera to mirror, which need only depend on the mirror's size.*

▷ *In a similar manner, when making interior pictures of small rooms, and where the camera is too confined for a reasonable view of the room to be obtained, a mirror can be placed or fixed against the wall and its image recorded by pointing the camera at an angle towards it.*

Such a picture appears to have been taken from a point outside the wall holding the mirror, and at a distance equal to the distance of the camera from it. Obviously, the larger the mirror the greater the distance from which the camera can work without including its frame or edges, and so destroying the illusion.

Visual experiment with a mirror and the focusing screen of the camera will make all these points as clear as the mirror's reflection, and may reveal many further possibilities.

Double and Triple Mirrors

One mirror makes magic, two mirrors multiply it not by two, but by repetition to infinity, or repetition in a circle.

Thus, out of one man, two mirrors make a multitude or a mystifying circle, two turn the world upside down, three turn it inside out and according to the relation of one to the other present an endless variety of repeated images.

For maximum success *the mirrors should be of approximately equal size, unframed and unbevelled.*

Two mirrors, placed parallel to each other, will repeat the image of any object put between them an infinite number of times. Such an effect is often to be observed in tailor's shops, theatre vestibules, and any room where mirrors occur on opposite walls.

By placing the camera adjacent to one of the mirrors and directing it towards the other at an angle, these effects can be successfully recorded. The mirrors, in this case, though strictly parallel, are not exactly opposite since the one next to the camera will be moved along to make room for it.

So placed, the camera sees a number of repeated images of any object between the mirrors, but a little adjustment will be necessary if you want to prevent the image of the camera being repeated and recorded also. This can be done by taking a ***high*** *viewpoint,* so that the camera points down towards the object and the opposite mirror, and placing a piece of plain card in front of the tripod legs; or by so arranging *the subject between the mirrors that part of it comes between the camera and the first mirror,* and thus prevents it from recording.

A greater number of repetitions can be included, and the camera effectively concealed, if a *hole is cleanly scraped in the silver on the back of one of the mirrors,* just large enough to permit the lens of the camera to look through.

A small mirror so treated is a useful property. The effective pictures so obtained will more than compensate for spoiling the mirror for any other purpose. The subject must be so arranged that the small dark hole, caused by the scraping, is more or less obscured or it also will be infinitely repeated.

Focusing should be contrived so that when the lens in stopped down the *depth of field includes the actual object and as many of the repetitions as possible.* Make no attempt to get them all sharp; at close quarters this will be almost impossible anyway, and the effect will be well captured if the further reflections recede to a fuzzy infinity.

By using the two mirrors meeting at an angle to each other as the background to any object, *repetitions are obtained in the form of a circle, of which the triangle containing your subject is a single segment.* According to the angle of the mirrors, so the number of the segments, or repetitions, will vary—*obviously, the smaller the angle, the more the segments,* and *vice versa.*

In this connection it is useful to recollect that the number of degrees in a circle are 360; thus, if you require a picture in which the image is to be repeated four times in addition to the actual object—five segments in other words—this number is divided by five. The resulting figure, 72°, is the angle at which the mirrors must be placed to give four reflections, or a total of five equal parts when the subject is included.

Similarly, six segments are obtained with an angle of 60°, eight segments with an angle of 45°, and only four with an angle of 90° and so on, the smaller the angle the greater the number, the greater the angle the smaller the number.

Odd angles can also be used, but it will be found most successful to use one that exactly divides into 360 as this gives equal compartments, with no odd pieces left over.

The smaller the angle the smaller becomes the space for your subject, and the dimmer become the further reflections, therefore, perhaps, *a minimum of 60°* is best created and adhered to.

Focusing, when using two mirrors, is best made on the point *where the mirrors join*, this being the centre of the circle. Other arrangements must be considered on their own merits, arranging the depth of focus to cover the extreme planes if these do not extend to infinity.

If the base on which the subject stands is formed by a *third mirror*, so that the camera looks down into the corner of a mirror box, a new and more complicated set of reflections will be obtained.

The effect now is not of a circle but of something like a half-sphere, the subject between the mirros being repeated below and under, as well as round and round—most attractive with certain objects, particularly if they touch the surface of all three mirrors.

By introducing a third mirror we increase our range of effects and reflecting possibilities, and a little visual experiment will enable you to discover much for yourself. In addition to forming the floor of a two-sided box, the third can be made into the third wall of a box with a normal base, the third side of a prism, or an imperfect triangle in which the camera can peep through a gap left in the apex.

In all arrangements, the camera can be prevented from reflecting, either by *directing the lens through a hole cut in a sheet of plain card*, which then becomes the reflected background of the picture, or by taking a *high viewpoint* so that the camera looks down on the subject over a piece of plain card placed against the legs of the tripod. The high viewpoint, of course, makes the most of the circular formation, or any other form of geometrical repeat.

Lighting should be arranged from above, and slightly behind the mirrors, so that light is directed on to those sides of the subject that face towards the mirrors—particular attention being given to getting an *evenly lit background, floor, and the two reflecting sides of the subject,* so that the pattern is unbroken by patches of deep shadow.

▷ *The uses of, and subjects for, repetition with several mirrors are limited by the size of the mirrors at your disposal. For economy, the majority of people would work on the table top and with subjects of small scale, where the mirrors need be no larger than twelve inches square, or a little longer in one direction.*

▷ *With larger mirrors at your disposal, however, portraits and*

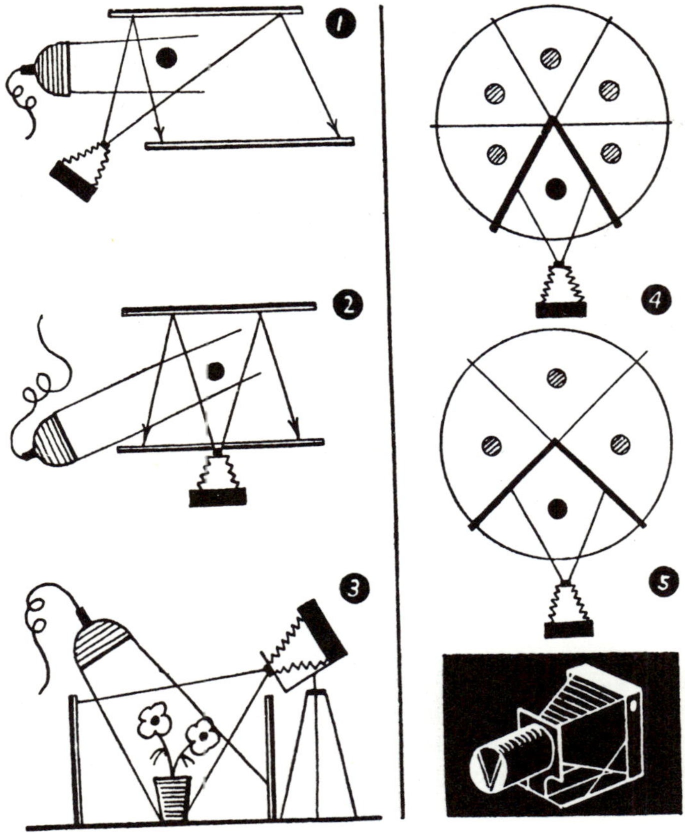

MIRRORS

Drawings *1, 2,* and *3* show alternative methods of using parallel mirrors to obtain an effect of infinite repetition—in *1* with camera at the side, in *2* looking through a small hole scraped in the back of one mirror, in *3* over the top of one of the mirrors. No. 2 is the ideal.

Drawings *4* and *5* show two arrangements of mirrors at an angle—of 60 degrees in 4, to produce a circle of 6 units—of 90 degrees in 5 to produce one of only 4 units.

The small drawing, white on black, shows a kaleidoscope gadget with two mirrors at an angle in a small length of tubing.

even full-length figure studies can be made in which five or more images stand or sit in a circular arrangement. The sitter is usually placed with back square to the camera, which is directed between the slit in two screens, and is thus prevented from being reflected in either mirror.

▷ *If the angle is set so that it exactly divides the degrees of a circle, the images will appear to touch in a circle when the fingers are rested on the glass at either side. Such an arrangement has many applications with other subjects, and is an ideal means of pattern-making.*

The Kaleidoscope

Pattern-making, and mirrors at an angle, have evoked the image of the kaleidoscope perhaps, in many readers' minds. These fascinating instruments alas, are not so common as once they were, yet their lovely patterns are but a repetition, in circular form, of objects placed beneath a segment made from two strips of mirror or black glass, and they can be repeated with any two mirrors so placed.

Kaleidoscopic patterns can be simply produced, as an extension of the previous method, by placing our two mirrors at an appropriate angle over any figured flat surface. If the camera or eye is applied to the top of the mirrors, or looks towards them at an angle of 45°, this small segment of actuality will be reproduced in reflection to form a circular pattern.

As explained on page 83, according to the angle of the two mirrors, so the number of *repetitions will vary, being greater when the angle is least and less when the angle is most.* The temptation to obtain an infinite number of repeats by the use of a very small angle should be avoided, since the *images lose their brightness the more they are reflected,* being never so bright as the original segment of reality.

A maximum of eight gives an adequate repetition with reasonably well-matched images, and such an effect is produced with two mirrors meeting at an angle of 45°.

The most commonplace pieces of a photographic print, as long as they show good contrast and animation of tone, can make excellent pattern material, and a little experiment will prove what fine patterns are yielded by the poorest material.

An actual kaleidoscope has space below the mirrors for the examination of three-dimensional objects, and your two mirrors could be so contrived, on a sheet of clear glass, that objects could be similarly placed beneath them. The improvised mirrors, and the actual kaleidoscope, have little to choose between them, both are excellent substitutes for the other. If you have a kaleidoscope, you have only to apply the lens of the camera to the eye-piece and focus on the objects below, to reproduce the effect in a photograph. *The eye-piece, however, is often smaller than the lens of the camera and so reduces its effective aperture.* This means either longer exposures or removing the eye-piece, if possible.

In every case, *you focus on the plane of the segment of reality,* whether it is in the flat or not, and ignore the reflection. Small apertures will not be necessary for flat patterns as these will be in one plane, but depth of field is necessary to cover the extreme planes of solid objects.

If the kaleidoscope, or a similar arrangement of two mirror strips set at an angle in a cardboard tube, is attached to the lens of the camera, three repeated images will be obtained of any object the camera is pointed at—whatever its distance. The images will be set at an angle to each other, controlled naturally by the angle of the mirrors, and will *slightly overlap* in all directions. Therefore, subjects containing *large bright surfaces must be avoided*, since these will tend to blot out the second and third images.

The mirrors can be simply stood against the lens, with an improvised support, but fitting mirror strips into a *cardboard tube* is much more solid and satisfactory. Such a tube can be rotated in front of the lens, until the images blend in the best manner, and then fixed with a wide rubber band or pieces of modelling clay.

The aperture of the lens will be effectively diminished by the use of this gadget. *Exposures must therefore be longer* than the subject would normally require—an extension by one-half will be a good rough basis for experiment.

▷ *The uses of the kaleidoscope, or a similar arrangement of mirrors at an angle, are confined to pattern-making pure and simple, but within this limitation there is still much freedom.*

Beneath the small segment formed by the mirrors can be placed an infinite variety of objects of strange texture, colour and contrast. In different planes and lit in various ways, the most trivial object or surface can give a rich effect in particular positions. Feathers, flowers, liquorice allsorts and objects that seem to offer no possibility whatsoever, should be chosen on principle.

▷ *Some examples will be sufficiently satisfying to justify printing individually, others can be repeated by printing several times, on a single sheet of printing paper, to form an all-over pattern.*

The use of a kaleidoscope attached to the lens, for recording objects further away from the camera than the end of the mirrors, is a matter of your own skill and taste. Strange and satisfying effects could undoubtedly be achieved, but most so far published have little more than curiosity value.

Prisms

A very similar effect, in essence, to that obtained with the kaleidoscope on objects at a distance, is given when a prism or a piece of prismatically-cut glass is attached to the camera in the manner of a supplementary lens.

A prism, when placed before the lens of the camera, causes the image of any object to be repeated according to the number of surfaces on the prism. Thus, a *prismatically-cut circular disc of glass with three surfaces gives three distinct images*, and one with five surfaces gives five—an effect which is to be clearly observed on the ground glass screen.

Unlike the effect of a kaleidoscope, *every prismatically repeated image is the same way round*. But, since they overlap each other considerably in all directions, care must be exercised in the choice of suitable subjects, so that tones will not blot each other out by superimposition.

The distance of each image from the other is always constant, though the arrangement and disposition on the plate can be controlled by rotating the prism before the lens. But a *lens of different focal length*—if the lens can be changed—*will alter the distance* of the separately repeated images.

Focusing is unaffected, and may be carried out on the screen of a reflex or plate camera or by estimating the distance and setting the lens accordingly.

▷ *The uses of a prism, whatever its multiplying powers, are best confined to isolated details on neutral backgrounds rather than complete scenes or pictures. Every image has a large area overlapped by those adjacent, and the edges consequently become rather confused.*

Black or dark backgrounds are almost an essential of the technique, as the merging of the images can take place in these neutral areas, where there is no detail or feature to be registered as a double or triple tone.

▷ *Portraits in dark clothes against black backgrounds, hands in surrounding darkness, artificially-lit groups of people in the open at night, or similar more or less isolated subjects, present ideal conditions and give the most satisfactory results. Each will be repeated separately and clearly, and with the minimum of overlapping, such little merging as takes place only serving to deepen the mystery of the effect.*

GHOSTS AND DOUBLES

The dimness of the darkroom, the camera's shuttered gloom, and the frequent necessity for avoiding strong light, might lead a less prosaic age to pronounce photography a black art and its effects as black magic.

But we, calling the camera an instrument of science, and with the customary credulity of the sophisticated, sometimes even credit its effects to the point of accepting a strange photograph as evidence to the claims of a spirit world.

How very right that there should be a supernature, but how wrong to hope that the camera, who has at heart the prior interests of its own strange children, could offer material proof of its existence.

The very transparency of a negative image instantly suggests the convention of a less substantial world. By turning to advantage the practical methods of photography, such as the combination by multiple exposure of objects seen separately by the eye, the camera can suggest the appearance of super-normality.

Black Backgrounds

If an exposure is made of any object against a black or non-actinic background, that portion of the negative that receives no image or light from the subject will remain in its original virgin state. That is, it will be absolutely transparent if the negative is developed, or it will normally record an image of the same, or any other object, in another position on the black background.

Taking advantage of this, it is possible to make as many separate exposures of as many different objects as we desire. Each object is recorded alone, without background or surroundings of any kind, and leaving the rest of the negative, whether previously exposed or not, untouched.

If the objects and exposures are many, and their relative

positions crucially important, such *positions must be marked, if possible, on the focusing screen*, or upon a tracing of it, so that the separate images may be correctly aligned and not overlap. Only the simpler doubles and triples may be achieved by merely sighting them in the viewfinder and cultivating a good memory; others must be registered in some manner.

The background itself can take several forms, of which the cheapest and most successful is that offered by the *open door of a darkened room*: this darkness is atmospheric and, lacking substance, will reflect no light and register no shadows. *Black velvet, black fabric, or black paint* will all serve well, but they are apt to register a slight difference in tone between the parts in light and those in shade.

It is necessary, therefore, to keep them far enough in the background to ensure their being *out of focus* as well as to *avoid the casting of shadows* on them. It will often be possible so to *screen the source of light that little falls on the back cloth*. And as the subject will be relatively much brighter, and the exposure calculated for it, the minute differences of light observed on the background will rarely be picked up by the emulsion.

It should be clear that if these pictures are developed without being twice exposed, they can also be simply combined in the darkroom with any other negative showing an object in another position against a black background.

The emulsions of the *two negatives are placed face to face* and projected in the enlarger together. Separate printing will not be successful unless the *paper is masked*, since the paper will be fogged by the printing light that produces the black tone of the first negative.

▷ *A little quiet contemplation will put many ideas in your head concerning uses for this technique: the following are among those that have already been made. Don't be discouraged if you thought of them first.*

Double or triple exposures of one person, arranged so that the model appears to be talking or reading to himself, eating with or serving food to his double, playing cards or drinking with himself and other odd conceits.

Separate exposures are made for each position, the movements being made by the model in preference to shifting the camera, care also being taken that any subsidiary properties such as table and chairs are not moved between exposures. These appear in all the separately taken shots and any slight movement will be registered on the film.

These properties, appearing often in the same position, will soon be over-exposed if the number of exposures exceeds two. This can, to some extent, be counteracted by subduing the light on such objects, or by avoiding furniture and table cloths of brilliant colour, in favour of the more shabby, dark, and subdued.

▷ A welcome variation can be contrived by using the camera at different distances. This implies a difference in scale and consequent size between the people and objects of each exposure. Thus your subject can lead a smaller edition of himself by the hand, converse with a dwarfed self stood on a table or chair, or even a midget stood on his own outstretched hand.

A few examples of this kind can, as before, be made by merely sighting the subjects in the viewfinder, but when the images are interdependent and yet intended to touch, their position in each exposure must be accurately marked on the focusing screen (if the camera allows it) or upon a tracing of it.

▷ Similarly, some pictures will depend for success on the two images looking each other squarely in the eye. Nothing reveals the deception more clearly than the separate gazes wandering above the head and over the shoulder. A piece of black thread can be marked with white chalk to give an unobtrusive visual point which, together with the position of the eyes, is marked on the focusing screen.

Joining these two points will indicate a line of vision, and adjusting the marked thread in relation to this line, for the second exposure, will give a point for the model to stare on.

▷ Multiple exposures need not be exclusively of the human subject. Interesting repetitions of a multitude of common objects can be obtained and the charmingly out-moded trick of the man in the bottle, that so amused our grandparents, gives a lead in the right direction.

The bottle—milk, medicine, wine, or spirit—is recorded as large as possible against the usual dark background. It should be so lit that its shape, contour, and substance are clearly revealed, but avoiding intense glassy highlights where the model's face is likely to appear.

After marking accurately the extent of the bottle on the focusing screen, the second exposure is made so that the unfortunate prisoner is kept within these marked limits. He can be

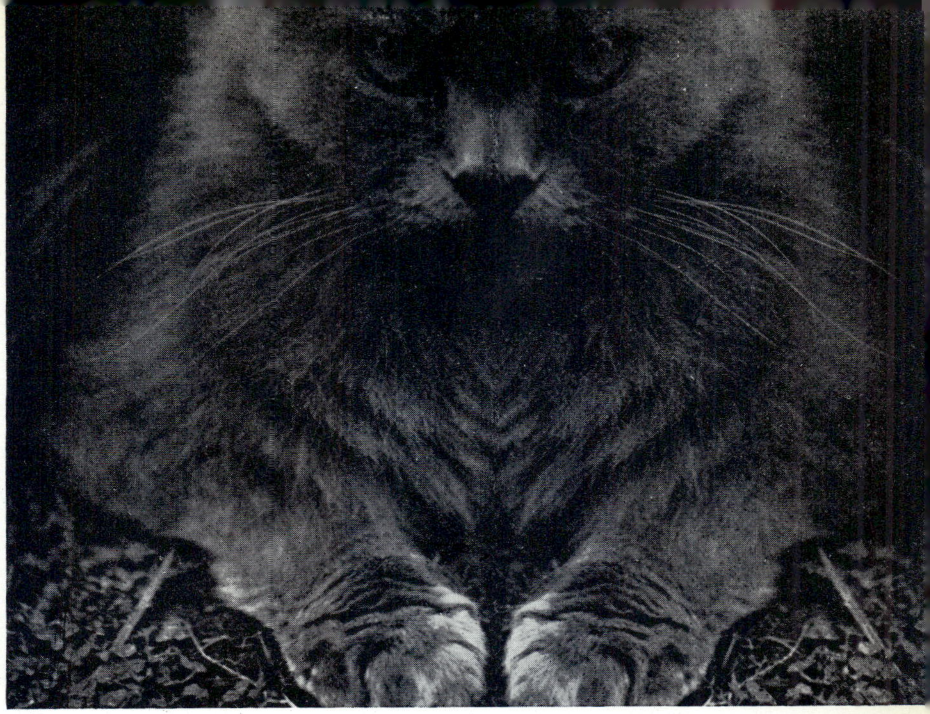

DOUBLING TRICKS

Above: The original negative shows only a little more of the cat than can be seen by obscuring exactly one half. The terrifying whole was created by printing the same half in reverse, turning the negative in its carrier, and accurately joining the two separate exposures with a sharply cutting mask over the paper—perfect symmetry.—*Edwin Smith.*

Page 94: A montage from three negatives. First negative—a white face on black background—double printed with background; notice how it prints through part of the image. The front face is a print from a separate negative cut and pasted into position.—*Cecil Beaton.*

Page 95: A normal print is partially overlaid by a negative print of the same image, the negative being applied to the positive print by simple cut and paste montage—the profile providing a simple cutting line.—*Scaioni* (*by courtesy of Rumble, Crowther and Nicholson and Josephine Kell*).

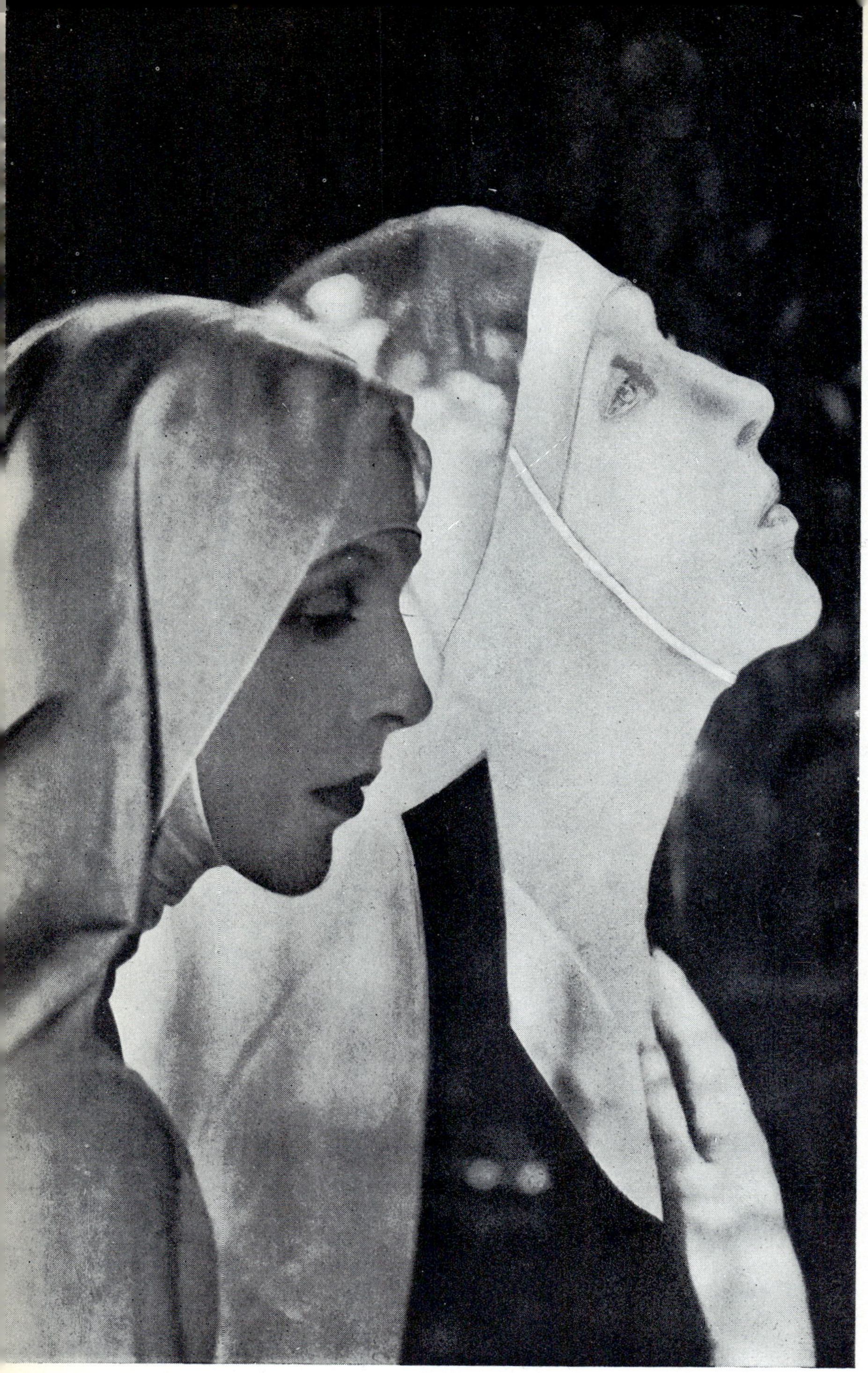

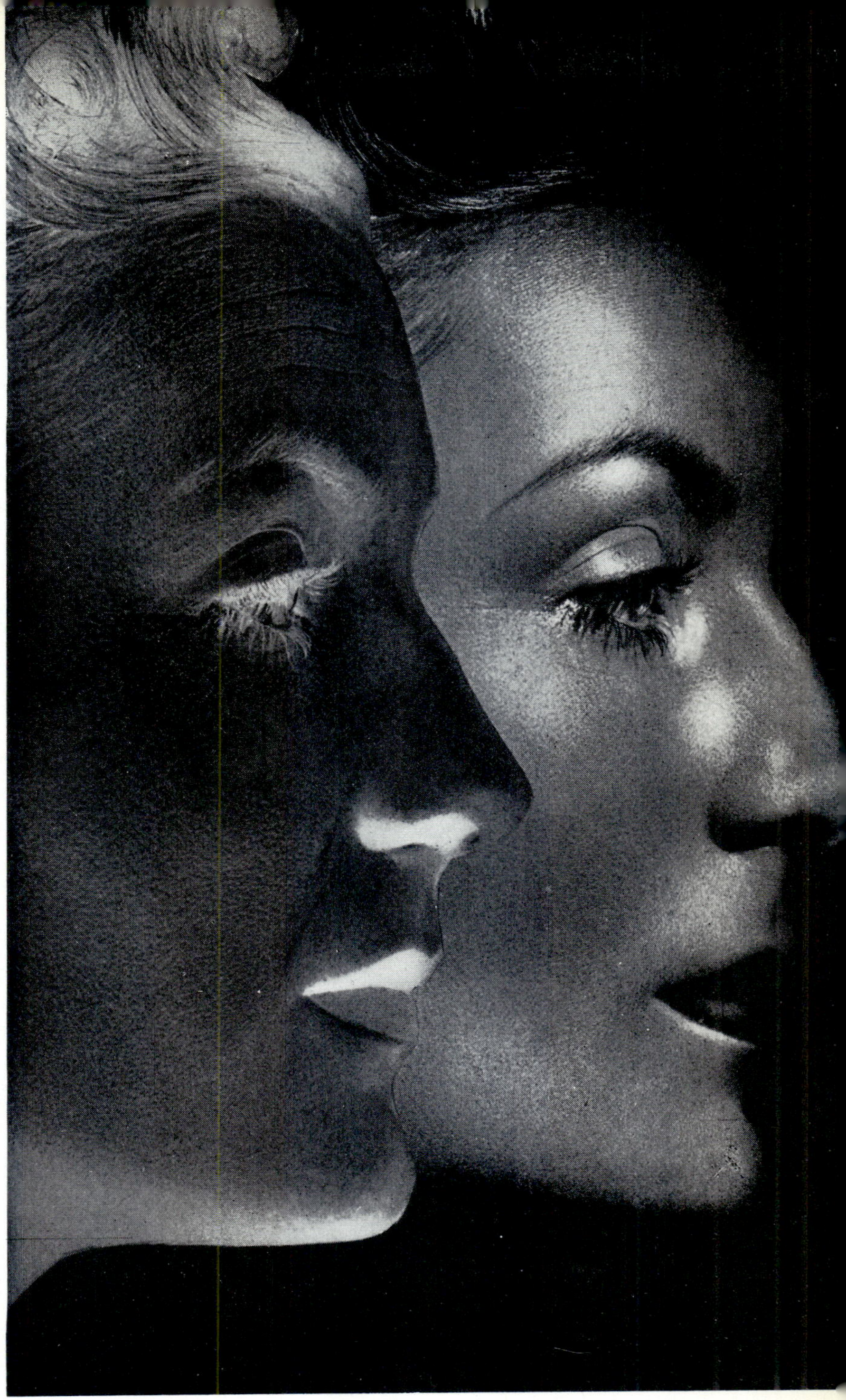

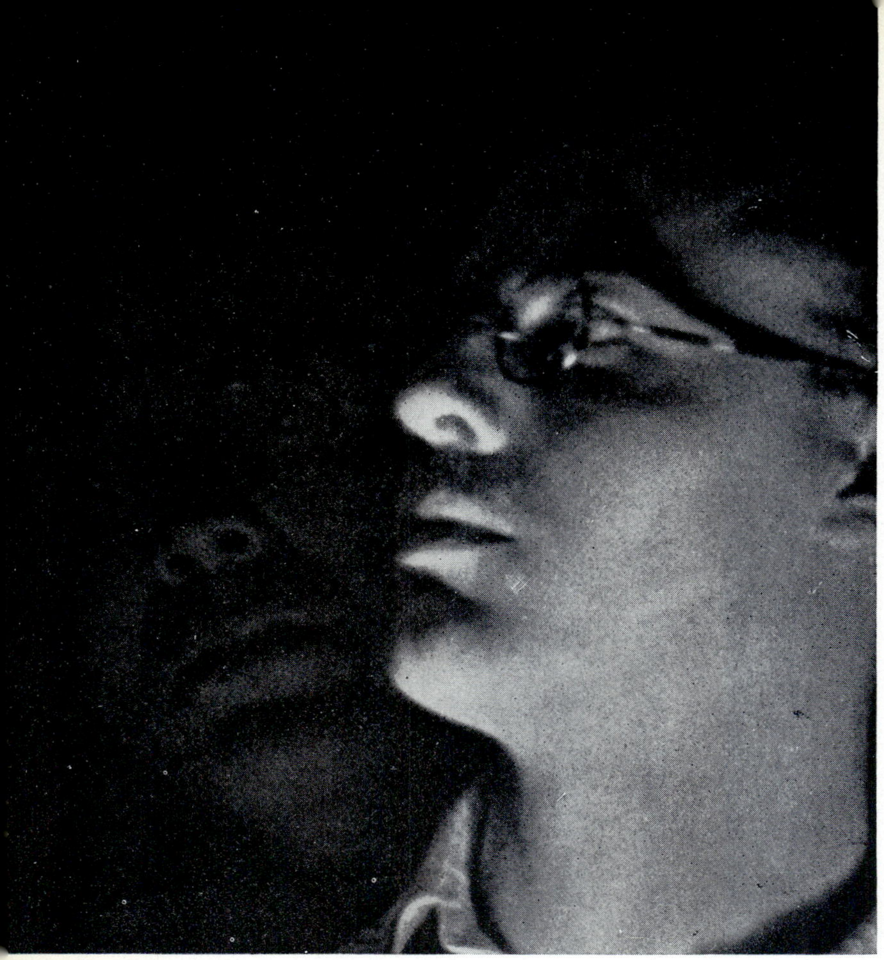

A mirror self-portrait against a black background. The full face was recorded first with a short exposure to produce its dark and distant tones, the profile next with a full exposure to place it on a seemingly nearer plane. Exposures made in a darkroom by switching on the light for the period of exposure; the juxtaposition of images is pure guesswork.—*Edwin Smith*

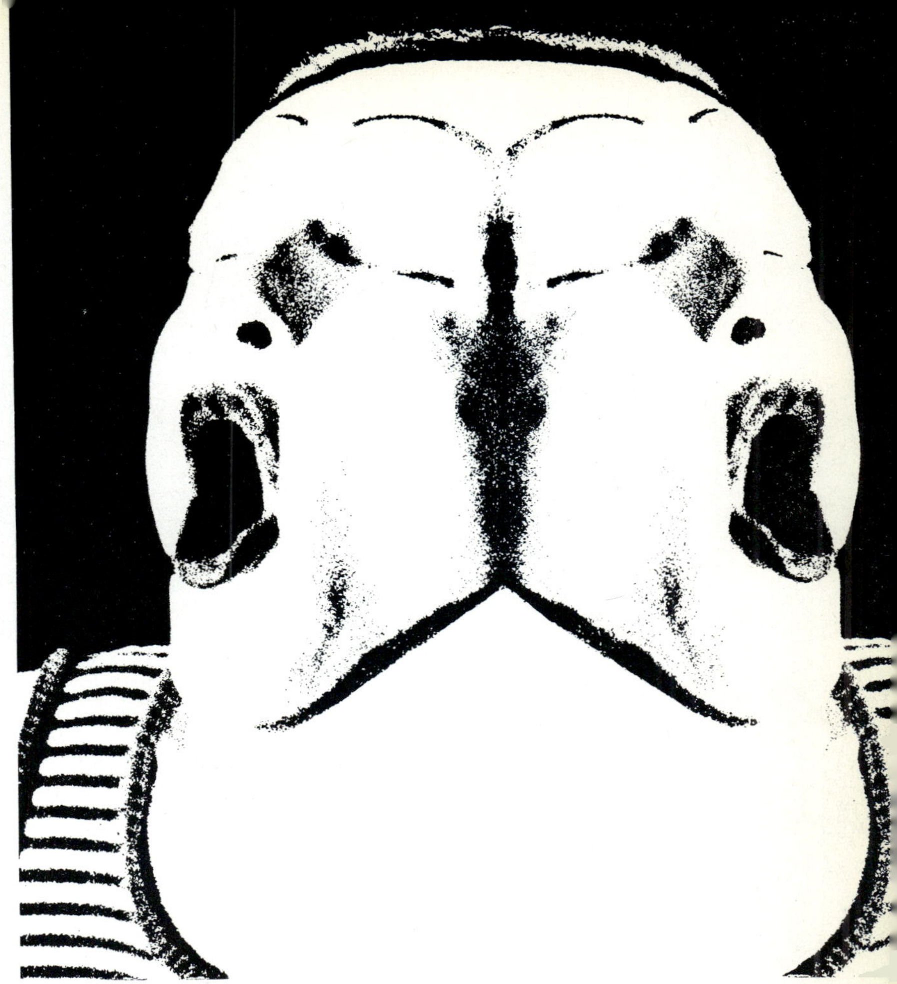

Double printed original, partly reversed, and copied on to lith material, eliminating detail to the extent that if this picture is turned upside down quite another sort of face appears.—*Rainer Kiedrowski.*

Page 98: Playing about with an old photo. The print was pinned up and copied twice. The two negatives, one a little denser than the other, were sandwiched with one inverted and then printed together.—*Edwin Smith.*

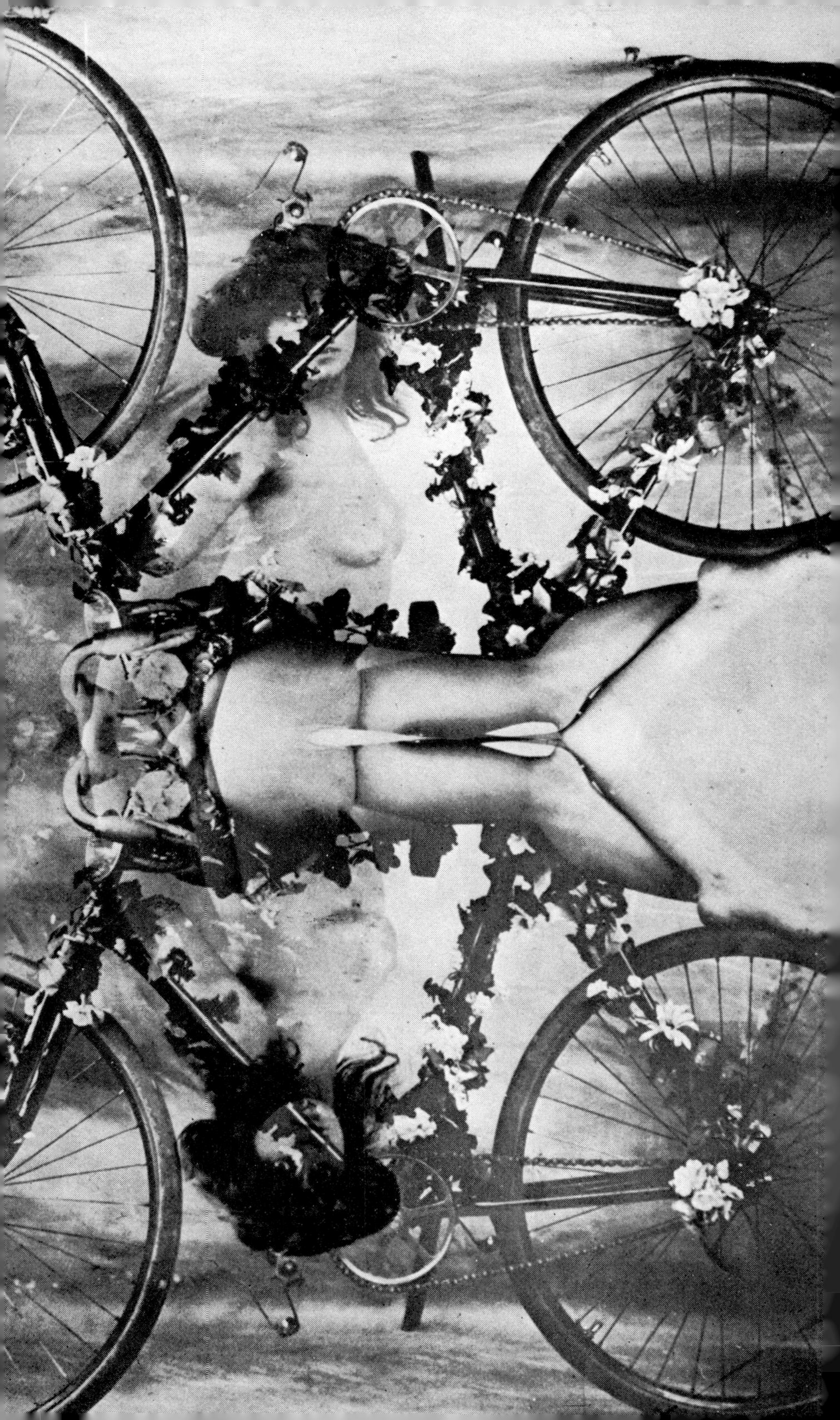

Symmetrical tree made up from two lith copy negatives, one reversed, trimmed and fitted together and contrast printed.

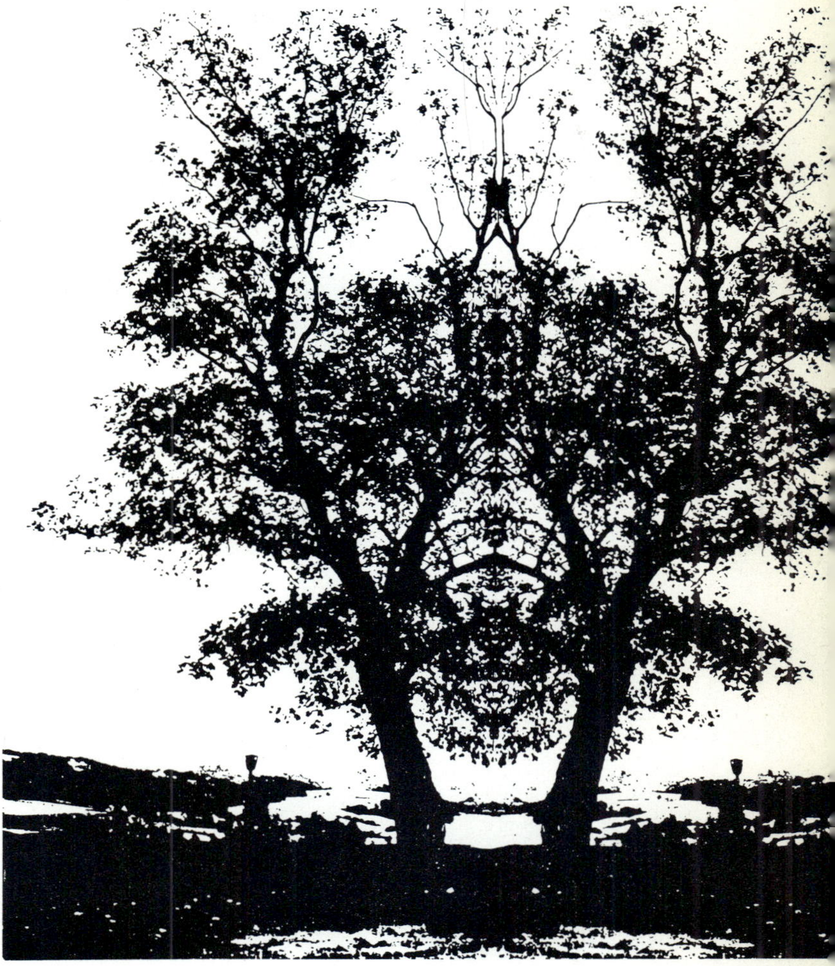

Page 100: Top left: Double exposure in the camera with the second shot taken after a short interval. Some subjects, and the camera itself, moved slightly. *Top right* and *bottom left* show separate negatives combination printed, and *bottom right* with a contact screen added.—*Edwin Smith, Ladislav Postupa, Janette Mussot.*

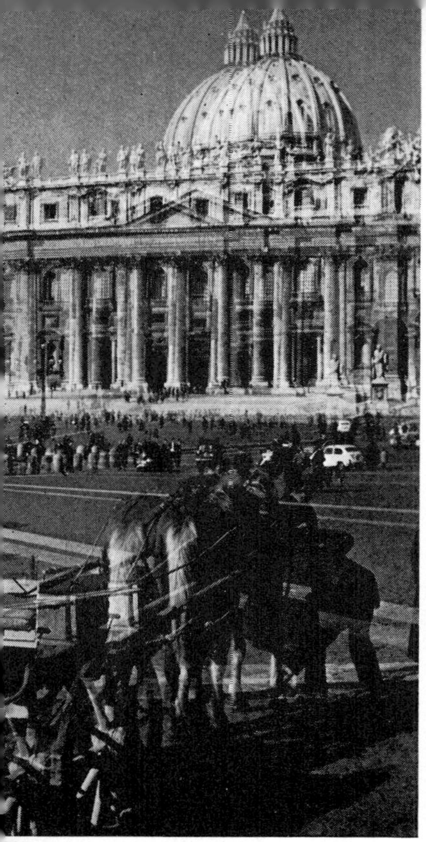
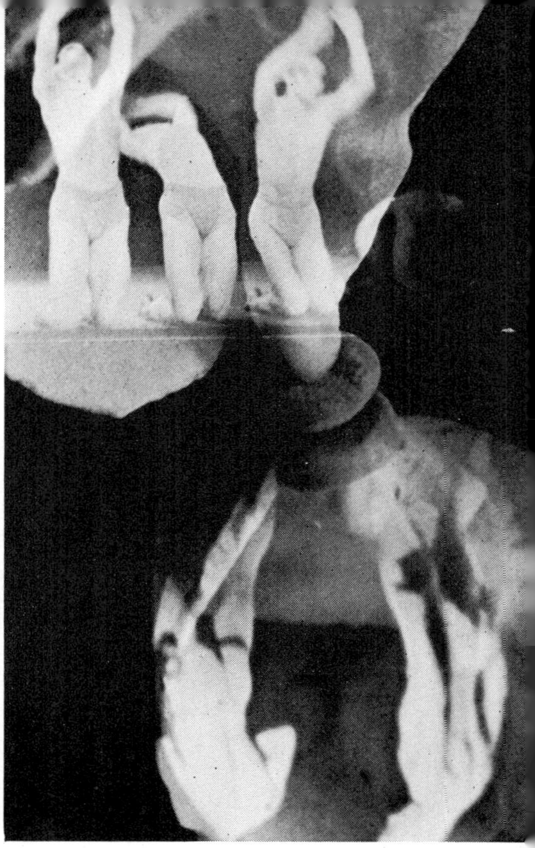
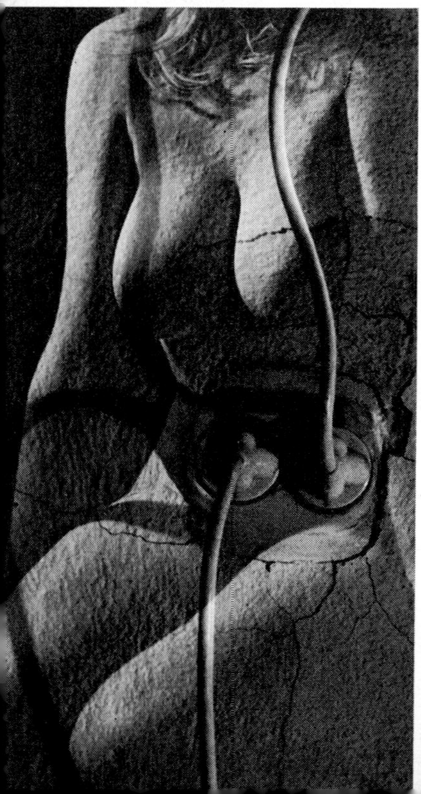
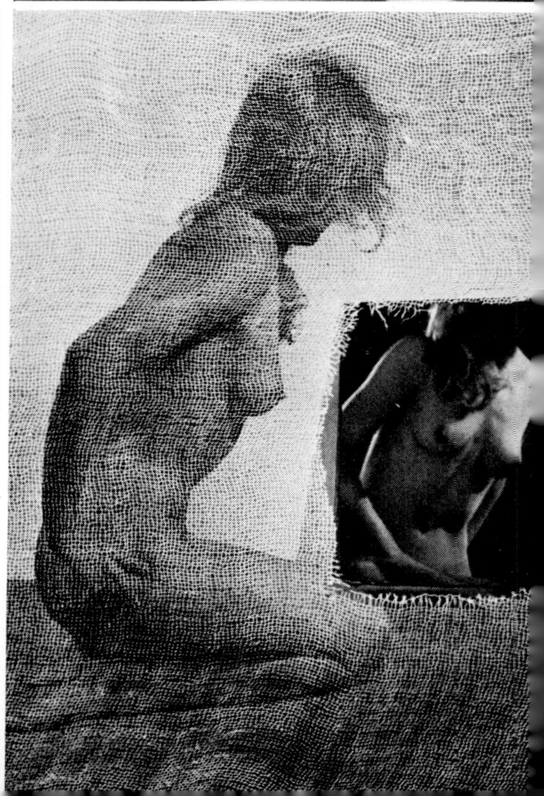

erect or struggling in some escapist contortion, or he could be as easily incarcerated in a glass chimney as the spirit of the lamp.

Black Background and Masking

In all cases of black background photography, the model must wear *light-coloured clothes.* Anything in the nature of dark suits or dresses tend to be lost in the surrounding gloom leaving you, most attractively, with a disembodied head and hands.

This gives the clue to a new range of effects and an extension to the black background technique.

Practical experiment with a black cloth will eventually suggest to you the possibility of making any *portion of the model invisible by masking in black material.* Thus, black gloves cut off the hands, or a finger-stall a chosen finger, a black hood will remove the head, black trousers or a long skirt sweep away the legs, and any small surrounded feature can be blacked out with black material patches.

If you find it more convenient, and more economical of black material, these curious decapitations can also be contrived by *masks within the camera*, though this is really only practicable with large format view cameras.

Masks must be cut from *black paper with a matt or non-reflecting surface*. Card covered with a *black velour paper is ideal.* They are inserted into the bellows at the back of the camera, so that they are not more than *two inches in front of the ground glass*, and arranged so that the openings in them disclose the required amount of the subject and cut it at the required point.

The openings should be just big enough to expose the required portion, and no more; being near the emulsion surface the masks will cut the objects quite sharply, and not with the blurred and ragged edge that would be effected by a mask outside the camera.

Masking is an invaluable help where the background at your disposal is not big enough for the desired effects. If, for example, your model is to occupy only a small corner or appear minutely in the middle of a dark space, and you have only an open doorway to pose him in, the surroundings of the doorway can be masked out in the camera.

▷ *Uses will soon begin to crowd in upon you and clamour for prior attention. Those that have already been suggested mostly dwell on the theme of decapitation, which is consequently wearing a little thin.*

▷ *An isolated head is recorded in a marked and predetermined position on the negative, either by using a black material cloak, or a mask within the camera that conceals all but the head and neck.*

The second exposure makes the head appear as the dish of the evening on the dining table, on a wheel-barrow, or balanced on the outstretched hand of a headless apparition, or any other position in which the head is seen against a dark background in the final picture.

▷ *If the head is recorded lying sideways on a block or some such improvisation, the second exposure can be made of the headless model in a number of gruesomely executed poses. The head appearing to have been chopped, sabred, or even sawn off, while the headless body kneels, lies abjectly across the work bench, or cuts a chicken caper in the background.*

▷ *The executioner will need to be portrayed by a second model, since the exposure showing the victim must include him standing by. An amusing effect of a man decepitated by his double can be achieved if the executioner is the same model whose head was recorded on the block. The second model takes the kneeling or other position with his head suitably masked.*

▷ *A little natural background should be included in the second exposure, to relieve the rather forbidding blackness. This can be arranged to the side, at the bottom, and even over the top, as long as the isolated head of the first exposure is seen against a patch of darkness of the required area.*

In practice it will be quite obvious that having used a mask within the camera to record the isolated head, no other mask will be necessary for the second exposure, since the head appears on blackness and cannot therefore be overlaid by another image.

Horizontal to Vertical

An interesting variation of the black background technique, and one which offers unrivalled opportunities to mislead, is the posing of a person or object on a dark-coloured floor and making the exposure from directly above. When viewed in the final print, such pictures appear as if taken in the vertical plane with no suggestion of their prostrate origin.

Since the eye is more accustomed to looking *at* things than looking *down* upon them, if no clue is offered to the plane of the original subject, the eye will tend to assume that any object shown is standing vertically. By spreading your model upon a

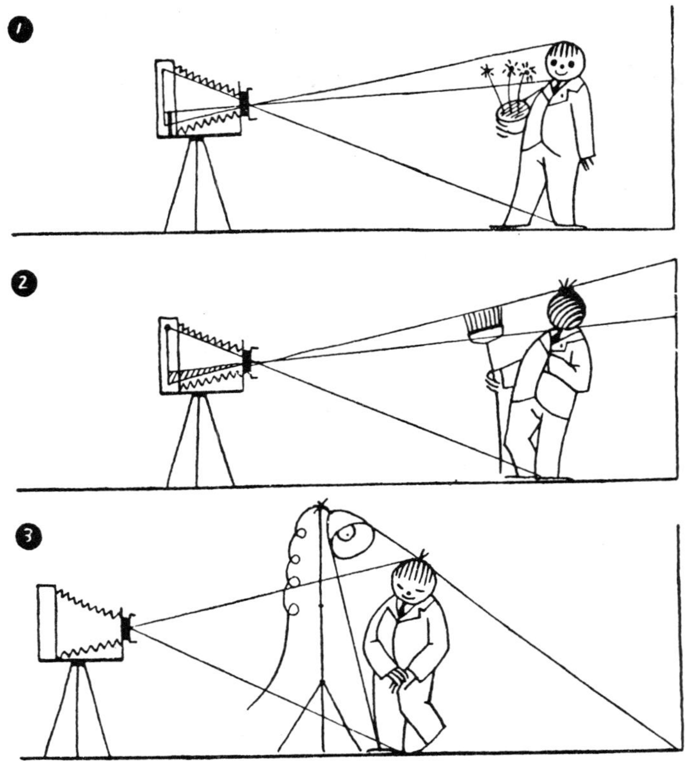

BLACK BACKGROUND MASKING

In drawing *1*, a mask within the camera is used to obscure the head of a subject posed against a black background. In *2* the subject's head is obscured by a black hood, which renders it invisible against a black background. In *3* an arrangement of lighting is shown ensuring that no shadows are cast upon the background.

dark floor, and recording him from above, he will appear suspended in animation against a theatrical darkness.

The floor should preferably consist of a large board or sheet painted a dead matt black. But failing this, a dark short pile carpet will serve if the lighting is arranged so that the pile is not given prominence. Plain dark linoleum is only suitable if reflections can be avoided, and this is rarely possible.

The height of the camera will depend on the extent of your subject and the angle of the camera's lens. *Wide-angle lenses are a great help* and can be used from no higher altitude than the top of a table or chair.

If the camera is *tilted upwards* from the foot of the model, the perspective in the final print will be that of looking up from the front row of the stalls, or some similar low view-point.

Reflex cameras could be arranged on a small plank so that the image can be viewed from the side, and the use of a small mirror as described on page 81 could be made to turn the view of other cameras—the image being seen at right angles to the subject and obviating the necessity of perching perilously over the model.

▷ *The most effective uses of this technique are always those that portray actions superhumanly acrobatic if actually performed in the vertical.*

Outrageous leaps, impossible falls, fantastic feats of balance, and every conceivable contortion, seemingly taking place in mid-air, can easily be contrived and will give your model a head-turning reputation. Juggling and balancing feats can simply be arranged by lying the plates, balls, and other impedimenta in more or less credible postions.

▷ *If the suggestion of a "floor" becomes necessary, this can be provided by a board stood upright on the background and rested against the model's feet. Similarly, a tight-rope could be easily simulated and will suggest many a circus pose.*

The possibilities of such false action shots are almost unlimited, and the probability is that you will be for ever after suspicious of any action picture with a black background.

▷ *An extension of such trickery is to make a photograph right way up—in the vertical plane—and present it to view upside down, arranging any subsidiary props to substantiate the illusion. Standing on the head and hands is an example that will immediately occur: others could be cunningly arranged.*

▷ *The opposite effect—to take a photograph upside down and*

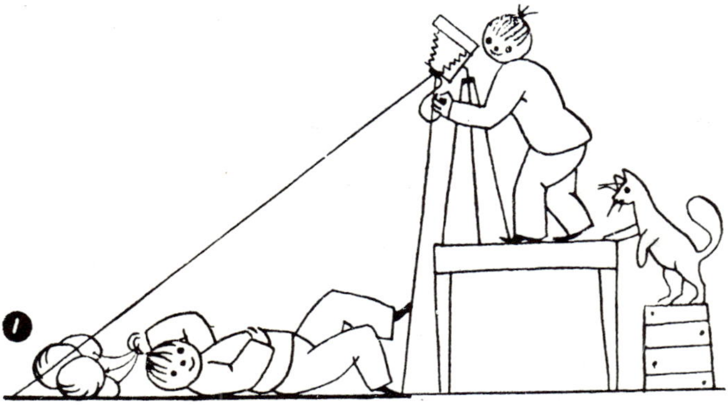

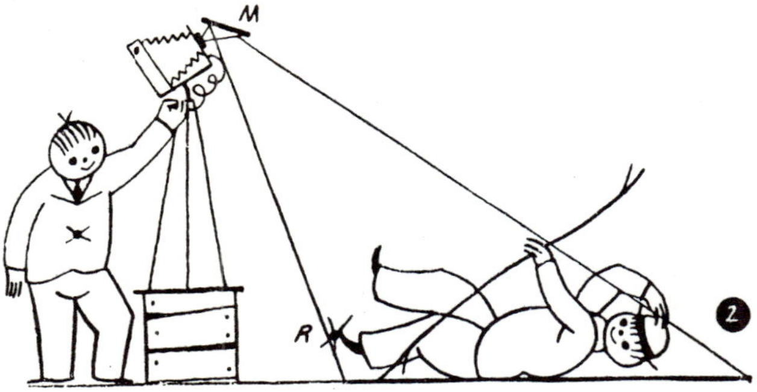

HORIZONTAL TO VERTICAL

The willing subject lies upon a black background placed upon the floor. In drawing *1* the camera and camera-man perch above him on a table placed at his feet, and make an exposure that appears to show the model descending gently to earth from a bunch of balloons—the viewpoint being from below.

In drawing *2* use is made of a small mirror (M) (as described on page 81) to turn the camera's view-point at right angles to itself, so that focusing and exposure can then be conveniently made from floor level. The subject, on his black background, does an apparent tight-rope act with a foot perched lightly on a stretched rope R.

present it normal way up—will seem a sophistry of little practical or fantastic value. But, we have before us a clever precedent—the elegant legs in stocking advertisements, at least one of which is made with the model's legs in the air, to produce a seductively swelling calf without muscular contraction. The shot is made with the camera normal way round, a light board being balanced or suspended above the model's feet, which becomes the unquestionable "floor" when the print is reproduced upside down. The method could undoubtedly be extended to produce other effects, and is worth storage room in the mind.

Natural Backgrounds

Black backgrounds are useful and all very well, but they are so rarely a natural condition of everyday observation, that they inevitably arouse suspicion in association with strange and exotic effects. Doubles and triples, and fakes with a natural and life-like background, are both more deceptive and disturbing.

Multiple exposures with natural backgrounds can only be contrived by interposing a *mask between the subject and the camera* to control the order in which the two halves, or other divisions, of a subject shall record.

Thus a mask can be used to obscure the top half of one side of the subject from the camera's vision, and then reversed so that these parts are revealed and half already exposed is concealed. By such means the subject and exposure are divided into two independent halves, which will appear normally combined in the final print without trace of a join.

The division can similarly be made into three parts across the negative in either direction, or into four parts by exposing one quartered corner after another, but these represent the maximum.

Masks are most conveniently arranged outside the camera, *a few inches in front of the lens*, ensuring that the *joint between the strips is diffused* and not sharply defined, and so that the images blend one with the other without a perceptible break or difference of tone.

The form the mask shall take depends on the complication or otherwise of your requirements, and a simple masking arrangement for dividing the subject into two equal halves—either top and bottom or down the middle—can be made in the form of a *hood or cap to fit on the camera lens*. Such a hood is easily contrived from a cardboard tube if you are lucky enough to find one the right size, or the collar can be made by wrapping a piece

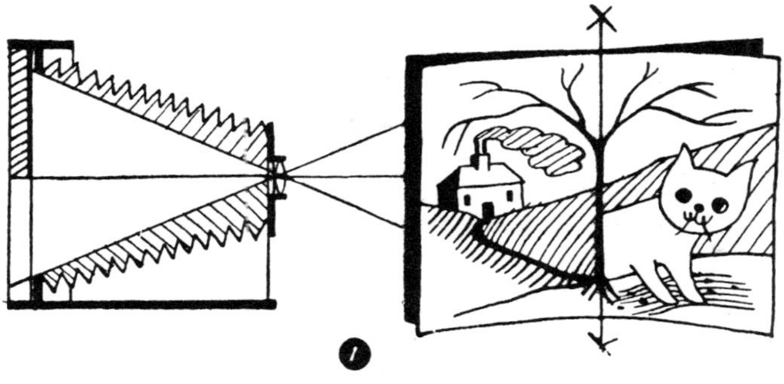

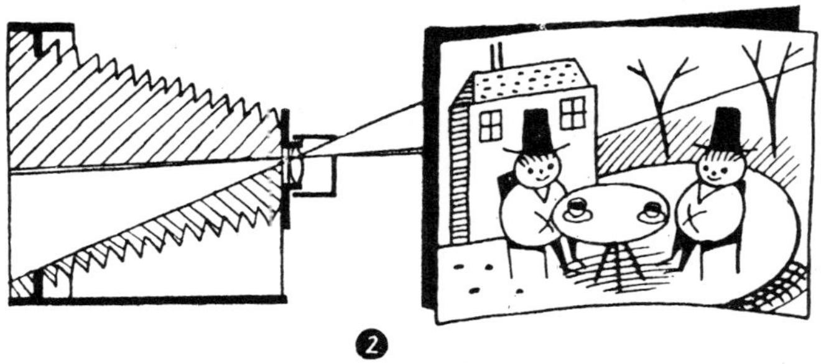

MASKING IN AND OUT OF THE CAMERA

The mask arranged inside the camera cuts with a sharp line, and has been used in drawing *1* to cut along the straight line of a thin sapling tree. If one-half of the result is obscured by the hand the production of this odd effect should be apparent—the cat clears off before the second exposure. This technique is really only practicable with a large format camera.

The mask outside the camera (2) cuts with a soft line, without sharp definition, and is suitably employed across any part of the picture. The subject appears to be having tea with a twin, whereas he only moved to the other half of the picture for the second exposure.

of thin card round the lens mount and gluing the ends together The length of the tube should be arranged so that the *front is about half an inch in front of the lens surface:* longer tubes may cut off the corners of the subject and darken the corners of the final print. Having cut the tube, masking is now performed by partially closing one end with a suitably cut disc of card, so that exactly half of the subject is concealed from the focusing screen of the camera.

It would be at first supposed that such an effect is given when exactly half the opening of the hood is obscured, but since there is a certain amount of diffusion behind the mask this is not so. *A mask that more or less accurately divides the subject into two is obtained not by cutting away one-half, but by cutting away about one-third.* So, if your tube and disc is one and a half inches in diameter, a half inch slice of the disc is cut off in a straight line and thrown away. The remaining piece is provisionally fixed in one end of the tube which is then placed on the lens mount of the camera. By so dividing the opening of the lens cap, the image should now occupy approximately one-half of the focusing screen, the division being vertical if the cut edge of the mask is truly upright, and horizontal if the cut edge is across the lens.

The accuracy, or otherwise, of your work can only be thoroughly tested by making an experimental exposure, exposing first one-half of the plate and then the other by reversing the lens cap. If the two halves blend without suspicion of a join you get full marks, and excellent doubles can then be made; but if there is an *under-exposed strip in the middle of the negative, the opening is too small* and must be slightly enlarged; if the strip is *over-exposed, the opening is too large* and must be diminished by cutting a new disc.

The aperture of the diaphragm has an effect on the success of the join, and if the opening has been cut a little too large, a smaller stop may help to correct the fault. It will therefore be best to *adjust the mask for one particular lens aperture,* and use this aperture with the mask consistently.

Having achieved an accurate and satisfactory mask, the disc may be glued permanently in place in the tube and the whole gadget painted a matt black, or covered with black velour paper, to prevent unnecessary light reflection into the lens.

Triple exposures with natural backgrounds are more difficult and need perhaps more care and trouble than the results are worth. The principal difficulty presented is one of successfully

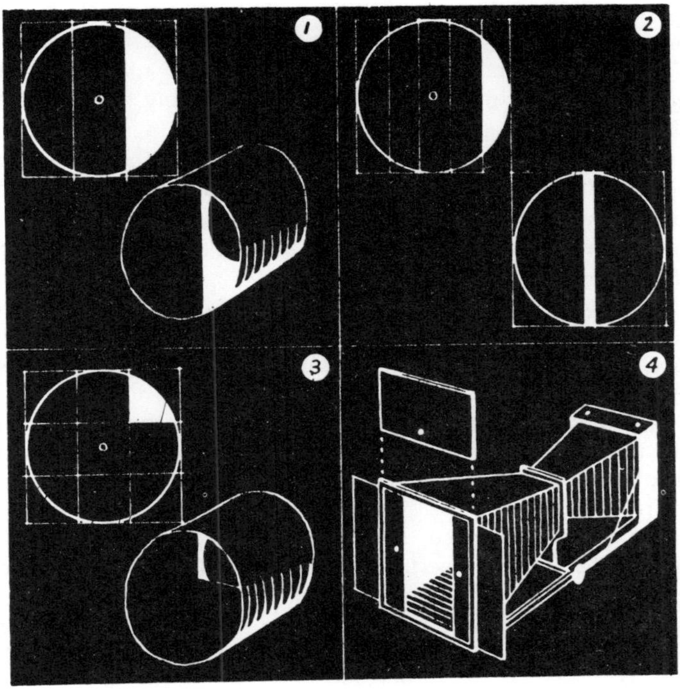

PARTIAL LENS CAPS

1 shows the opening, as a white space, necessary to separately expose one-half of the plate at a time—an opening of one-third the diameter. *2* shows the two openings necessary to expose a third of the plate at a time. the top—a fifth of the diameter, is used for each of the sides by reversing; the bottom—approximately one-twentieth of the diameter, is used for the centre. *3* shows the opening necessary to separately expose the four quarters of the plate—a third of the diameter in each direction. *4* shows an effects box in the form of a framed opening connected to the camera by adjustable bellows, in which can slide masking panels—from either side or from top and bottom.

masking the two sides of the image so that only the centre third is recorded; masking the two-thirds of each side is reasonably simple, but there is so much diffusion of the image from the centre third that over-exposed areas are inevitably formed either side of it.

A lens cap similar to that constructed for doubles can be adapted for triple exposure, and it will be found that the width of the opening necessary to expose only the middle third of the picture will be a surprising fraction of an inch, the side openings also being very small.

It has been ascertained elsewhere that if the lens cap is one inch in diameter, the central opening in the mask will be a slit only .012 of an inch wide. The side opening on the other mask will be .2 of an inch from the rim of the cap.

Obviously two caps will be necessary, one with a dead central slit for the centre of the picture, and one for the sides, with a side aperture which can be used to expose each opposite side in turn by reversing.

As will be expected, such small openings will considerably reduce the effective aperture of the lens, and exposures will need to be increased to approximately four times normal.

Quadruple exposure, where the four quarters of the plate are separately exposed, is effected by cutting a notch out of a circular mask, a little less than one-quarter of the circle.

If two discs from which a third of each has been removed (to produce a double, as previously described) are placed on top of each other so that the cut edges form a right angle, this will indicate the approximate area of the notch; it will be one-third of the disc in each direction at right angles to each other.

Adjustment of the cutting by experimental exposure, as recently described, will ensure that exactly one-quarter corner of the picture area is exposed at a time, the cap being turned in either direction so that the other three corners are consecutively exposed.

The reduction of light caused by this small opening also necessitates prolonging the exposures approximately three to four times.

In all kinds of masking—double, triple, or quadruple—it will be best to adjust the mask to one particular aperture of the lens, and always use that aperture with that particular mask. As already described, varying the aperture will usually affect the extent of the image and cause under- or over-exposed strips at the various joins.

The cut edge of the mask, whatever its shape, can be used to divide the picture at all angles, the division not necessarily being consistently vertical or horizontal. Any diagonal division can be obtained, of course by adusting the cut edge of the mask to that particular angle. However, it is of vital importance to the success of any divided exposure that the edge be kept precisely at the same angle when the cap is rotated for the second, third, or fourth positions.

Needless to say, all multiple *exposures on natural backgrounds must be kept identical for each picture*, the separate strips or corners all receiving equal intensities of light. This is particularly important if the dividing lines cut across an even surface, or the separate divisions show objects which must print the same tone. To this end it will be best to avoid arbitrary time exposures, which can rarely be exactly duplicated, and employ those speeds that are automatically given by the shutter mechanism, and which can be relied upon for absolute consistence.

Since it is imperative that the camera should not be moved by the least fraction of an inch between any double or triple exposure, a very *solid and sturdy tripod* is an indispensable part of the equipment—unless the camera is bolted to a heavy table.

For the sake of simplicity a lens cap has been made to serve for all the multiple exposures described, but these effects, and others of greater complexity, can be achieved by the use of an *effects box*. This could consist of a framed opening, about 10 in. x 8 in. (25 cm. x 20 cm.), connected to the lens panel of the camera by bellows or a similar light-tight contrivance, and in which two masks are arranged, like sliding doors, to form an opening of any width or position.

Oddly-cut masks can also be arranged in the opening of such a box, so that the subject may be recorded in any strangely divided fashion. The centre of an image can be masked by a patch held in position by black thread, the second exposure being made through the mask from which the patch was cut. Exposures made of people against black backgrounds can be combined with exposures of natural backgrounds by such suspended masks, marking the accurate position of the person on the focusing screen, and arranging a patch mask in the frame of the effects box so that the image is not overlapped by the second exposure.

▷ *The uses of multiple exposure against natural backgrounds have been for the most part restricted to the duplication and triplication of a single person in different parts of the plate, to suggest twins, triplets and the like.*

The operation is obvious, the model merely moving himself to that part of the scene recorded by each separate exposure, in such manners and positions that indicate that he is entertaining or talking to himself, or any other preconceived conceit.

A little thought, or no thought at all, will suggest many situations and odd occupations for the person so duped or triplicated, the variations involved being entirely subjective and involving no special technique beyond the masking lens cap.

▷ *The obvious isolation of the figures into three or two compartments can become rather tedious, the vertical line, though quite invisible, becoming a consciously felt barrier by the fact that no parts of the separate figures overlap.*

This can to some extent be avoided by adopting a diagonal rather than a vertical dividing line, the effect of which is to place a part of one division vertically over another. By such means the model can lean over the shoulder of his second image, or extend an arm apparently into the other half of the plate, the two images seeming successfully to invade each other's territory and the effect of rigid vertical division is broken up.

▷ *Backgrounds for these double and triple exposures, being natural, should show variations in form, tone and texture, and not be plain and unbroken. Indoors, parts of curtaining, mouldings, pictures and other naturally occurring objects should be encouraged. Ourdoors, trees and folliage of all kinds could be particularly suitable.*

Small variations in form tend to disguise any suspicion of tone difference occurring at the joints, and, to further assist this end, the divisions of the picture can be arranged on some background object which shows lines or tones running in the same direction—such as the folds of a curtain or the many repeating lines of a moulding.

▷ *The mask can be used, not to repeat a person or object, but to cut portions from a single image. By such a use the upper or lower half of a person can be removed and left oddly isolated in a normal scene; legs, arms, heads and hands can all be severed if they are extended into the masked portion of the picture and the second exposure made of an unobscured background.*

▷ *Similarly, a series of welcome variations are revealed if the dividing line of the double exposure is regarded as the centre line of a symmetrical figure, if you place an unframed mirror across a print you will observe the possibilities of such a strangely-placed division.*

One-half of the film is exposed to the image of a person arranged so that the cutting line of the mask cuts off some part of them, either an odd slice or just either side of the centre of the body in a vertical direction. The second exposure is made of the same person, cut in exactly the same way, but on the other side. If the two halves are correctly aligned the complete negative shows a curiously-joined figure of fantastic shape.

An easy example, and one which should make the method clear, is the creation of the Siamese twins. The model standing with back to the dividing line so that the mask obscures that position of the anatomy that is intended to join to the other twin.

For the second exposure the model turns t'other way round so that the mask cuts in an identical manner across the same place. By carefully marking the focusing screen so that the two cuts coincide, the final image reveals a person inextricably, and inexplicably, joined to himself. Twins joined at the side, instead of the back, can be likewise obtained if the model faces the camera and the mask cuts off a slice of the hip on each side.

As long as the position of the two cut portions is arranged in the same position on the centre line, there is no necessity for the two images to be identically occupied, each can easily indulge an individual fancy.

▷ *If the operation is clear to you, other applications will soon be apparent, and the human figure can be endlessly severed and rejoined in a variety of unholy ways, depending how and where the mask cuts.*

Strange double profiles in which the model has two fronts and no back, or two backs and no front, double-headed monsters and bodies compressed or enlarged by omitting or duplicating a strip of their torso either side of the centre line. As before suggested, practice on flat prints with an unframed mirror will reveal the possibilities of the process.

▷ *By cutting across the picture in a horizontal direction the bottom half of the film can show a rear view, and the top half a front view of the same person, who thus appears in the finished combination to be oddly twisted about the middle.*

▷ *Again, if, after recording the bottom half, the model raises himself on a box or lowers himself by bending knees, the finished print will show a strange effect of elongated or compressed anatomy, providing the two points on the masking line are made to combine successfully.*

▷ *Separate exposure of the four quarters of the film area can produce an image in which the top half of a person is in one half of the picture, and the bottom in the other. The legs being recorded in one bottom corner, the torso and head in an opposite top corner, and the two remaining corners exposed to unobscured background.*

▷ *By cutting a figure at odd points, as described a few paragraphs ago, the four corner mask can be made to produce figures with odd junctions on both its centre lines; a little thought will reveal this to you better than a multitude of words.*

▷ *Double exposure without the use of masks can be used to produce transparent images of objects and people in a very ghostly manner.*

The effect is contrived by removing the person or object from the scene before making the second exposure, so that they, and the background they obscured, are only half-exposed.

According to convention the ghost may be draped in a sheet or hung about in light-coloured clothes—he will be just as transparent either way. When the exposure is prolonged, and not just a fraction of a second, the model can walk out of the picture without interrupting the exposure—he will probably leave a few spiritual streaks, but this is all in the right tradition.

With these specimen examples as your guides, the direction and first few steps of many new roads should be clear. These early yards are well trodden, but way ahead you will find no more than a few infrequent footsteps faintly preceding you.

Doubles in the Darkroom

The principle by which one side of an image is recorded separately from the other makes it possible to produce double exposures with natural backgrounds in the darkroom, by masking alternate sides of the printing paper beneath the enlarger.

Double exposures with normal surroundings can be achieved by the combination printing of two negatives on the same sheet of printing paper.

The negatives are obtained by making two separate exposures in the normal manner, without the use of a mask, and without shifting the camera. Both, when developed, will show an identical scene with a different disposition of the person intended for duplication—in one-half of one exposure, and in the other half of the other.

The negatives are projected in a normal manner using the englarer, one side of the image being obscured by a mask over the printing paper, and the mask being reversed for the exposure of the second negative. A print is obtained in which the opposite sides of two negatives are obtained on the same print, the two sides naturally being those that contain the person.

Masking is achieved by placing a *sheet of black card over the printing paper, about one-quarter to one-half an inch* (0.50 cm. to 1.25 cm.) above its surface, and so arranged that it obscures the empty half of the scene of each negative by being reversed for the second exposure.

The successful merging of the two sides will depend entirely upon the accuracy with which the two negatives are registered along the cutting line of the mask, and it will be necessary to use a sheet of paper, identical in size and thickness to the printing paper, as a *register* on which can be *marked* the main feature lines of the images and the position of the mask above.

After the first exposure, the half-exposed paper is temporarily returned to its dark box and the image of the second negative manoeuvred into correct place with the aid of the marked sheet of paper.

When the mask has been accurately placed, the half-exposed paper is returned to the paper holder, taking care to get it right way round, and the second exposure is made of similar duration to the first.

If the operations are successfully carried out the two images should blend without trace of a join, both halves will have the same printing tone, and there will be no clue to the double origin of the finished print.

The nearer the mask to the surface of the paper, the sharper the cut edge, and the greater the consequent need for accuracy of masking and registering the two halves. A distance of half an inch (1.25 cm.) on a 10 in. x 8 in. (25 cm. x 20 cm.) enlargement will permit a slight diffusion of the image beneath the mask, which thus permits the two halves to blend without a line of hard definition.

This *diffusion inevitably implies slight over-exposure* of that area and a darkening of tone in the region of the join. With backgrounds of varied detail, form, and tone this could pass unnoticed, but in the case of plain, flat-toned objects and grounds, the defect cannot be ignored, and the mask must be moved nearer to the paper.

If you can attain the requisite skill, there is no reason why triples and quadruples, or any similar division, should not be managed in a similar fashion, the method will be as obvious as the accuracy and patience required.

By an extension of this last method it is possible to obtain the effects of curious duplication about a centre line that were described on page 112. They are here contrived by printing the same half of a negative on both halves of the paper—by reversing the negative in the carrier for the second exposure.

The operation is the same as the two-negative method, including the use of the paper for registration-marking and the black paper mask reversed for each exposure. Except that instead of the second negative being substituted for the first, the negative is turned over in the enlarger so that the same portion of its image occupies the other half of the paper in reversed form.

In some cases, particularly with thick film, the *displacement of the emulsion when the negative is reversed* brings it either larger or smaller than its former size and will necessitate *re-focusing the image.*

Under these conditions, getting both images of identical size is a very ticklish job, even with the aid of the marked paper. A more successful arrangement is to doctor the *negative carrier*—by strips of paper used as packing—so that the emulsion of the negative occurs in the same plane whichever way up the carrier is turned.

▷ *Masking a negative in the darkroom is not essentially different to masking the film in the camera, and the effects obtained by the one, as described on page 111 are easily duplicated by the other. It is an alternative, and not a separate method.*

Effects which involve the use of strange shaped masks, however, are much more easily accomplished in the darkroom than with the aid of an effects box before the camera. A sheet of good clear glass, without flaws of any kind, is placed above the surface of the printing paper and masks of any shape can be laid upon it to conceal or reveal any parts of the image.

Thus, in the production of a normal double, the cut edge of the mask can be made to follow some feature in or about the centre of the picture—say, down the side of a door, along the top of a table, and down one of its folds to the floor—so more effectively disguising the joint than if cut in a straight vertical down the picture. The cutting would be done in the middle of a

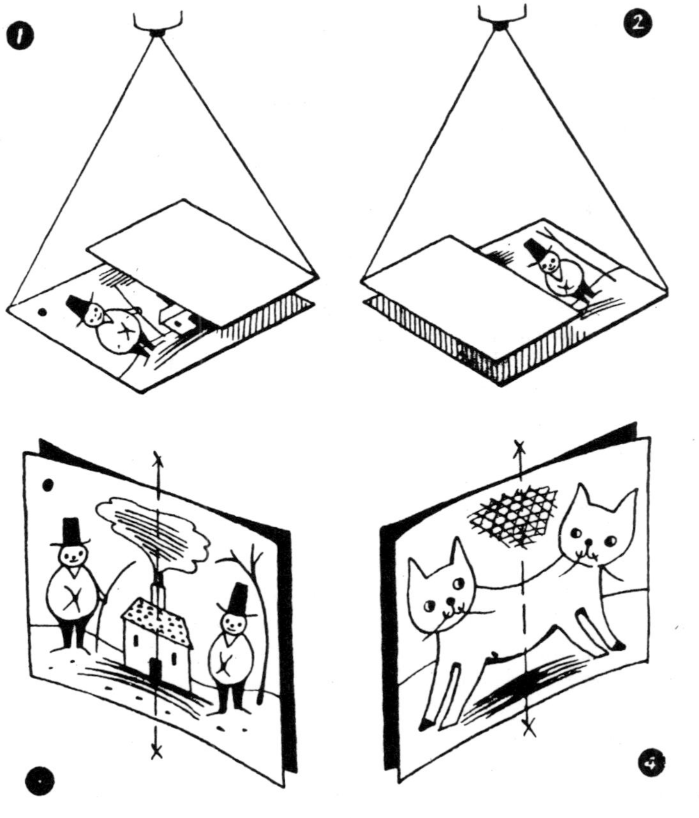

MASK BENEATH THE ENLARGER

Two negatives have been made of the same scene—the same person occurring in an opposite half each time. The negatives are so printed on the same sheet of paper, by masking opposite sides during both exposures (*1* and *2*), that a single print of the scene is obtained, inhabited by twins or two separate images of the original person—*3*.

As a variation, a single negative can be half masked and reversed for the second exposure, so that one end is repeated twice to make a whole picture—the half of the picture showing the cat's tail has been masked away in each exposure.

large mask, and the two sides alternately laid on the glass for the successive exposures.

▷ *Reversed duplications in the enlarger can imitate effects of the same kind achieved by masking in front of the camera, and* such as are suggested on page 112.

In the enlarger, however, the method may be extended to include many other subjects, for example animals, that would be most difficult to treat by double exposure in the camera.

Thus, by duplicating one side of a horizontal negative showing the side view of a cat, dog, horse or other quadruped, an animal with two ends and no head, or two heads and no end can obviously be created.

▷ *Reversal of a complete image, rather than an oddly-cut part, gives the effect of a true reflection, and suitably chosen scenes can be printed as if relected in water if the dividing line is arranged in a natural position. Prolonging the exposure of the lower half will produce a deeper printing tone, which enhances the reality of the effect.*

If the dividing line of the mask is arranged exactly down the middle of a full face portrait, faces can be printed which are composed of two right or two left sides. It will perhaps surprise you that there can be a great difference in the two sides of many faces, and that strange effects can result from duplicating either side to complete a new face. Thus, three faces can be made from one.

▷ *First-rate abstract patterns can be created by reversed duplication of appropriately shaped and cut images, and the placing of an unframed piece of mirror at various angles across a collection of prints, will reveal the effects that their negatives are capable of producing in this direction.*

▷ *Dividing the image and exposure into four corners will produce patterns reminiscent of the kaleidoscope, the reversed duplication occurring on each side of the two centre lines.*

▷ *The ghost that appeared in the closing sentences of the last method can be raised in the darkroom if its shape is cut from a black mask and laid in the appropriate position on the surface of the printing paper.*

The mask holds back the light from this part of the paper: the longer it is left the lighter the tone of the ghost, though it should not be left for too long or the spirit will be a disappointing bleak silhouette without transparency.

Such an apparition is not so successful as the half-exposed person previously described, but the effect is possible.

PHOTOMONTAGE

Photomontage is the simultaneous presentation of a number of images in the form of a complete picture, combining on one print objects, information, and suggestion that were in reality removed in space and time, and that would otherwise take several separate photographs to convey.

The combination can take several forms, the images overlapping each other, merging into one another, or occurring in separate conjunction, and they are achieved in the camera, in the enlarger, or by simply cutting and pasting.

Multiple exposure, in one way or another, is the basis of all montage effects, and the term photomontage is often exclusively claimed for combinations that only show a separate conjunction of separately taken pictures. Territory, however, in these suburbs of photography is not distinctly defined, and the point where one clearly becomes the other lacks definition.

From the spectator's, rather than the producer's, point of view, a photomontage is of two kinds, according to whether deception is intended or not.

In one, the separate images are grouped in such a manner that would lead the spectator to believe the picture a straight and honest print of a single negative. Composition, lighting, perspective and proportion are kept consistent throughout, and joining by pasting or double printing is arranged so that its presence is not easily detected.

The other intends to convey information or sensation without illusion, to suggest an idea without seeking to conceal that the final product is anything but an assembly of separate views. Perspective and normal proportion need not be strictly adhered to, and composition is directed towards abstract design rather than natural effect. The joins, and any other artifice, are not disguised here but openly proclaim themselves as part of the effect.

Cut and Paste

This is the basic and most primitive method of montage, and since it is almost impossible to conceal its presence the technique is best used to produce those effects in which the joins are either unimportant or part of the design.

As the title suggests, the method consists of cutting out parts of one or more prints and pasting them over parts of another print, a photo background, or on a plain neutral sheet to form a design.

All prints to be so treated should be made on *thin or single-weight paper*, and on papers of identical surface. The *contrasts* and density of each, unless particularly desired otherwise, should be the same—one should not be noticeably lighter or darker than another. The prints should be of consistent *sharpness* so that a hard cut edge does not appear too harshly among a collection of fuzzy outlines.

Cutting should be done with a sharp knife having a thin blade, a *mount-cutter's knife* or *a razor blade* in a cutting holder is most suitable. These will permit one to follow more accurately the often complicated outlines of the picture, without leaving the furry edges or points in corners that are often produced by even the sharpest scissors.

The cutting operation should be performed *on a sheet of glass or metal* so that the cut is made cleanly and the edges should be slightly bevelled inwards, towards the back of the print.

Even the thinnest printing paper has a quite substantial edge. This must be reduced by *sandpapering* the back of the print until the margin is of wafer thinness and beds down evenly on the print below. The sandpaper should be of a gentle grade, and to minimise the risk of torn edges it is perhaps best to cut the print, the first time, with a rough margin of about one-sixteenth of an inch all round, the final accurate cutting being performed after the edges are thinned. (The special 'document' printing paper though suitably thin for montage may not be opaque enough to paste over dark tones without some show-through).

When the margins are successfully reduced there should be no white edge around the cut portion when it is laid on the final print. If you have not succeeded in wearing them down far enough, and are afraid of tearing the print, the slight *white edge should be painted black* or tinted to match the tones adjacent to it.

"Pasting" is not meant to be taken literally, as memories of soggy scrap-books might suggest, and paste is actually the last thing that should be used. If the prints are glazed the water content will dull them, and even if they are of matt surface the stuck portion will usually bulge and blister.

Apart from the dry mounting press, the ideal photographic adhesive is *rubber cement*, which can be obtained in small tubes and tins from any sizeable artist's material dealer. This substance will not affect the glaze of the picture, and, should any spread out from edges on to the print's surface, it may be simply removed by rubbing it with the finger until it crumbles off, without leaving a trace. Should you change your mind about the positions of the mounted parts, they may be removed with a little care and re-stuck in another position without damaging the lower surface.

The rubber cement is best applied in a thin even film with a *palette knife* or a similar flexible blade, the print being placed gently in position and firmly pressed with the hand, or by rolling a rubber squeegee over a protecting sheet of paper laid on the print.

If successfully accomplished, the edges of the mounted print should not catch the light or cast a shadow, and though the presence of the patch can be detected when the print is seen by side light, a *flat-on light* should not clearly reveal its existence.

When the desired effect depends upon deception and disguise, the finished pasted-up product should be *copied on to a new negative,* the print being evenly lit from all sides. To keep the stuck portions rigidly flat, and without the slightest wave, it is often desirable to copy the print *under a sheet of glass,* so weighted that it presses the parts into close contact.

▷ *The craft of cut and paste is older than photography, and in earlier centuries it was a popular pastime to cut pieces from the prints of the day to form new combination pictures on screens, trays, and other surfaces; to make lovely bouquets, and similar still-life pictures, from odd scraps of coloured material, paper, and printed stuffs.*

And, though not in the cut and paste manner of course, nobler examples of the montage manner are provided by Breughel and other Flemish painters, who combined in a single picture incidents which, though not in essentials disconnected, rarely occur together in the boundaries of a single scene. Thus, on one delightfully crowded canvas, Breughel has depicted a busy scene, each occupant and incident of which amusingly illustrates a popular proverb of the day. The picture includes as many as ninety—nearly all of which are immediately recognisable and many in popular use to-day.

In one of its first appearances in photographic history, montage was used tendentiously, purporting to show the flight of the Empress Eugenie from Paris in 1870, by pasting prints of the heads of the Empress and her maidservant upon the shoulders of two other women in a group specially posed, with a carriage, before the entrance of the Tuileries. A pictorially more ambitious attempt of 1857 by O. G. Reijlander, "The Two Ways of Life", is a large composition skilfully constructed from many separate negatives, mostly multiple printed, showing on one side the primrose, on the other the thorny, paths—neither very appetising in the Victorian version.

To-day the method survives as "collage" and "decoupage" to create fantastic pictures from separate cut images. Strange pictures which outrage all formal order or conventional sense, and which, apart from the paste-up, could only find form in the imagination.

There are clues to the uses of cut and paste montage. Clues only can be given, for the material and its uses are limitless and stretch almost to a patched and sticky infinity.

▷ *The cutting of any print can be whole or partial, and a horizontal picture of a landscape can be cut merely along an edge that follows the horizon, be it hills, hedgerows, or clumps of trees. This top-cut print can be mounted on to yet another landscape, or upon the picture of a busy street which in turn has been cut along some natural profile, such as the tops of the buildings. The two can then be mounted over a print showing sky, water, or what you will, in endless planes.*

Cutting along natural contours is a most successful method of joining several small-scale scenes—ranges of hills, groups of thickly-foliated trees, long lines of roof-tops or single houses, the straight horizon of a lake or ocean. Any scene or group of objects that offers a straightforward cutting line is ideal. The process can be likened to the cut-out scenery of the theatre, which is cut on a natural line, each wing screening the beginning of the other until the backcloth is reached.

Such combinations can be frankly fantastic and purely imaginative, or they can aim at some kind of reality by keeping perspective and relative proportion more or less within the bounds of credibility.

The prints, preferably, should be varied in tone so that the several planes are made apparent, each cut-out contrasting effectively with the next, the darkest plane in the foreground and the others getting lighter as they recede, or vice versa.

If the product aims at nature, the effect of a consistent direction of light should be maintained by arranging that the shadows shown in the separate pictures all fall the same way, which can often be simply achieved by making reversed prints of any offenders, by inverting the negative in the enlarger and printing down though the back of it.

▷ *Complete cutting, in which the object is severed from its original background is another mode of operation. The cut-out figures of persons, animals, birds, buildings and vehicles, or any other self-contained unit can be pasted on various backgrounds to serve several ends.*

Such isolated figures can inhabit the montage scenery, just described, in a rational manner or so that they appear to walk in water or on air. A collection of such figures can form a tableau on a normal photo background of a room, a street scene, or even a neutral background of clouds or sea. They can be effectively composed on a plain white or black paper background, and connected, in perspective, by a few well-placed straight lines either drawn or pasted on.

▷ *Kaleidoscopic patterns, as described on page* 86, *can be contrived by cutting out the same portion of several prints from one negative, pasting them up in the form of a circle or star of which the images form the separate segments. Several enlargements, all of even printing tone, of a single negative showing varied detail and contrast, will yield many such patterns from its various parts. An equal number of reversed prints will be necessary to provide the alternating reflected image of the kaleidoscope pattern.*

▷ *Impossibly monstrous, but lovely, bouquets can be brought into being by cutting out the images from separate flower negatives and pasting them up in more or less natural conjunction.*

▷ *Strange and fascinating towns can be built from the repeated and suitably pasted image of a few houses. Variations in the printing tone of the separate pieces will be found a great help in suggesting colour and avoiding monotony of tone.*

▷ *Photographs can be cut to shapes that ignore the contour of any image they contain, flower shapes or letters cut from any part of the picture, so that details appear in strange places, will suggest the possibility. Plain backgrounds are best.*

On the unimaginative the best suggestions will be wasted, and this method will yield but meagre results if there is no sense of fantasy. With imagination and patience, cut and paste will yield rich results in the very best and noble scrap-book, scrap screen tradition.

Just think of the oddly embarrassing situations in which you can paste your least attractive acquaintances and relations, the dubious company you can cause them to keep, and in what suggestive surroundings.

This is a territory of which you are sole master and creator, and you will either love or loathe its anarchic freedom.

Double Exposure

Fantasy is the forte of cut and paste. It *can* be done to deceive, but the labour which seeks to conceal itself is often tedious, and effects which aim at truth to nature are best reserved for methods more suitable to that end.

Multiple exposure is all five aces of photography's trick pack, and the basis of naturalistic montage in the camera or enlarger.

Before the age of double exposure prevention devices on cameras the double exposure was every amateur's first unwitting trick, and it is more than probable that the first freak photograph was a double exposure.

Successful accidental doubles were rare, but the best had an air of rightness and authority that only the happy accident can ever aspire to. The remainder suffered from too much confusion and chaos, as do many intentional examples.

The varied densities of a negative are products of the action of light upon the silver salts of an emulsion, those parts of the subject displaying bright tones or colours, or brilliantly lit, creating the greatest density; those parts of low tone or colour value, or poorly lit, creating the least. If two exposures are made on the surface of a single piece of film, the features of the second subject will record with most success on those parts of the negative that contain the lower tones and shadowed parts of the first image, and with distinctly less success on those parts that received the brilliant tones and highlights.

Obviously, the shadows of the first exposure leave the emul-

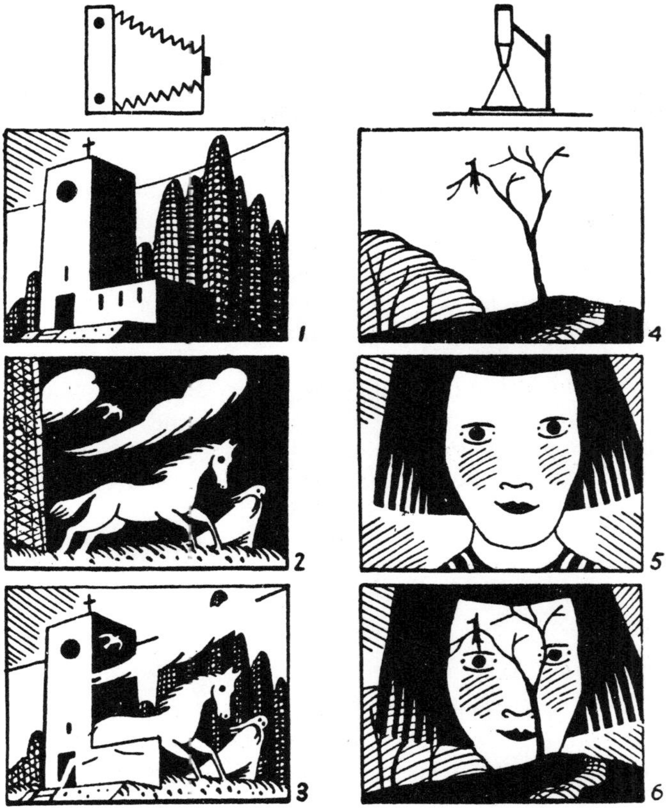

DOUBLE EXPOSURE

Through the camera, the second exposure records best on those parts of the first that contained the shadows and darker areas. *1* being the first exposure, *2* being the second, and *3* being the developed result—*2* appearing clearest in all the shadow areas of *1.*

Through the enlarger, the second exposure records best on those parts of the paper that registered the lighter areas of the first. *4* being the first exposure on the printing paper, *5* the second, and *6* the developed result—*5* appearing only on the lightest areas of *4*.

sion relatively unchanged and in its more or less original sensitive state, whereas the lighter parts create a tone, more or less opaque, according to their relative intensity. The shadows therefore can record a second image with an almost full range of contrast between shadow and highlight, whereas the parts already affected by light can never register a second shadow, and the second highlights only serve to increase their density to a point of ultra over-exposure.

To make successful doubles, then, it is essential that particular attention be paid to the disposition of the areas of light and shade in each exposure—*seeing that the shadows of one occur over the highlights of the other, and avoiding an intense brilliance in the same place twice.*

To this end, it is best that one subject should be of low general tone value, or with a dark neutral background. People with dark clothes, dark trees or foliage, dark stretches of water or wet streets—all will produce low densities and leave the film with a full near range for the second exposure.

Under-exposure will greatly assist in keeping down negative density, so that if the two exposures are made to share the required time—or each gets only half its ideal requirement—most subjects, whatever the disposition of light, will be suitable.

In the Enlarger

It is clear that if the under-exposed film, or a normally exposed one that contains many low tones or shadows, is developed without being exposed a second time, the resulting thin negative can be printed in combination with another, either simultaneously in the enlarger, or one after the other on the same sheet of printing paper.

Should the two negatives be combined in the enlarger, the two *emulsion sides must be placed face to face in the negative carrier,* or focusing difficulties will arise. The effects of this simultaneous combination are identical to double exposure in the camera, and it is often a more convenient and controllable means of getting a desired effect.

Printing one negative after another, whether by contact or enlargement, however, has a very different effect. Instead of the second image appearing through the shadows of the first, it now prints through the *highlights*—the shadows being already affected by the first exposure and incapable of registering another image.

When a double exposure involves a dense negative or any

brilliantly-lit subject, such as a bright wall, a snow scene, or, say, a nude that fills the plate, the best and only method of successful combination will be separate printing of one negative after the other on the same sheet of printing paper, and not combined negative printing or double exposure in the camera.

▷ *The uses of double exposure in camera or darkroom are manifold. It is the broad basis of many effects to be subsequently described under other headings.*

Selection and particular combination of the two subjects or negatives is the basis of the method and its effects, and your choice will naturally be guided by the ultimate end in view.

The two subjects may be selected for their pattern-making possibilities, where the two are combined to make a rich abstract design, interesting for its own sake, and without subjective motives.

They may be combined as a comment one upon the other, so that the second image extends a story-suggestion hinted at in the first.

Thirdly, they may be combined on a plane of pure fantasy to suggest the atmosphere of a dream, or to enhance the mood created by one of the pictures.

▷ *Pattern-making combinations can be carried out with many subjects. It has been done successfully with parts of the nude human figure superimposed one on the other, by separate printing; popular material is geometric objects or parts of machines. The parts of a clock or other mechanism may be placed on neutral or black backgrounds, and recorded one after another to make a pre-designed pattern arrangement.*

Such combinations can obviously be made with any collection of surfaces, or separate objects, that your imagination suggests as good designs. The effects are very rich and almost without end.

▷ *Story-telling or moral-pointing combinations have been responsible for much tedious symbolism of a painfully obvious kind, lean and grasping hands printed over a large loaf of bread, glasses of evil liquor over the distorted portrait of some happy inebriate, piles of notes and coins over bearded misers or bloated capitalists, and similar devices for explaining a picture out of existence.*

These may be emulated or eschewed, according to taste.

Effective use has been made of print in all its various forms from books, newspapers and hoardings, to give literary aid to a pictorial invention; a race card or the sports page of a newspaper over the image of racing horses, the headlines announcing a murder over the picture of a screaming face; these give the idea—a little obvious, but since print will always give a quickly-read clue this is more or less inevitable.

The combinations can be made in the camera or the darkroom. Print, as it is usually dark on a light ground, however, gives a dense negative and will best be combined with any other image by separate printing on the same sheet of paper.

▷ The fantastic, or free association of ideas method, in which the combination is on the plane of imagination, produces the most consistently satisfying results. Here nothing is impossible, and it becomes more than difficult even to suggest a specimen example.

Subjects should be chosen whose combination is unusual and not stereotyped, not to convey a wordy or literary idea, or hammer home a hackneyed symbol, but to suggest pictorial poetry rather than pictorial prose.

Verbal descriptions of such a combination are, in essence, impossible since the intention is to transcend words and convey more than a mere description of the effects would contain. They are best paralleled by those happy accidental doubles that used to be created without our bungling assistance, and where faces appeared suspended strangely in groups of trees, or where a horse strode magnificently across a faint family group—the reality not of the pedestrian, but of the plane where parallel lines meet.

▷ Apart from these montages which exploit the duality of the double image and frankly admit duplicity, there are a number of possible uses in which the negatives can be combined to produce a result whose double nature is difficult to detect.

Thus, negatives of night or evening scenes, in which the sky portion is almost clear gelatine, can be double printed with negatives that show various phenomena of the night.

The moon, for instance, is difficult to record in successful conjunction with a moon-lit scene, since the exposure for the scene will be long enough for the moon's movement to be shown. But, such an evening scene can easily be combined with a negative in which the exposure had been adjusted for the moon, and which shows it in the required position.

This moon negative is preferably made with a longer focus lens than the other, which will show it relatively larger than nature on the finished print. A correctly proportioned moon looks more *than a little lost in a photographic night sky. The negative should show no detail of landscape or surroundings but only the moon on a perfectly clear emulsion.*

It is only necessary to combine the two negatives face to face, so that the moon occurs in a suitable part of the scene, and enlarge them simultaneously in the normal manner. The result will be most effective when the moon has an atmospheric ring round it, or a few clouds nearby.

▷ *Other nocturnal phenomena which, like the moon, record as black densities on a clear negative are bursts of fireworks and flashes of lightning. A negative which has been exposed to several rocket bursts can be effectively combined with attractive night scenes of towns, showing illuminations, or a foreground of dimly-lit people, both taken separately.*

▷ *Lightning, recorded at night, produces a clear negative except for the wriggling rivers of the flash, and such a negative can be double printed with any number of different scenes, both day and night, that show a more or less clear gelatine sky in the same position.*

▷ *Rainbows, which because they are unpredictable, are notoriously difficult to capture in a truthful manner, can also be produced by combination printing, if the bow is suitably drawn on a large enough piece of film that has been developed, fixed, washed and dried without exposure, and is therefore quite transparent.*

The bow is formed with a compass and pen which has been charged with neococcin solution, red ink or any opaque paint. Take care that the point of compass or pen does not damage the emulsion, by sticking the point in a piece of thick card or india-rubber, and letting the solution flow from the pen without the point coming into actual contact.

The arc is drawn in a suitable position on the negative in relation to the second image, and should consist of two or three arcs with a slight space between each, care also being taken to maintain suitable scale so that the bow does not look too heavy.

The second negative, of the same size (and it is easier to work this effect with large format materials) show an image, the greater portion of which consists of dark storm clouds, with a suitable space for the rainbow to span the sky and merge each of its ends in the landscape or houses below.

In this case the negatives are not combined face to face, as this will give a sharp and harsh rainbow quite uncharacteristic of the actual phenomenon; they should be separated with a glass plate, the back of one being placed in contact with the front of the other.

When a wide aperture is used on the enlarging lens the bow will not be in the same sharp focus as the other image, but the more the lens is stopped down the greater must be the separation.

▷ *Exploiting the same principle of a transparent negative treated with opaque pigment, any scene can be filled with artificial snow flakes of a most realistic kind. The flakes being simply produced by spraying the clear film with opaque colour from an old tooth brush, rubbing the finger along the side or surface of the bristles.*

The "flake film" is separated from the other negative so that the flakes are not sharply defined but suitably out of focus. If three clear films are so treated with flecks of various size—by reducing or increasing the distance between film and toothbrush—a stereoscopic effect can be achieved.

The film with the smallest dots is placed in contact with the emulsion of the principal negative, the others being further removed according to the size of the dots—being made on film they can be separated with glass sheets.

Such a concoction is worth its trouble, giving the authentic appearance of large and fuzzy flakes in the foreground, getting sharper as they approach the plane of focus. Don't make too many dots with the brush or nothing of the scene will be visible.

Flakes can be given a streaky appearance, suitable to a heavy and fast fall, if the colour is lightly wiped in one direction before it is quite dry. The effect in all cases will be at its best in conjunction with evening and night scenes, or where the street is very dark, to give the necessary contrast to the flakes. And it should be done on large format materials, 35mm flakes would be disproportionatley large compared with the scene.

▷ *If the water drops, trickles, and streaks on a glass pane are recorded so that the glass retains its transparency and no objects behind are registered, the resulting negative can be combined with a wet weather or umbrella scene to suggest the view through a rain-streaked window.*

The effect is best produced artificially on a portable sheet of glass, by spraying it with waterdrops and encouraging them to run in the customary fashion. The picture is then made with the glass against a black background, and back-lit as if seen against the sun or an artificial light.

This gives the necessary transparency to the negative and enables the other image to successfully print through it.

▷ Yet another kind of effect can be obtained by double printing a single negative, and shifting the paper between exposures. The negative should show good contrast, preferably of a silhouetted nature, such as a line of trees whose trunks are seen against the sky, roof-tops and chimney-pots, or people seen against clouds or other light background.

These dark images, when the paper is shifted in any direction to the necessary extent, will print on adjacent portions of the paper that are relatively unexposed, with a full tonal range and a convincingly double manner.

If the dark accents are widely spaced, the shift can be performed three or four times before one begins to overlap the other. The different exposures should not be equal, but gradually diminished for each extra image, so that they get successively fainter and fainter in the manner of receding planes.

By this means a silhouetted image of a few widely-spaced trees can be made into a large mysterious forest, and a few stray chimney-pots bewilderingly repeated like the nightmare of a smoke-abatement society.

In practice it will be apparent to you that enough of the negative image must be left to one side of the printing paper, in the direction of the shift, to absorb the necessary movement. The paper will otherwise be fogged by moving outside the borders of the negative.

Double Exposure with Masks

The powers of double exposure in the camera or enlarger are considerably extended if masks are employed to screen parts of the subject, or negative image, during each exposure. Thus, instead of printing over one another in an obvious manner, the images can be made to merge without a perceptible joint and with maximum deception.

Instead of total combination, parts of each image are combined, without overlapping, by screening the unwanted portions with a mask in or outside the camera.

Photomontage in the camera, in addition to the effects of superimposition recently described, can be also contrived by masking opposite parts of the image during each exposure.

The partial lens cap described on page 106 for the propagation of twins and triplets, can be employed, where the subject is cut into two or three simple areas by straight dividing lines. A glance at that particular page, will show you how the mask is used to produce its effects, and spare here the necessity of repetition.

For masking lines of less regular shape, where the image is divided into oddly-shaped compartments, the effects box tentatively described on page 111, and the mask within the camera as used for decapitation on page 101, will be found the most satisfactory means of blending the two images. Both methods can employ masks cut to follow some contour of the subject, or to obscure an isolated part of its centre, though with varying accuracy and precision in each case.

The *mask outside the camera,* as a lens cap or in the effects box, *cuts with a soft and out-of-focus line,* the edges of each division are vignetted into each other, and care must be taken that these diffusions properly merge and do not overlap to form an area of over-exposure around the join.

The diffusion is considerable and makes it quite impossible to use masks of complicated outline and small scale, or isolated patches of minute area. We have previously observed that *two-thirds of the lens must be covered by the partial lens cap before half the plate is obscured,* and it follows that a mask of any shape or size will always obscure less than the area it occupies before the lens, owing to diffusion behind it.

Observation of the partial lens cap will reveal that there is a part in the centre of the lens that remains obscured during both exposures, the successive positions of the cutting line of the mask overlap, occurring alternatively left and right of the centre line. This must be arranged in the two positions of a mask of any shape, or there will be *an area of unpleasant over-exposure between the two halves.*

The *mask inside the camera,* however, when it is placed not more than one inch (2.5 cm.) from the surface of the film, or plate, *cuts with a sharp and firmly defined line;* there is little or no diffusion, and masks of any shape and complication can be used.

The cut line on the negative accurately follows the area and extent of the mask, so that a mask which covers exactly half of the picture opening will obscure half of the image, and so on. Obviously, the necessary skill and accuracy in joining two images cleanly cut by a mask within the camera is considerable: the joint is sharp, with little margin for error, and failure to register the two masks renders the negative useless.

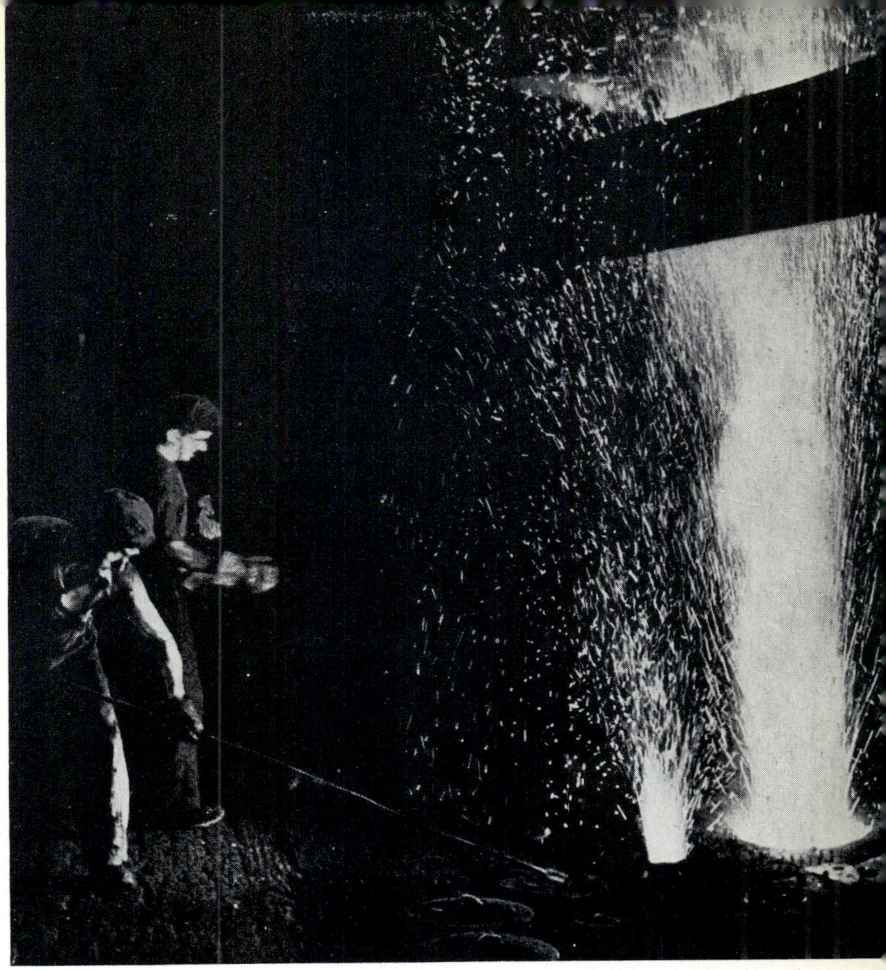

MONTAGE

Montage by double exposure, the first a shapshot of the figures taken with flash in action. The second, on a separate negative, of the furnace "blow-outs" in a brief time exposure. The two combined by separate exposures on a single sheet of paper beneath the enlarger.—*Lancelot Vining.*

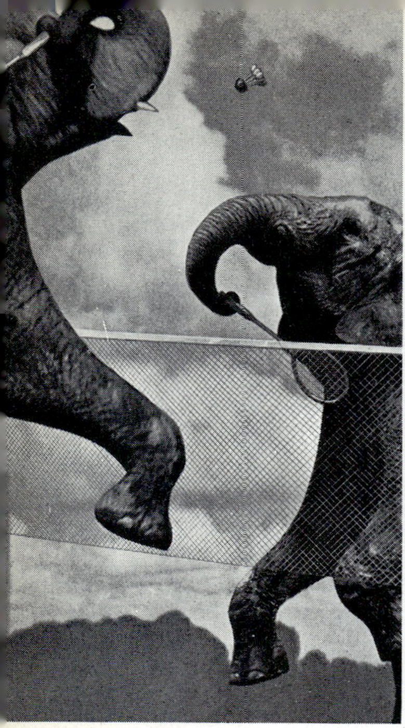

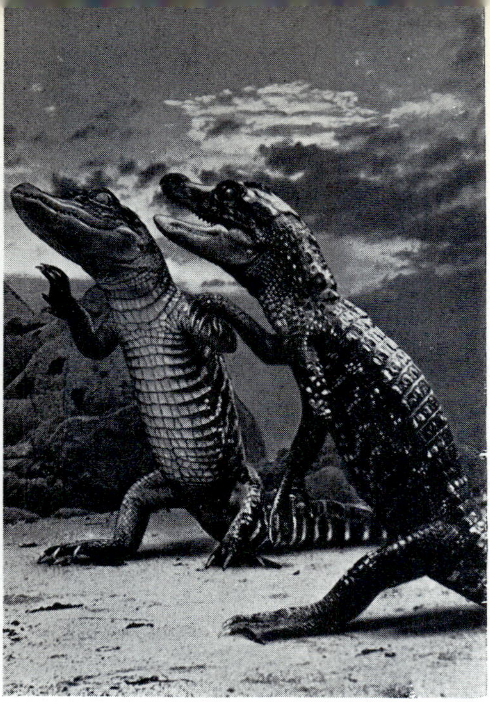

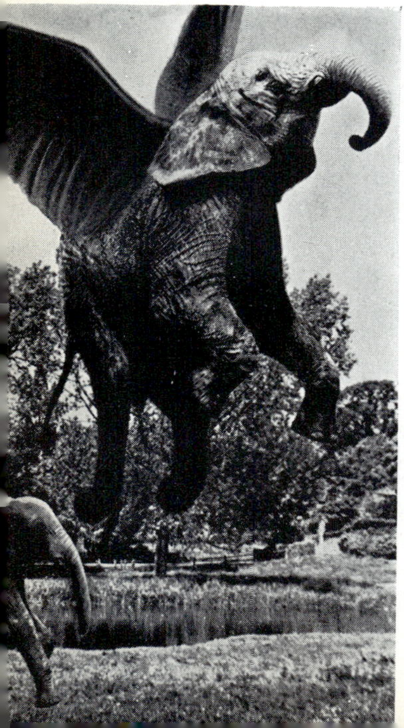

Three cut-and-paste montage pictures assembled from zoo photographs. *Top left* from three negatives—one each for background and each elephant—net, racquets, and shuttlecock being painted in. *Bottom left* from three negatives, the wings cut out from a picture of flying gulls. *Top right* from four negatives—background, foreground, one each for the baby alligators.—*C. A. Bromley.*

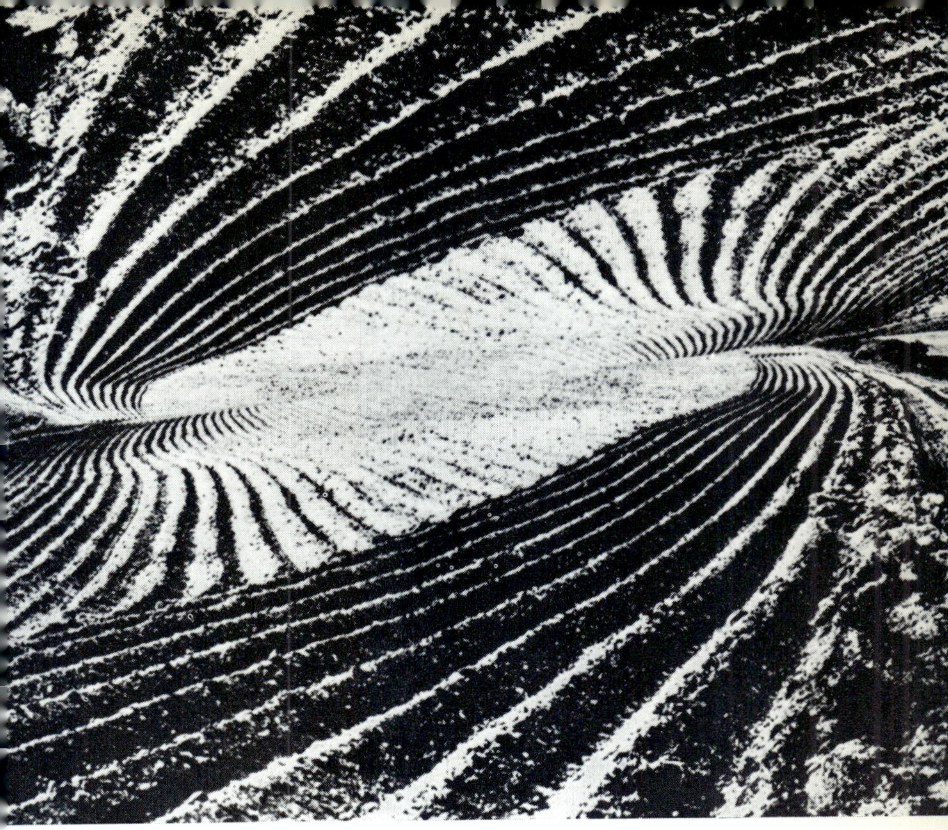

Simple two-part cut-and-paste montage of a ploughed field where two separate identical prints were joined by a diagonal cut across the centre.—*Miroslav Spurny*.

Page 136: Multi-join-up montage. Numerous frames from a sequence of an escalator in a large store joined together in a mosaic.—*Anita Kloten*.

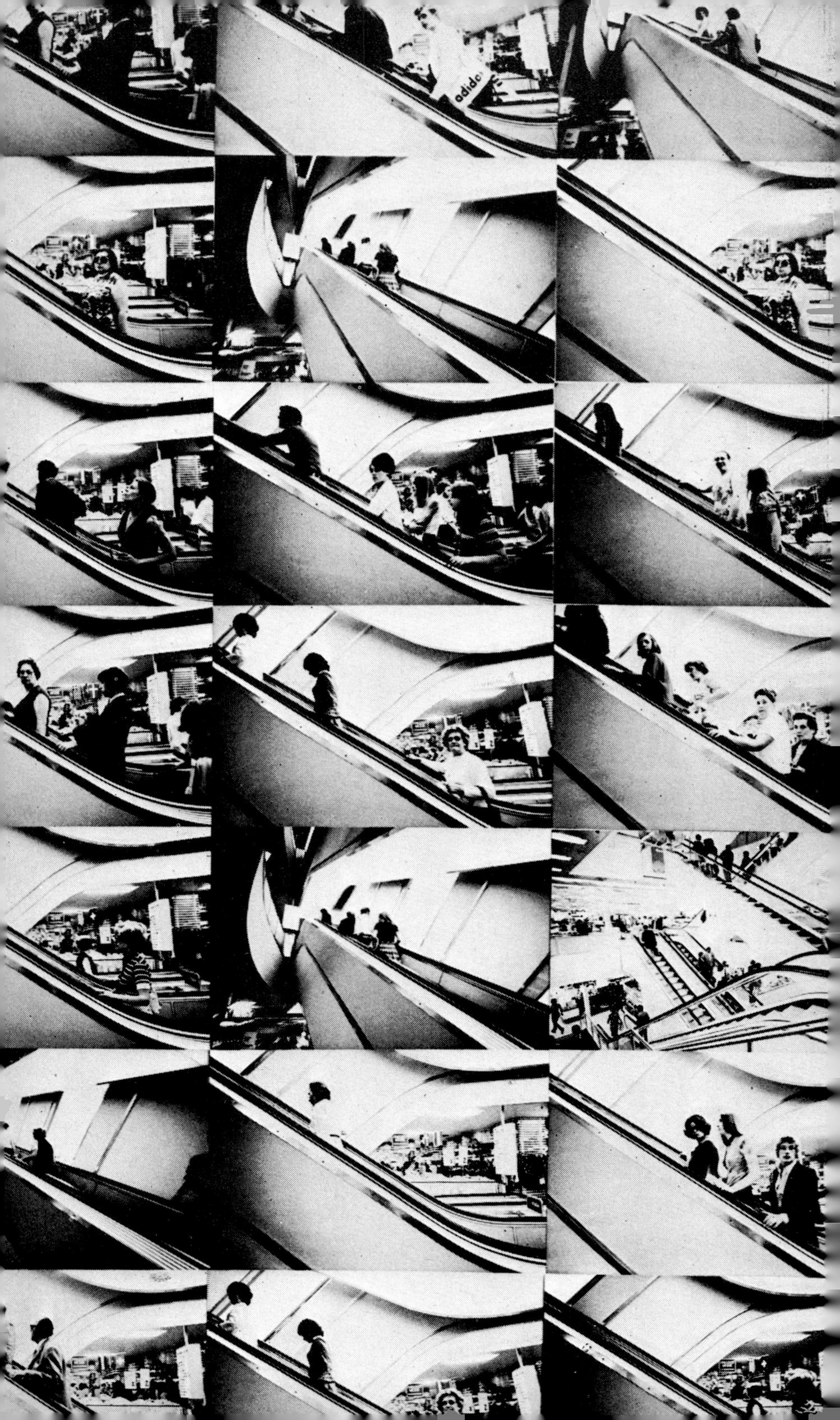

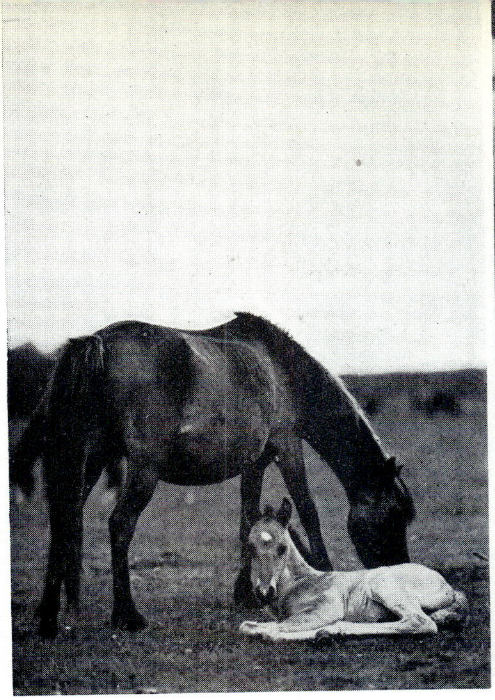

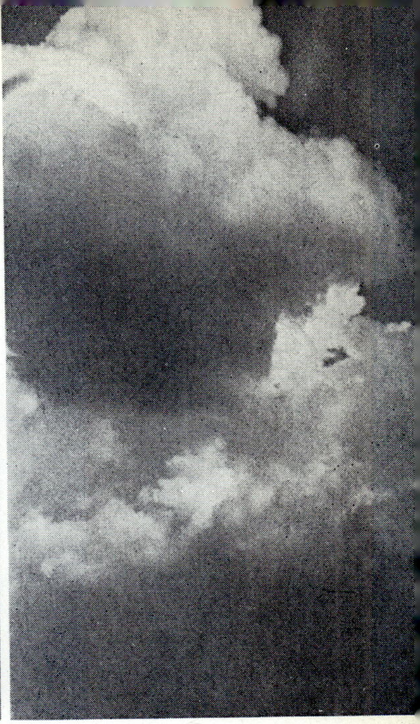

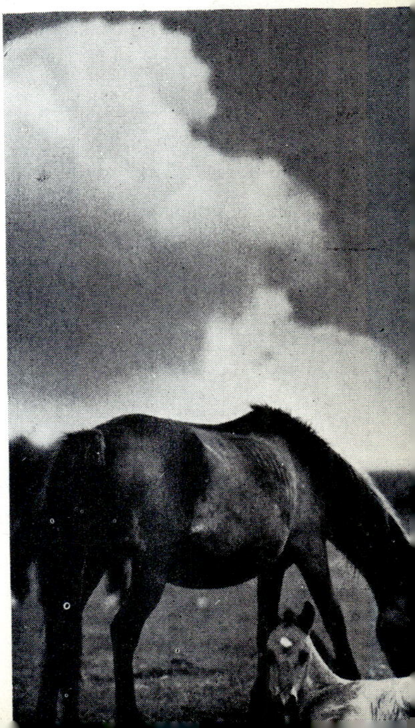

A nice picture with a dull, empty sky is improved by printing a cloud formation of suitable tone and shape, making a normal printing exposure of the subject but screening the subject half of the picture when making the second cloud exposure. The clouds have been printed slightly out of focus to conform to the fuzziness of the subject background.—*O. R. Croy.*

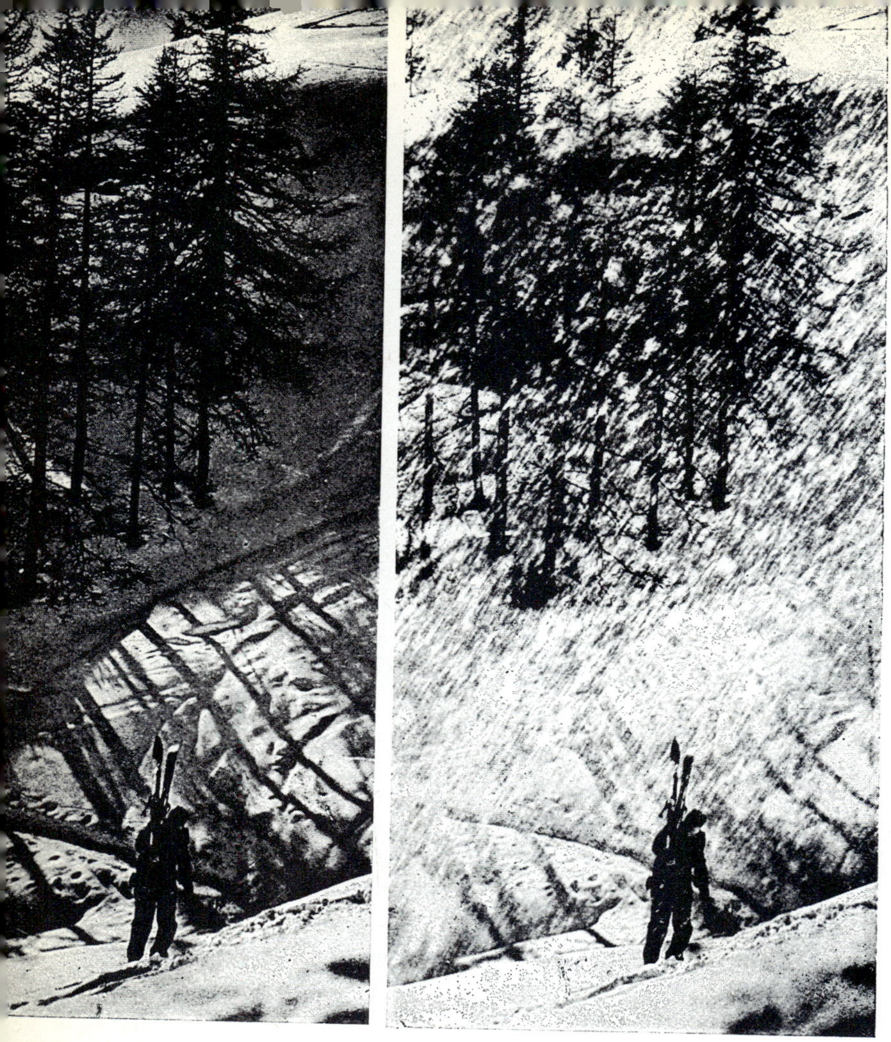

Two versions of the same scene from the same negative. On *left* a straight print, on *right*, a print from the negative after artificial flakes have been added from a toothbrush.—*H. Gorny*

Photographic forestation through moving the paper whilst printing by enlargement. *Above*, a straight print from the negative, and *below*, a print in which the exposure has been interrupted half-way to shift the paper in a horizontal direction. With such widely-spaced units the paper could have been shifted several times more, and an unequal division of exposure times would have produced images of varying tone with more suggestion of recession.—*Edwin Smith.*

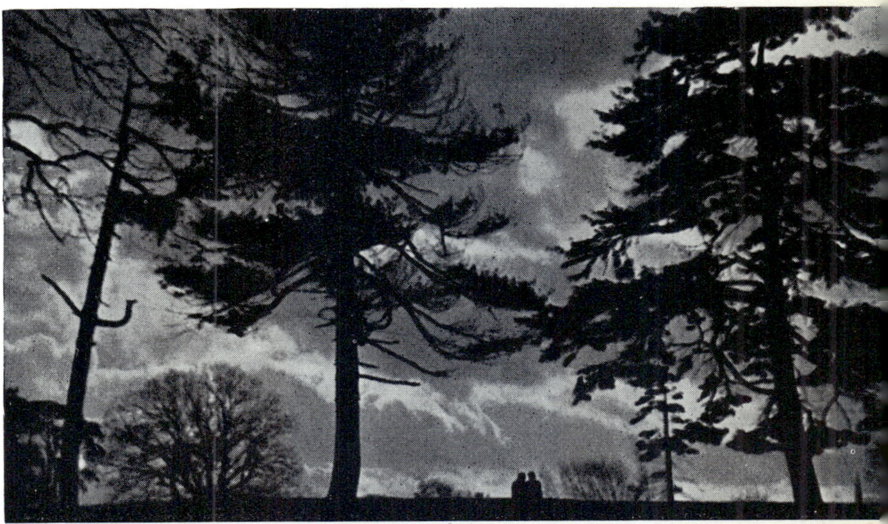

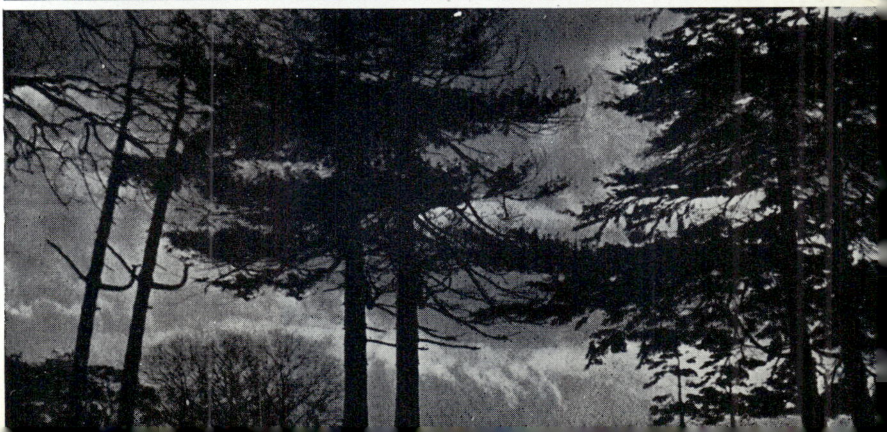

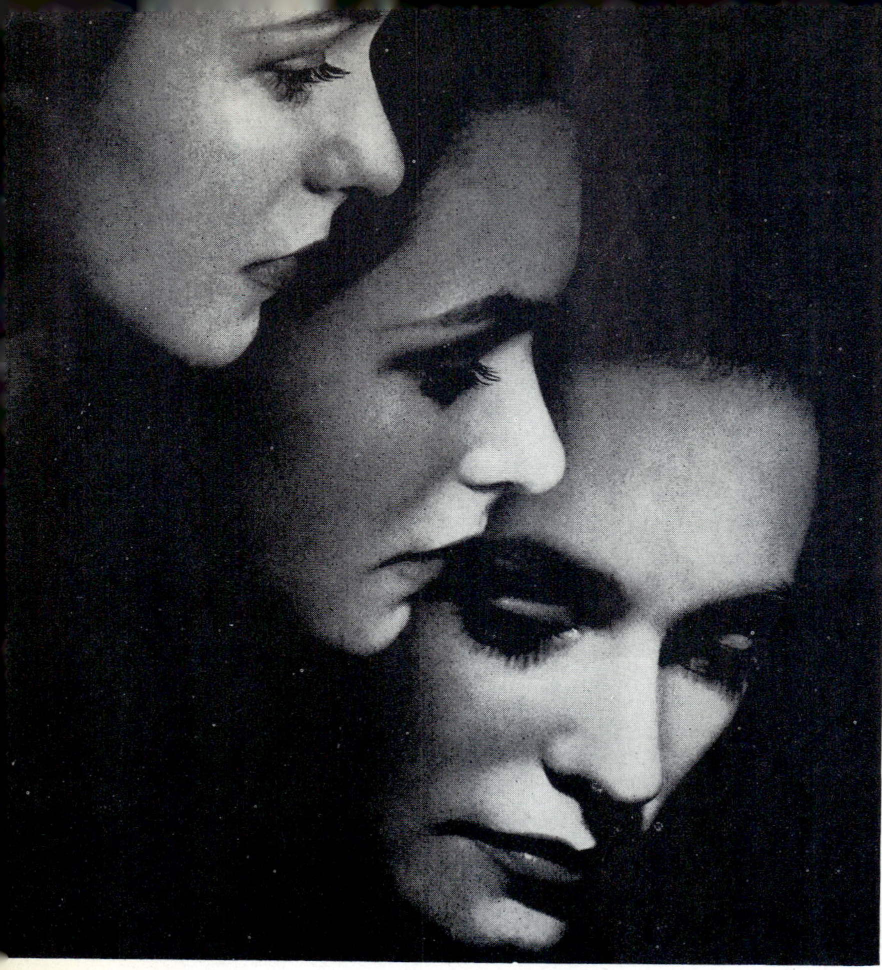

The head of a single model, repeated three times on the same film by triple exposure against a black background. The top left head is taken first, the bottom right taken last, each being arranged on the film so that the shadows of the face and dark tones of the hair occur next to the light profile of the previous exposure, and are thus not registered. Careful planning and a tracing on the focusing screen is necessary.—*Hurrel.*

It is best to form the *cutting line in the middle of a mask large enough to produce the two necessary halves;* in this way the contour of each mask is identical, being cut along the same line. After the first exposure, it will only be necessary to fit one into the other, in the manner of a jig-saw, and remove the mask already used, to ensure accurate registration.

Masks within the camera can be fixed in many ways, depending entirely on the particular construction and topography of the camera back. In some view cameras stout masks could be propped or *pinned on a convenient ledge,* thin ones might even be *fixed in the picture opening* without interfering with the movements of the dark slide.

Masks of complication are best *gummed lightly on to a sheet of good clear glass,* plate for preference, of a size that will conveniently fit into the camera back and remain rigidly in position. A contrivance, such as thin strips of wood or card, should be provided for the glass to slip into, so that it always occupies the same position.

After the first exposure the glass is removed, the second mask fitted into the first, lightly gummed in position, the first mask removed and the glass replaced for the second exposure.

A carefully planned arrangement of this kind is very little trouble to contrive, and will render the most complicated problems of masking reasonably simple.

Masks, whether in the frame of the effects box, or within the bellows of the view camera, should have a *matt non-reflecting surface*. Shiny black paper is quite unsuitable since stray light may reflect from it and partially fog the film.

The ideal material is *black velour paper* which has a dull matt surface that effectively swallows all light striking it. It is too flimsy to be used alone and should be pasted both sides of a stiff card, and then cut to the required shape.

Masks in the Enlarger

Apart from a single drawback: that the business is repeated for each extra print, the enlarger is far and away the best and simplest means of producing many effects of montage, with and without the aid of a mask.

The popular cameras of to-day are, of course, mostly very small format (usually 35mm) types and their pictures are enlargements. In any camera smaller than a quarter plate, a montage involving masks of complicated contour can hardly be successful, even with superhuman patience. But it is more within the bounds of common ability when making a whole-plate or 10 in. x 8 in. (25 cm. x 20 cm.) enlargement.

In most cases of darkroom masking the *mask is arranged between the enlarger lens and the printing paper,* so that parts of the projected image are intercepted and prevented from registering.

As with the mask within the camera, and as more meticulously described on page 115, *the nearer the mask is to the surface of the printing paper the sharper is its cutting effect, and the nearer to the enlarger the softer.* Thus, a mask laid directly on the surface of the paper leaves a patch of identical area and clear definition, whereas a mask held a foot away will obscure less than its own area, owing to diffusion of light beneath it, and with a cutting line of soft definition.

Obviously, and as previously pointed out (page 132), more accuracy and patience are needed to join two halves with a sharply-cut division, than two which have diffused edges that blend one with the other.

A similar situation obtained with masks in and before the camera (page 132), and, as there, we here arrange that masks whose shapes are broad and simple should cut with a soft and diffused edge, above the paper's surface, and those whose contours are cut about in confusion should cut with a sharp edge as near to the paper as possible.

Simple problems of montage can often be solved by the basic *shading process* described on page 68 where the shadow of the hand is used to obscure various parts of the paper while other parts are printing. The hand, or the two combined, can be shaped to fit many different circumstances by bending the fingers and inclining the hand at various angles to change the area of its shadow. The *size of the shadow can also be varied by changing the distance of the hand from the paper,* the nearer the smaller, the further the larger.

Such easy means are particularly suited to those instances where only a part of one negative need be obscured, as when printing clouds on an otherwise blank sky. The negative of the landscape is printed unmasked, since its white sky leaves the paper relatively unexposed, and it is only necessary, when printing in the clouds from a second negative, to obscure the landscape portion from any further light by shading with the hand.

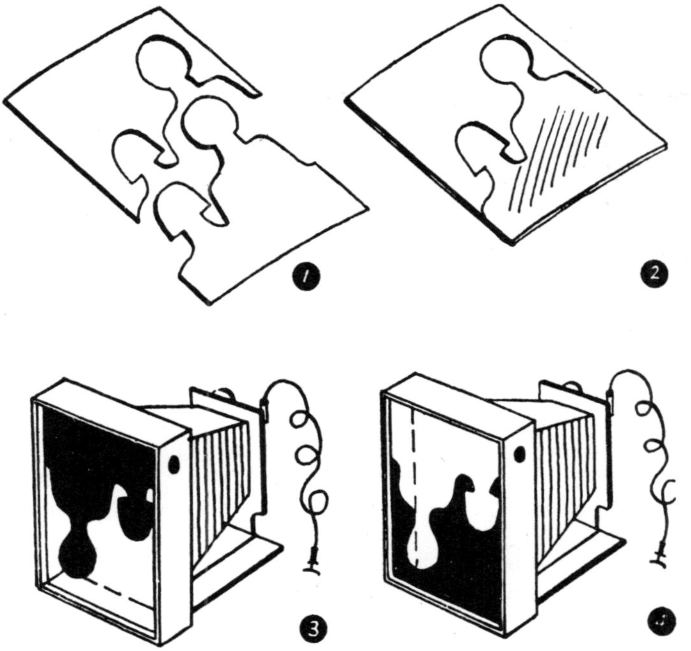

MASK IN THE CAMERA

1. The desired masking line is drawn, in its relatively correct position, on a sheet of masking paper and accurately cut. *2.* The top half is lightly gummed to a sheet of clear glass. *3.* Arranged upside down in the camera.

After the first exposure the glass and mask are removed, the second half mask gummed into position, the first half then removed, and the glass replaced in the camera for the second exposure—*4.*

Masks of simple shape, but which are, nevertheless hard for the hand to assume, can be cut from a sheet of stiff card or paper, the negative being projected upon it and the desired outline marked in pencil and subsequently cut. This shape is used in place of the shaped hand, and in the same manner, being held some three or four inches (7.5 cm. to 10 cm.) above the paper's surface and gently rotated about a quarter of an inch (0.75 cm.) in each direction. This slight movement helps to blend the images and prevents the formation of sudden differences of tone.

Spot printing too, described also on page 68, can be used for many simple montage effects, any isolated image being printed in the middle of the paper through a hole made with the cupped hands, or cut in a card mask. Such a hole need not be cut to fit the printed image, like an orthodox mask, but can be a *small circle or any irregular shape,* its size obviously depending on the area of the image to be exposed. In practice the mask is used between the paper and the enlarger so that the small beam of light passing through the hole only exposes the desired portion of the image.

The spot will be small and sharp if the mask is used near to the paper, large and diffused if near to the enlarger, and care must be taken that the movements of the spot are regular over the whole image so that all parts are equally exposed, and that the spot does not move outside the limits of the particular image to form a dark halo round the subject.

The montage whose parts do not merge but meet together with a sharp joint, not intended to be detected, involves a mask much nearer to the printing paper and with more accuracy of alignment than is possible with the hand, or a rough mask held in the hand. Here one makes use of a sheet of *good clear glass supported on small wooden blocks* as near the paper as possible, and on which may be placed the masks, one after the other.

The line that forms the cutting edge of both masks is accurately obtained by *focusing the image on a sheet of masking paper laid in position on the glass.* The relevant contour is then traced on the paper and cut in such a manner that the two halves obtained can be used for each successive exposure. When the negative is re-focused on the printing paper below the glass, the image of the mask should be enlarged just the right amount, and with an edge that is just sufficiently unsharp to gradate the joint.

Having made the first exposure through one half, the second mask is fitted into the first one the surface of the glass, like two pieces of a jig-saw, and should be weighted into position before the first half is removed prior to the second exposure.

If the *glass sheet is so fixed that it cannot be easily disarranged,* the paper holder sufficiently weighty to withstand normal jogs, and the printing paper kept accurately in the same position for each exposure, this method should not be beyond an average standard of ability.

The necessary movements for adjusting the two or more images should be made by *moving the negative in its carrier* rather than by shifting the paper holder. A sheet of spoiled and undeveloped paper can be used to mark the respective positions of the images and ensure that each registers accurately with the other.

▷ *In its capacity for making double portraits against natural backgrounds, the mask before the camera has already been dealt with on page 90, where the use of a partial cap before the lens to obscure the opposite sides of a scene in two successive exposures was described.*

If both exposures record the same scene or background, and the camera is not moved, the two halves of the picture, though taken separately, will blend into a seemingly single product. Where such effects are intended this is the basic, and the best, use of any mask before the camera.

▷ *If, however, the two images do not represent an extension of the same scene, or part of a scene, and the camera is moved to another location for the second exposure, though the joint is soft and diffused there will be no disguising the double origin of the finished product.*

Such use of a mask can be made to combine any two images of a composite montage consisting of a number of separate pictures merging into one another. The final effect is made from, say, three negatives each showing two merged images instead of six separate negatives that must be merged in printing.

Nevertheless, it is not always possible to combine on one negative two objects that are considerably removed in space and time, and to combine them in just such a manner that best suits the particular montage in mind. Such mergings, therefore, are probably best made in the darkroom unless circumstances, or a specific need, suggest otherwise.

▷ *The mask before the camera, in the frame of the effects box, or a similar substitute, can be made to place isolated objects and persons in strange and unnatural conjunction with a natural background, the object being first recorded against a black or dark background, in a noted position on the plate.*

When making the second, natural background, exposure that part of the plate or film already exposed is obscured with an appropriately-shaped mask held before the camera.

Since it is impossible to get a clean, sharp joint with a mask before the camera, that part of the natural background against which the object or person is seen should be relatively dark in tone. By this means the halo of darkness brought by the person from his original background is more or less swallowed up.

▷ *All the odd effects of decapitation, dwarfing and doubling described under Ghosts and Doubles (page 90), and there confined to a black background, can, by adroit masking of the second exposure, here be displayed in surroundings more congenial and less open to suspicion.*

▷ *Further oddities are possible, without the use of a black background, if a mask is used for each exposure. Thus a head or hand, or other isolated fragment, if on a large enough scale can be recorded against any natural scene through the small hole in a mask placed in the frame of the effects box. If the second exposure is made of the normal scene, without moving the camera, and with a small "spot" mask concealing the already exposed area, the head or other disembodied feature floats confidently in the midst of an otherwise impeccable picture.*

Within the camera the mask cuts sharply and precisely, and, unless you have much more than the average share of skill, the contour of the mask should be kept simple and made to follow as far as possible an easy natural contour of the subject.

▷ *A straightforward mask that cuts vertically down the middle of the film can create intriguing situations if arranged to cut down the middle of a slender isolated obstacle, such as a flag pole, a lamp post, a thin column or narrow tree.*

The first half exposure may show a person emerging from behind half of the pole, or other slender substitute; the second is made minus model and shows only the other half of the obstacle against its unobscured background.

Thus, in the final combination, a person may appear to be emerging in some mysterious manner from behind an isolated obstacle too small normally to conceal him. The model should be arranged, of course, so that parts of him would be visible both sides of the obstacle in a normal exposure.

Such a means is capable of several applications. Hands and heads may strangely protrude from behind the thin isolated upright of a chair back, or, with a horizontal mask, over the top rail of a ladder-back chair, or a five-bar gate.

▷ *The mask within the camera can follow any contour of the picture, but the skill and good fortune required to join successfully two halves of complicated contour is often far more than the result is worth.*

The most common use for which such masks might be needed is to bring together two objects, or an object and a background, that could neither conveniently nor possibly be brought together in reality for a single exposure. This can be just as well achieved by the ingenious use of a single mask cut from a photographic print of one of the images.

The object or person is recorded against a plain dark background so that the parts to be subsequently occupied by the image of the second exposure are more or less unexposed. The negative is processed in the usual manner and a rough proof-print taken.

This rough print is used as the mask for the second exposure, the object or person being cut from its dark background by accurately following the contour with a very sharp knife, care being taken to leave no rough edges or pieces of paper fluff in the corners.

The cut-out print is fixed face outwards to the sheet of clear glass used to support the masks within the camera, the glass and print attached being placed upside down as near to the plane of focus as possible.

If the camera is now focused on the required background, and the exposure made so that the two images will occur in the desired relation, the developed negative should show blank parts corresponding to the image portion of the other negative, and can be successfully combined with it to make either contact prints or enlargements.

The negatives will be placed face to face so that the densities of one are seen through the transparencies of the other, and adjusted until the two separately taken images meet without a visible join and form an apparently single image. A pin-prick through both, in each corner, or a tiny spot of adhesive will secure them together in accurate register.

The background, of course, can be either actual or copied from another photograph, painting, drawing, or magazine illustra-

tion. In most cases it will be best if it is just slightly out of focus, and either under-exposed or under-developed to keep the tones softer and more subdued than the original object, intended to be seen in front.

Such a method is relatively simple, and endlessly useful, it being possible to successfully combine any isolated, or partly isolated, object with any background whatsoever. The first masking negative can be made, not from reality, but from another print in which all but the figure or object has been painted black, by which means people can assume fantastic attitudes in mid-air, or in any other isolated position.

▷ *A vertical enlarger can be used for most montage-effects, and, given skill in the two or three methods of masking and blending, there is no end to the number of possible combinations of two or more negatives. If the means, as recently described, are clear, opportunity for their use will soon be found.*

The most elementary use of montage is the printing-in of clouds from one negative on to the blank and featureless sky given by another. This has been common pictorial practice from the infancy of photography, and the enlarger provides an ideal means of combination.

Clouds can be borrowed from any landscape negative or outdoor scene that shows the desired composition or formation that you require, or they can be specially recorded for the occasion. A collection of negatives showing nothing but clouds of various types and with different directions of light is a useful part of any printing equipment.

The particular sky chosen should be suited in every way to the landscape or other scene it is to accompany. A common fault is to mix the directions of light, so that the shadows on the subject fall one way and those on the clouds fall the other. This must be watched, and care should also be taken to preserve relative scale so that the clouds are not enlarged a considerably greater amount than the landscape, or vice versa.

The simplest state of cloudy affairs is represented by a cloud negative completely transparent in all places where the landscape or other images are to print through. Here the two negatives are merely placed face to face in the enlarger and printed simultaneously.

▷ *Almost as simple is the landscape negative whose horizon cuts more or less straight across the picture without complicated projection of any kind. Here it is only necessary to screen with the shadow of the hand that part of the paper already exposed to the landscape, so that the clouds do not print in the lighter tones of the earth.*

Objects or persons that project themselves into the clouds from the flat plane of the landscape are, for our purpose, of two kinds: those that are dark in tone, such as trees or other foreground material seen more or less in silhouette against the sky, and those that are lighter in tone than the darker parts of the sky, such as a face, a light building, or any object painted white.

The former need no masking since the paper on which such dark objects occur will already have been fully exposed to produce their rich blackness. The second exposure of the clouds will not therefore affect these masses and they can be ignored.

Light or white objects, on the other hand, leave the printing paper relatively unexposed, and unless they are protected with a mask during the second exposure dark portions of the cloud negative will print over them in a far from satisfactory fashion.

A cloud negative could be chosen with a strong white area large enough, and in the right position, to cover all the white parts of the first exposure, but where this is not possible a mask must be used.

Projecting objects of simple and compact shape can often be well enough masked with the shadow of the hand, in combination with a straight-cut mask to obscure the flat landscape. The paper must be marked with a couple of unobtrusive pencil dots, or some such registration marks along the side of the printing frame, to guide the correct placing of the masking shadow.

Objects of complicated shape, consisting of thin white verticals or other narrow areas of light tone, must be protected with a cut mask either held above the paper with the hand, or placed in careful position on the surface of the glass. In either case it is advisable to keep the mask moving with a slight rotating movement, to prevent the formation of hard edges and so that the sky diffuses successfully into the other parts.

If the sky of the original landscape or other negative is very dense, and its clouds only thinly defined, no mask will be needed for the first exposure. It is a very simple matter to obscure with the hand any tones that might register in that half of the negative.

▷ Spot printing is an excellent device for printing-in isolated objects that are intended to appear in the foreground of any combination picture, being particularly suitable when the objects are of simple shape and intended to be dark in tone.

The method will also produce effective repeat patterns if the spotted image is repeated at some regular interval all over a large sheet of printing paper.

Success here obviously depends on the accurate disposition and tone of each successive printed image, any one or two printed out of alignment or out of tone completely ruining the pattern, and it is advisable to plan the whole operation carefully in advance.

The number of repeated units must depend on the nature of the chosen negative and the size of printing paper it is intended to cover, and to avoid overcrowding or the use of minute images it is as well not to work smaller than 12 in. x 10 in. (30 cm. x 20 cm.) or 10 in. x 8 in. (25 cm. x 20 cm.) at the very least.

Many subjects may be suitable, but it seems well to choose some naturally self-contained image, such as the human face, the single bloom of a flower, or something along those lines. The subject can be light in general tone, with dark accents, or it can be light on a dark ground. In one case the finished pattern will be light in effect with regularly repeating points of dark tone, and the other will consist of a generally dark ground on which occur repeating images of lighter tone.

A trial print should be made of the selected portion of the negative, exposing it through the appropriately shaped hole in a card mask, slightly rotating the mask during exposure so that the edges are vignetted and are at no place sharply defined.

With this specimen print as your guide, a blank sheet of paper of the right size is marked out with the accurate position of each successive image, which can, according to choice, be set out in adjoining squares, on diagonals, or any of the usual pattern arrangements.

The vital points that indicate the position of each exposure are measured off this guide, or transferred by pricking through with a small sharp pin from one to the other, on to the final sheet of sensitive paper.

Such marking, if you are careful and have a good memory, need consist of no more than four faint dots indicating the total extent of the image in each direction. A hole is then cut in a sheet of masking paper, just larger than the area indicated by these dots, and which will fit into position over each group of four dots in turn. This protecting and guiding mask is used to cover all parts of the paper except the small area to be exposed beneath the hole in the exposing mask.

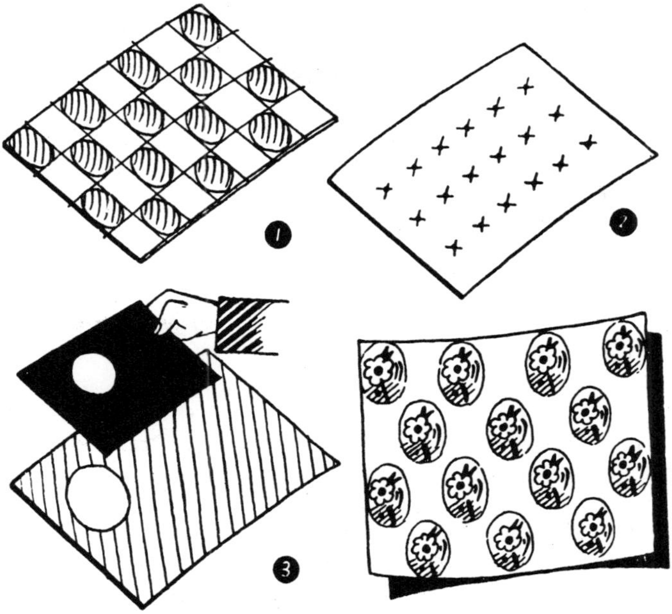

PATTERNS

1. The original layout, marked clearly with the number and accurate disposition of the repeating units. *2.* The sensitive paper marked lightly with the bare essentials necessary to place the images during printing—in this case a pin-prick at the corner of each rectangle. *3.* The printing operation, with the paper protected by a large mask, and exposed through the hole cut in a smaller. *4.* The developed result.

Printing of the separate images should be done in strict rotation, as each unit is successively exposed it being crossed through on the guide, so that no blanks are left and no parts are treated more than once.

The light falling through the exposing mask, should be allowed by rotating it with a circular motion to fall for a small part of each exposure on the edges to be occupied by adjacent images, which will just be visible inside the cut line of the protecting mask.

In this way each image will successfully merge into the other, each unit having a soft edge that slightly overlaps its neighbours on all sides. Thus no parts of the printing paper will be left a blank white, and if the object is seen on a dark ground the background of the pattern will be a uniform black.

Simpler, unvignetted, patterns could be made through the holes in a protecting mask, if the hole is cut to some definite geometric shape that will successfully repeat. The cut mask is merely laid in position on the surface of the paper, correctly aligned by means of the light pencil dots, and the exposure made directly without a diffusing mask or other complication.

Similarly, of course, each image could be printed separately on small pieces of printing paper, and joined together in patterned form by the cut and paste method previously described. Larger areas could be covered by this means than is usually possible or convenient in the darkroom.

The pattern field is a rich one, and can yield fine results with a little imagination and a lot of patience.

▷ *Multiple montage, or a picture honestly made up of a number of images merging one into the other with no attempt to conceal the joints, implies a technique that is ideally suited to the enlarger and the cut-out mask.*

Such pictures are usually built around a single definite theme, idea, or motive, and each separate image included should justify its place in the picture by contributing something towards the total mood of the finished print.

Subjects range from pictorial interpretations of Industry, Agriculture, and similar abstractions, to the more homely impressions of the various aspects of your house, holiday, your garden or your child.

The streets, monuments, landmarks and public buildings of a town or city can be brought together in one picture to suggest such a total impression as might be left on the memory from a hurried afternoon's sightseeing.

Many towns do, in fact, offer for sale picture post-cards in which a number of separately-taken views of its principal attractions are combined in one picture. They are, of course, rarely blended or montaged together, but occur in individual frames "artistically" drawn, or tied together in some arrangement of ribbons or other dusty charm though nowadays the design, as such is generally more simplified.

The units may be combined in a frankly fantastic manner, so that perspective and relative proportion are obviously discounted. Objects which would normally be found at the top of a picture being put at the bottom and vice versa.

The alternative is to observe a natural order, and, whilst in no way attempting naturalism, keep large things in the foreground, and background things in the distance, sky at the top and the heavier earthy things at the bottom; observing if not all the rules of perspective at least those of diminishing size and tone.

Choose your subject, select your negatives, and begin by roughing out your ideas on a sheet of paper of the required size. If you are reasonably skilful with a pencil and can afterwards identify what your own drawings represent, this rough plan can consist of a combination of pencil sketches made from the separate prints or negatives by tracing the main outlines of each from the image projected through the enlarger.

The alternative, a little wasteful of printing paper but otherwise more satisfactory, is to cut into rough shape prints from all the selected negatives and lay them about until a satisfactory composition is achieved.

Joints will sometimes be arranged on a natural contour of the subject, so that one image cuts sharply over another; or, if the adjoining areas are similar in depth of tone, the two can be diffused imperceptibly into each other; again, the images could overlap so that one is seen through the other in the vicinity of the join for a variable distance.

All three variations can be successfully employed on a single montage, but it will often be an improvement to make use of only one type of joint throughout any one picture for the sake of unity and to avoid unnecessary confusion.

Having decided upon a satisfactory combination of the images, and having a clear mental conception of the manner in which you intend to mask each separate one and effect a join with its neighbours, the necessary masks should be cut, using your drawn or photo composition as a guide.

This preliminary composition is of great importance as a permanent guide through the gloom and mystery of the dark-room operations. It is placed in the printing paper holder beneath the enlarger and there it remains throughout the complete process, acting as a guide to register correctly the image of each separate negative, and being covered by the actual printing paper when the exposures are being made.

The method of masking depends on the complication of the montage, it being quite feasible, if the units are large and simple and the joints diffused or overlapping, to hold the separate masks in the hand a few inches above the paper, rotating them slightly in the approved manner.

For less simple combinations, however, it is advisable to work as near to the surface of the paper as possible, either on a sheet of glass acting as a rigid support, or on the paper itself.

It is an excellent plan to mark the various masking lines on a sheet of stiff card similar in area to the guiding composition, cutting off each piece as its counterpart on the paper needs to be exposed, and rejoining it to the other with adhesive tape when the exposure has been made.

In this way the mask is always complete except for the part being actually printed through, and if used in contact with the printing paper, being very slightly rotated for any diffused edges, it provides a very accurate means of masking and joining the separate parts.

The adhesive tape or paper used for piecing the cut portions of the mask together again should extend along the whole join, and should be absolutely opaque or light streaks will penetrate through it and fog the paper beneath.

In order to give adequate time to effect any diffusion or other screening, the exposure times should be regulated by reducing the aperture of the lens the required amount so that they are not less than thirty or forty seconds.

Similarly, it is well to dilute the developer so that the image comes up slowly, giving time to adjust the various tones and control their depth.

▷ *Further uses for enlarger masking have already been described on page 66, where a method of producing distorted effects of elongation and compression was suggested, and on page 115, where the mask on a sheet of glass was used to produce the effects of twins and triplets.*

▷ *When and where necessary, lettering can be incorporated in any photograph by montage methods, using cut-out letters to mask the print, or using a mask from which letter shapes have been cut. In one case the letters will be white, and, in the other, a dark tone whose depth depends upon the exposure given.*

With the necessary skill you may construct and cut letters of your own design, but they may just as easily be cut from the large display type-faces that make the heading of many newspaper and magazine advertisements. A few specific types are in common use, appearing again and again in different forms, so that it is not impossibly difficult to collect a complete alphabet of several different kinds.

If the paper on which the letters are printed is reasonably thick, the letters may be cut and used just as they come, but they must otherwise be pasted on opaque masking paper before cutting.

The choice between light or dark lettering will obviously depend on the position the letters are to occupy on the print, and the nature of the surrounding tones. If the lettering is to be seen at all clearly, good contrast must be kept—white lettering against a dark ground, and vice versa.

White letters are the simplest, since they are quickly formed by lying the cut-out letters on the surface of the printing paper in the desired arragement. For black letters, the mask from which letters, in correct order and spacing, have been cut is laid in contact with the paper and the exposure made through it.

It is a good plan to cut the individual letters in small black squares so that words can be formed by laying the squares alongside each other, any gaps between, caused by wide spacing, being obscured by small pieces of masking paper. This obviates the boredom of having to cut every title and word separately for each occasion.

Letters with isolated centres, like the O, P, Q, B, etc., can either be cut in stencil form so that the centres are held in position by paper "straps," or the centres can be separately laid in position on the surface of the paper.

Diapositive Masking

The powers of the cut mask are necessarily curtailed by the limited powers of human patience and ingenuity with scissors or knife. It is clearly impossible to follow such narrow and complicated contours as, for instance, the delicate fronds of foliage, with sufficient accuracy to ensure an invisible joint.

In such cases, therefore, some means relying less upon the imperfect human element and more upon the automatic efficiency of optical mechanics must be employed, and such a means constitutes the next method.

The mask within the camera, consisting of a cut-out print of an object or person recorded against a black background, and as described on page 147, is the best method of masking and joining when the masking line is not too complicated or small in scale. When such is the case, however, and where the cutting skill required and the labour of patience involved is not in proportion to the value of the result, you proceed as follows.

The exposure is made of an object against a black background in the normal manner, the film is changed, and a second exposure made without shifting either subject or camera.

For this *second* shot *the black background is replaced by a white one,* the *lighting* being arranged so that it *falls on the background,* the object being seen in complete *silhouette*. Such an effect can be achieved by directing a strong light on to a sheet of white paper, so that the subject remains in deep shadow, or by placing the light behind a stretched white sheet so that it forms a uniformly luminous background. Any means may be used as long as the subject records on the negative as absolute clear gelatine, and the background as an absolute density.

From this silhouette negative is made a *diapositive*, a positive transparency or lantern slide, by placing it in contact with a contrasty film, *emulsion to emulsion*, and exposing it to the light beneath the enlarger, or other light source.

This film could suitably be a *process* material, or similar slow-speed emulsion giving a contrasty result, and should be *developed strongly* to produce an appearance similar to the subject during the second exposure: a dense black subject on a perfectly white background, the whiteness being registered on the diapositive as an absolute glass-like transparency.

This, then, is a mechanically-produced mask, showing all the complication of the original subject's outline, with less labour and infinitely more accuracy.

The *diapositive is placed within the camera*, in the manner of the cut mask method previously described, and the *exposure of the desired background made through it*, so that the objects of the background are registered in the desired conjunction with the outline of the subject.

Place the mask as *near to the plane of focus*, or surface of the film, as possible; indeed, it is an excellent plan to place it in actual contact—emulsion to emulsion.

Since the image produced by the lens is *upside down* on the film's surface, see that you place the mask that way round or you will be faced with an eventual combination in which the background will be topsy-turvy.

The background negative will be quite blank and unexposed in all those parts obscured by the densities of the diapositive, and when developed these parts will be as transparent as the clear gelatine.

It is therefore only necessary to combine the subject and background negatives so that the blank portions of one fit precisely over the dense portions of the other, and enlarge them as if they were a single negative, which the finished effect should lead one to believe they are.

To summarise briefly, we have (*a*) the subject taken against a black background; (*b*) the same against a white background; (*c*) a diapositive or lantern slide of *b*; (*d*) the desired background taken through *c*; (*e*) the united subject and background obtained by combining (*a*) and (*b*).

By using the diapositive mask with its emulsion side towards the back of the camera, the silhouette of the subject on the background negative is reversed, which permits you to combine the two final negatives, with their emulsions touching, bringing them into the same focal plane and solving the difficulties of focusing in the enlarger.

Depending, of course, on the nature of the subject and the desired effect, it will usually be advisable to keep the contrasts of the background negative as subdued as possible, reducing the time of development or suitably diluting the developer. This keeps the two planes nicely separated and prevents confusion when the foreground subject is cut about with varied detail.

▷ *Subjects suitable for this technique will be limited to those which have, or can assume, complete immobility. The method depends, almost entirely, for its success on the fact that absolutely no movement of camera or subject takes place between the substitution of white for black background.*

With a steady model, and reasonable good fortune, it may be possible to use the method for people if some means of support is provided, something for the person to lean or support the head against, for example. But absolute success cannot be guaranteed, and you must be prepared to do a little retouching work round the edges if the model so much as breathes deeply.

People, anyway, can usually be treated with the cut-out print mask, so that, broadly speaking, the method is best confined to the still-life and subjects of that nature.

Detailed portraits of flowers, combined with soft-toned backgrounds of gardens and other scenes, are the kind of material for this method, and other combinations will frequently occur when the subject must stand strongly from its surroundings.

▷ *It is not always so much a means of combining objects with fantastic backgrounds impossible to reality, as of obtaining a concentration of interest on the foreground plane, mixing the strong light of the subject with the subdued contrast of the background in a manner rarely possible under normal lighting conditions.*

▷ *By placing the mask, not upside down but right way up in the camera, either the subject or background will appear topsy-turvy in the final combination. This effect has not, I believe, been exploited and it might amuse you to show brimming glasses of liquid suspended, apparently upside down, before a normal background, or other gravitational impossibilities. On the other hand, it might not.*

The Wet Method

A rather messy method of montage, but one which could be used to satisfy the cravings of a messy mood common at some time or other to most photographers, is known aptly as the "wet" method, and consists of the second exposure of a partly developen, but unfixed, negative (preferably a plate) or print.

The *first exposure* is made of any subject against a *black background*, the negative normally developed, rinsed, *not fixed,* rapidly dried and returned to the camera.

If the *second exposure* is made of the *desired background*, in the normal manner and without troubling to mask those parts of the plate already exposed, the background image successfully registers on the still sensitive parts of the plate that saw nothing more than the black background of the first exposure, and that have been relatively unchanged by development.

Having been twice exposed the plate is now *developed for the second* time, then fixed, washed and dried as normal.

The success of this method depends on *developing to an extreme density the subject image of the first exposure*, so that the negative silver image receives no impression from the background of the second. This can usually be achieved by developing the negative as for very harsh contrast, in strong developer or for a longer time than usual.

If, however, the subject contains dark tones or shadows that leave the negative more or less unexposed, the *subject image*—not the background—should be treated with a normal *uranium intensifier applied with a brush;* this produces a deep brown image that effectively prevents any further tone from registering on the emulsion beneath. The alkali of the second developer will remove all traces of this intensification without injury to the emulsion.

Apart from the extreme density of the first image, the second development produces a negative whose harsh tones will defy any grade of printing paper. Before it can be successfully printed the negative should be *reduced with an ammonium persulphate reducer, or bleached* in a solution of 130 grains potassium ferricyanide, 45 grains potassium bromide in 2 fluid ounces of water.

After such a bleaching the negative may be *redeveloped* by daylight in a *soft-working, fine-grain developer* until the desired density and gradation are achieved. If it is now fixed, washed and dried in the normal fashion the resulting negative, besides being a miracle of chemical ingenuity, will show the subject against a separately-taken background in the manner of a single exposure, without visible joints or other artifice.

One point to remember is that the *sensitivity of the emulsion is reduced by the first development,* and exposure for the background must therefore be prolonged as if for a plate of slower speed.

Again, it will be best, unless you have unbounded darkroom confidence, to use an *ortho emulsion* rather than panchromatic, since a darkroom illumination can then be used during development and the relative densities watched. In fact it will be essential if partial intensification is employed. If available *plates* rather than film are preferable, as the latter are inclined to look a little limp and worn out after so much hard work, and are not half so simple to handle as a firm plate.

A similar technique can be applied to the *positive process* in the enlarger, by the use of the bleaching solution mentioned above. This is brushed on to those parts of a partially developed, and blot-dried but unfixed, print that contains the unwanted image.

The solution bleaches the paper to which it is applied back to its original sensitive state, and exposure of a second negative can be made upon it and developed in the usual way.

Once again, the first development and bleaching reduces the sensitivity of the emulsion, making the paper much slower in speed; it is therefore advisable to treat two prints and use one as a guide to ascertain the correct duration of the second exposure.

▷ *This method has no unique uses of its own, but is an alternative method of producing all those effects of montage that consist of recording an isolated object against a strange and separate background, and such as have been set forth in the uses of other montage methods.*

To those for whom an occasional wet mess is pleasant, and any form of complex cutting painful, this method is dedicated and specially included.

Photo Backgrounds

Apart from slight loss of brilliance and contrast, it is rarely possible to distinguish with any certainty whether a print is a direct photograph of the actual scene, or a photographic copy of another photograph of that scene.

Since the eye finds difficulty in separating the two once they have been photographically fused, it is possible to create a number of effective montages by combining three dimensional reality with the two dimensions of a print.

The photographic background to a real object or scene is a method of montage that has long been exploited by the cinema and laterly by television, where the effect of an expensive set or exotic surrounding is frequently obtained by projecting a moving film, or still lantern slide, from the back of the set on to a translucent screen, before which the actors and properties are placed.

Effects on so ambitious a scale are a little beyond our scope, but a photo background of an area sufficient to absorb a half-length figure or two could be managed by projecting the desired scene through a slide projector.

The wall or screen on which such a background is projected must be kept in shadow if its image is to attain any body or contrast, and *lighting* for the objects or persons arranged before it should be set so that it *shines away from the background* and towards the subject at a diagagonal . . . say from the S.E. or S.W.

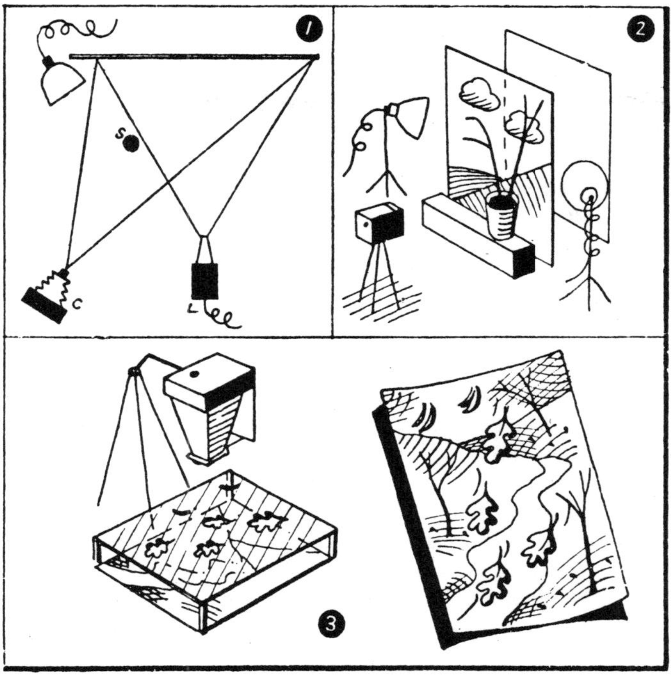

PHOTO BACKGROUNDS

Drawing *1* suggests an arrangement of lighting for a projected background—*C* being the camera, *L* the lantern or projector, and *S* the subject—so lit that no shadow is thrown upon the wall.

Drawing *2* shows a large transparency used as a photo background to an actual object, lit in such a manner that only reflected and no direct light shines towards the camera.

Drawing *3* uses a print as a photo background, objects being arranged on a glass sheet a few inches above the print's surface. In this case leaves are used, over a suitable scene, to suggest the gusty effect of a windy autumn day.

when the camera is pointing towards the subject and projected background in the south.

The large areas of shadow facing the camera that such a direction of light will give can be relieved by *local reflection* from metal foil or white paper reflectors, directed so that they have little effect on the background.

A simpler method, for more modest effects, is to use for the background a print of the subject or scene desired. Here the range of combination is obviously limited by the size of the print at your disposal, and combinations will mostly be confined to small-scale effects contrived on the top of a table.

The print should be so pinned on a drawing board, or other flat vertical support, and the actual objects so arranged upon a raised platform, that space is left *below and at both sides of the print for artificial sources of illumination*. This ensures a luminosity of the background print, and helps it to stand stereoscopically away from the foreground objects.

If the effect intended is worth the effort, the background can be formed from a *transparency of the desired image*—an enlargement made on to a large plate—and this plate set up before the subject lit by reflection from behind. By this means the background image has maximum luminosity, since its tones are made direct by light instead of reflection from paper.

The background need not, of course, be confined to a single picture in one plane but could easily consist of one or more cut-outs placed before the background in the manner of the wings of theatrical scenery, or as ranges of mountains.

In all combinations of reality with a printed image, care should be taken that the principal directions of light are roughly the same in both cases. A considerable latitude is actually possible, it being only necessary to avoid the extreme absurdity of shadows falling in opposite directions in the two separate planes.

▷ *The effects peculiar to this technique, when the combination consists of a print showing a large expanse in small scale, with foreground objects shown in a scale relatively much larger, are similar to those given by the wide-angle lens. Actually superior, because there is no unpleasant distortion of perspective, merely an intriguing divergence of scale.*

Infinite combinations are possible, and particularly good opportunities are provided by subjects that provide portable material such as the sea shore with its various weeds, pebbles and shells, or the countryside with its many twigs, leaves, berries and fir cones which can all be collected and made into strangely fascinating foregrounds for pictures of sea and country.

▷ *If the background picture is laid in the horizontal instead of in the vertical plane, natural objects can be arranged above it on a sheet of clear glass, supported a few inches above the surface, and the effects of falling leaves and feathers, or hanging blossom and berries simply simulated.*

Here the real objects are not confined to the base of the picture but can appear as if hung from above or isolated in mid-air in the centre of the picture.

Unless your background is large, objects in the natural plane are restricted to a certain size and scale. Humanity is largely ruled out, though perhaps a hand could be included holding a flower before a scene of sentiment, of a glass before one of festivity.

Part of the fascination of the finished effect is the equality of definition over the whole picture, from objects under your nose to hills and clouds which are apparently in the far distance, though in reality of course no farther than a few inches on the background print.

Thus the lens of the camera should be stopped down so that both planes are pin-sharp. If, however, you wish to emphasise the effect of rigidly defined planes, the background print may be left just the tiniest bit out of focus, to suggest its distance. A background print could be made very pale and in high key to the same end.

▷ *An amusing inversion of the method is to pose photographic cut-outs against natural backgrounds, cutting the isolated objects, or figures, from prints of the required size and setting them up in some natural scene.*

The prints should be applied, with rubber cement, to stiff card before being cut, or, if you have the facilities, glued to thin plywood and cut with a fretsaw.

If these cut-out figures are arranged in a small natural scene, and placed so that the cut edges are not visible, the effects of the final print are deceiving and puzzling. The figures set the scale for the rest of the picture and made any natural objects such as grass, leaves, twigs or stones look truly enormous.

The isolated cut-out is most successful when the print shows a person or animal. Thus, a cat cut-out a few inches high, when placed among pebbles and grasses of a suitable corner of the garden, changes the apparent scale of the surroundings to jungle proportions.

Care must be observed not to show any object among the surroundings whose size is a too definitely known quantity, such, for instance, as a cigarette end, a match or match-box, which will destroy the illusion though, of course, it may add to a nightmare idea.

TONE TRICKS

How a cautious public, habitually suspicious of any "artistic interference with nature," ever reconciled the grey monotone of a photograph with the colours of its natural original, and accepted them without audible comment, is moderately mystifying.

For many years after its first birthday the camera insisted on its version of yellow objects in dark tones and blue objects in light ones. Just how the common spectator reacted to this flagrant distortion has not, I believe, been recorded, but I fancy that, so great was his faith in the mechanical vision of the camera, he pushed it all into the pattern and made peace with himself somehow.

Similarly, to-day, he fails to consciously observe how pale the pillar-box appears on panchromatic films, how wan the strident red omnibus, how dark the pale-blue eye.

If, then, the common spectator is anything more than a tedious but necessary fiction you can be assured that, short of turning white to blatant black, he will not boggle if you decide to change any tone of your subject, either when making the original exposure, or the finished print from a normal negative.

Only a pallid purist could for long deny the necessity of controlling or adjusting the tones of a subject. However careful and selective the operator, life, being the chaotic and over-abundant thing it is, offers few subjects not marred by some over-insistent detail impossible to avoid—a tone too bright here or too dim there. And again, however expert its creator, the negative that yields its best print without manipulation, and whose tones are not improved by judicious dodging, shading or spot-printing, is as rare as a camera in a fortified area.

The methods of tone control and alteration, though sometimes tricky, are not altogether tricks in the proper sense of that word, and though all can be pushed to such an extreme that interference is inevitably suspected, most can be used so unobtrusively that the presence of special means is not readily or easily detected.

Filters

Apart from the choice of film, which, according to its classification as "ordinary," ortho or panchromatic, implies precedence of one or of two particular colours over others, filters represent the principal means of tone control or distortion at the time of original exposure.

This is not the appropriate volume for a lengthy explanation of the colour filter, and a nodding acquaintance between you both must be assumed. They are discs of optically-ground glass, or wafers of thin gelatine, mounted in the form of a supplementary lens to slip on the lens mount of the camera, and dyed in various strengths of the three primary colours—red, yellow and blue, and the secondary colours green, orange, etc.

Their effects are based on the fact that the *filter will grant priority of passage through the camera to that colour of the subject identical with itself, or of the same colour family, and obstruct the passage of those which are opposite, or what is known as complementary.*

YELLOW FILTERS are best disposed towards yellows of the subject, least friendly to blues—the complementary colour of yellow, and, since a little yellow is present in most reds and in all greens, these two colours receive a tolerable attention and a reasonably correct tonal rendering.

Providing, therefore, that the film is yellow sensitive, yellows, recorded through a filter of that colour, will register in the highest key—the stronger the filter the whiter their printed effect. Blues will register in the lowest key, the deeper the filter colour the nearer they will print to black.

GREEN FILTERS are partial to the greens of any coloured scene, hostile to red, and tolerable to yellow and blue. Given a highly green sensitive film, through a filter of that colour, green will record as a light tone—the deeper the filter the nearer to white it will approximate. Red will register darkly—the deeper the filter the nearer to black it will appear in the final print.

RED FILTERS, on the other hand, are unfriendly both to green and blue, both of which they insist on describing as very dark tones. It dotes, inhumanly, on the colour members of its

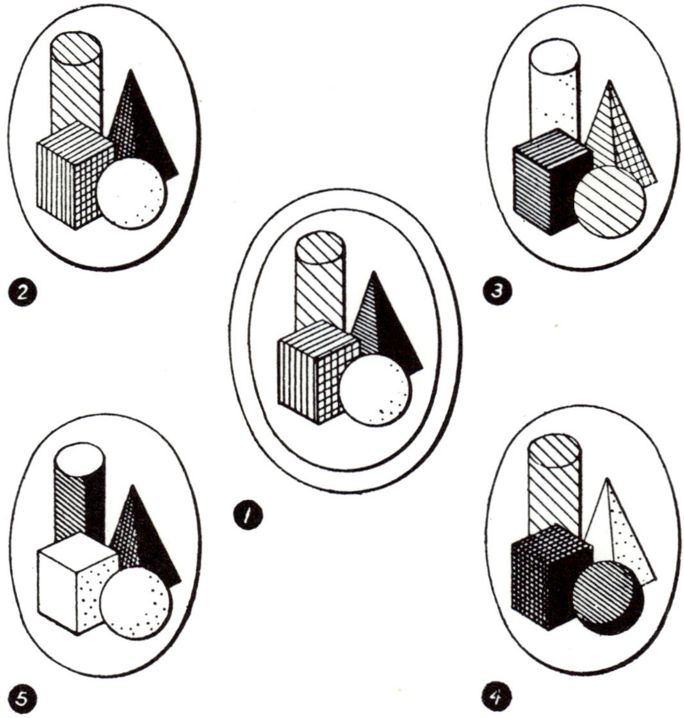

COLOUR FILTERS

The sphere is yellow, the cylinder is green, the cube red, and the pyramid blue—all at spectrum strength. To the eye (*1*) the colours appear in that order of brightness—yellow lightest, blue darkest. Through a yellow filter (*2*), blue becomes a little darker but the rest remains unchanged. Through a green filter (*3*) green is now the lightest and red the darkest. Through a blue filter (*4*), blue is light, yellow and red the darkest. Through a red filter (*5*), yellow and red are the lightest, blue and green the darkest.

own family—calling them white if its own shade is deep enough, and permits a reasonable amount of light from yellow objects to enter the camera.

BLUE FILTERS, according to strength, have a bias against yellow and a prejudice in favour of any colour in the subject similar in hue to themselves. Greens, since all but the lightest contain a goodly proportion of blue, are rendered normally, but red, unless it tends towards the blueness of the range between crimson and violet, is held back from the film inside the camera and consequently fails to be adequately recorded.

In every case, of course as much will depend upon the nature of the film emulsion, it being foolish, for instance, to use a red filter with an ortho, or "ordinary," film in the hope that it will register reds in high key, since these special films are themselves just as "selective" and only partial to blues and greens.

Apart from the existing basic colours, it is quite possible to combine any two filters to obtain a secondary colour of any desired kind. Thus, with a red, yellow and blue filter it is simple, by using any two together, to obtain the effect of an orange, green or violet filter to encourage the light-toned rendering of any of these shades existing in your subject.

It must be realised, of course, that the use of any filter, by excluding rays complementary to its own colour, reduces the total amount of light entering the camera—an increase of exposure is therefore involved.

Every filter has a factor, denoted in terms of a number, by which the normal exposure time must be multiplied. Thus, a filter whose factor is x2 doubles the exposure, x4 will quadruple it, and so forth. Combining any two or more filters will entail an exposure increase equal to the sum of the two or more factors, and the examples just given, if combined, would increase the exposure six times.

The normal use of colour filters scarcely constitutes trickery, in fact, the orthodox function aims at concealing their use by a more truthful and natural rendering of colour than is possible by the unaided emulsion of the film.

But, the use of the filter to unnatural ends—to conceal something in the final print that was strongly evident in the subject, or to emphasise something that in reality was scarcely visible to the eye, or to create a special effect, is a use uncommon enough to justify mention here.

▷ *The basis of minimising, or concealing, areas or objects of a certain colour depends upon the quality that deep filters have of recording areas of their own colour as strongly as they record white.*

So, freckles or other irregular patches of red-yellow pigmentation, if the sitter finds them less becoming than the susceptible photographer, can be removed from a protrait if the exposure is made through a filter similar in colour to the markings, which are, in most cases, a yellow or pale orange.

▷ *Similarly, the stained and yellowed pages of old books, drawings, and manuscript can be copied as clearly as the day they were executed if a filter similar in colour to the stain is employed—something usually in the deep yellow, orange or light red scale.*

▷ *A manuscript or any document or drawing that has been over-enthusiastically corrected in blue pencil or a pronounced blue ink, can be copied cleanly, with little or no trace of disfigurement, through a blue filter of appropriate strength on to a blue sensitive film such as the special orthochromatic or "ordinary" emulsions available for large format cameras.*

Indeed, any colour, for whatever reason, can be more or less concealed among white surroundings, or on a white background, if a strong enough filter of that colour is used for the exposure, in combination with a film material that is sensitive to that colour—accepting the rough basis of ortho or "ordinary" for the greens and blues, and panchromatic for the reds and yellows.

▷ *The basis of the opposite condition—to emphasise objects or coloured areas that are already concealing themselves among areas similar in tone, though different in colour, depends either upon choosing a filter of similar colour to emphasise the object as a light tone on darker surroundings, or choosing one of complementary colour to emphasise it as a dark tone against light surroundings.*

Thus, to reverse our recent examples, freckles or other irregular pigmentations of the skin can be emphasised to a cruel degree if recorded through a blue or deep green filter, since these complementary colours prevent them from recording on the emulsion and make them print almost black.

▷ *Faded ink writing on yellowed parchment can be copied with greater contrast through a filter of deep red to lighten the parchment and darken the script.*

Blue prints, or drawings and documents in pale or faded blue inks, can be registered in contrasts as clear as black on white if recorded on panchromatic film through a yellow or orange filter.

▷ *The use of yellow filter to give contrast between a blue sky and its white clouds is a common practice, and the stormy over-filtered skies obtained by the use of a filter too deep in colour are also well known. When, however, a deep blue sky is recorded through a strong red filter, the blue is held back from the film to such a degree that those portions of the negative receive almost no exposure and consequently print nearly as black as night.*

In such a manner the effect of moonlight pictures is frequently faked, care being taken to avoid the presence of tell-tale clouds, which, with their excessive contrasts, would destroy the illusion.

For these "moonlight" pictures strong sunshine is needed and ideally there should be enough reddish-brown tone in the buildings, or other landscape parts of the negative, to register lightly and add the necessary contrast to the depth of the sky.

The sun should be kept well clear of the boundaries of the camera's field of view—well to either side or preferably right behind, so that the sky has the authentic even tone of the true night sky without lighter gradations to the sides or the top.

▷ *The use of a deep red filter, in combination of course with a panchromatic film, will facilitate the recording of distant views and capture on the film details that were quite obscured, by aerial haze or mist, at the time of exposure, and therefore, invisible to the eye.*

In haze and mist the normal, visible, rays of light are scattered by the water vapour and never come to focus on the plane of the film. The deep red rays of longer wavelength, however, penetrate water vapour and can be recorded on the film if a deep red filter is used to hold back the scattered rays of other colours.

▷ *The red-yellow nature of artificial light has a similar effect on colour to the use of a yellow filter in daylight, it is partial to the reds and yellows and neglectful of the greens and blues. These tones can be changed back to their day-time appearance if a pale blue filter, like a daylight bulb, is used during the exposure.*

Infra Red

A few sentences ago something was said about the penetrative powers of red rays through mist and haze, and the way this assists the recording on a plate or film with a panchromatic emulsion, distant objects which are otherwise invisible.

Light rays of still greater wavelength, to which the eye is blind, penetrate still further and bring to a sensitive recipient details of objects so *distant in space that under no favourable condition of weather could they ever be observed by the eye*—naked or otherwise.

Such sensitive recipients are the materials with an infra-red sensitive emulsion, usually available in roll film, cut film or 35mm form to special order only. In combination with a filter so deep that it is known as *black* red, these films will successfully record all the various phenomena produced by the infra-red ray.

One special point for the camera loaded with infra-red film or plate concerns focusing. Deep red rays come to focus at a point further behind the film's surface than rays of normal light; the amount is minute, but enough to be a serious consideration if the lens is of long focal length, such as the telephoto, or if the lens is used at a large aperture.

In these cases the lens to film distance must be increased, the average amount of such extension being usually assumed to be *1/200th of the focal length*. A series of test exposures should be made, marking the position of each on the focusing scale of the camera. The sharpest negative will indicate which mark was correct, and this will be constant for all work at that distance.

Some cameras, notably of the 35mm type, have markings on the focusing scale for infra-red work. But the displacement of focus is not a serious drawback and will not be thoroughly effective for distance work if the lens is of short focal length, of small aperture, or stopped down to *f*/11 or beyond.

The scientific and, so to say, legitimate uses of infra-red photography, besides the popular recording of distant prospects, includes the deciphering of ancient documents, detecting forged signatures and manuscript, and many branches of medicine and surgery.

▷ *But, with our present interest in tone distortion, infra-red concerns us here chiefly with the strange manner in which it treats the tones of the wooded landscape.*

Like the deep-red filter with panchromatic film, infra-red materials pick up no light from blue skies, which reflect no such rays. These, therefore, record as black tones, on which any clouds stand out as clearly as a white cat on a coal heap. But, and this is unique to the process, the green fields and foliage of the trees record as brilliantly white as if they had been newly laden with snow, but with infinitely more detail.

This transformation is said to be due to a substance called chlorophyl—the green colouring matter of grass and leaves, which is a strong reflector of infra-red light and therefore builds up considerable tone on the sensitive film. The effect is fantastically unreal, not to say unnatural, but who, embracing beauty, asks for truth?

As might be expected, the snowy appearance is at a maximum when the subject is lit with a flat-on light—sun behind the camera, and at its least when the sun is directly shining from one side or the other. Against the light, only the tops and top-sides glow like leafy haloes.

▷ *One point always to remember, like the Mayor without his corporation, or the policeman without his boots, infra-red film has no special power without its filter.*

Polarisation

Polarised light is no more a trick than the infra-red ray, though no less either, perhaps. But, since by its use we can obtain in the camera a result that is often totally different to that seen by the eye at the time of exposure, we'll let it go; the process has a place in the repertoire of trick photography.

The vibrations set up by any ray of light have no consistent direction, proceeding not only directly between subject and camera, but by way of reflection from polished and other reflecting surfaces. The disturbing glare and reflection from water, mirrors, highly-glazed china, picture glass and shop windows, are instances of this multi-directional quality of light, a quality that makes it often impossible to obtain either a clear picture of objects behind any of these surfaces, or of the surfaces themselves.

A pola-screen, or pola-filter, *attempts to reduce the many directions by which light may reach the camera to a single direction only*—that directly parallel to the plane of the polarising device.

This plane can be changed at will by rotating the filter. The result of rotating the filter can be seen if you look through it as you do so. Any effect arranged visually through the filter can be recorded by the camera if the device is placed before the lens at exactly the same angle. Alternatively, with single lens reflex cameras the filter can be rotated, and, observed through the viewfinder until the desired effect is achieved.

TONE TRICKS

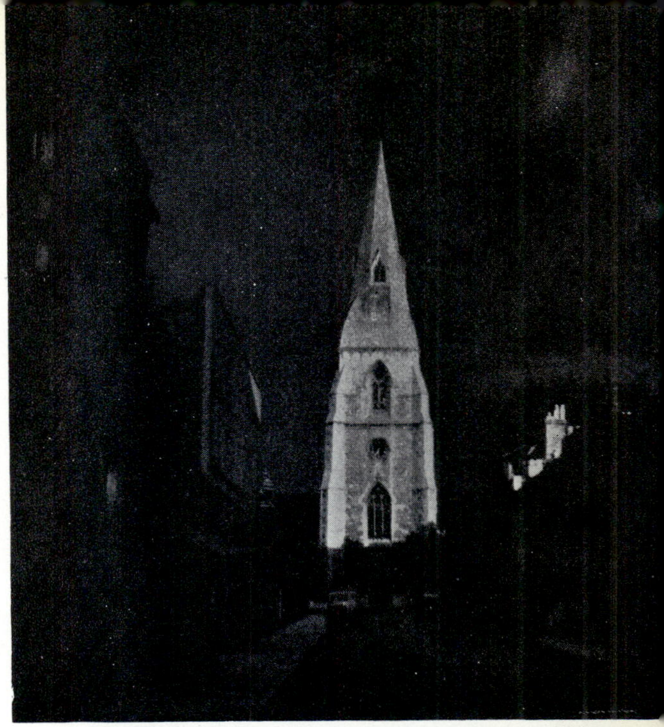

Low evening light picked out this steeple for particular and exclusive attention, and a low, cunning photographer picked out an orange filter to record it though subduing all other tones and producing an effect of fascinating exaggeration.—*Hugo van Wadenoyen.*

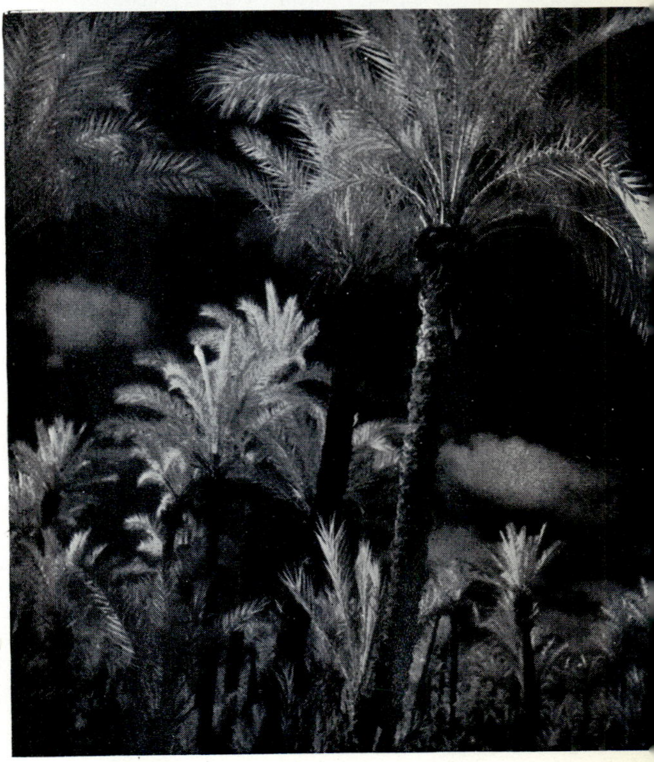

Palm trees improved and their fronds turned to feathers, by the imaginative use of infra-red film and a black-red filter. Chlorophyll, the colouring pigment of foliage, strongly reflects infra-red rays and is an important conspirator.—*P. Boucher.*

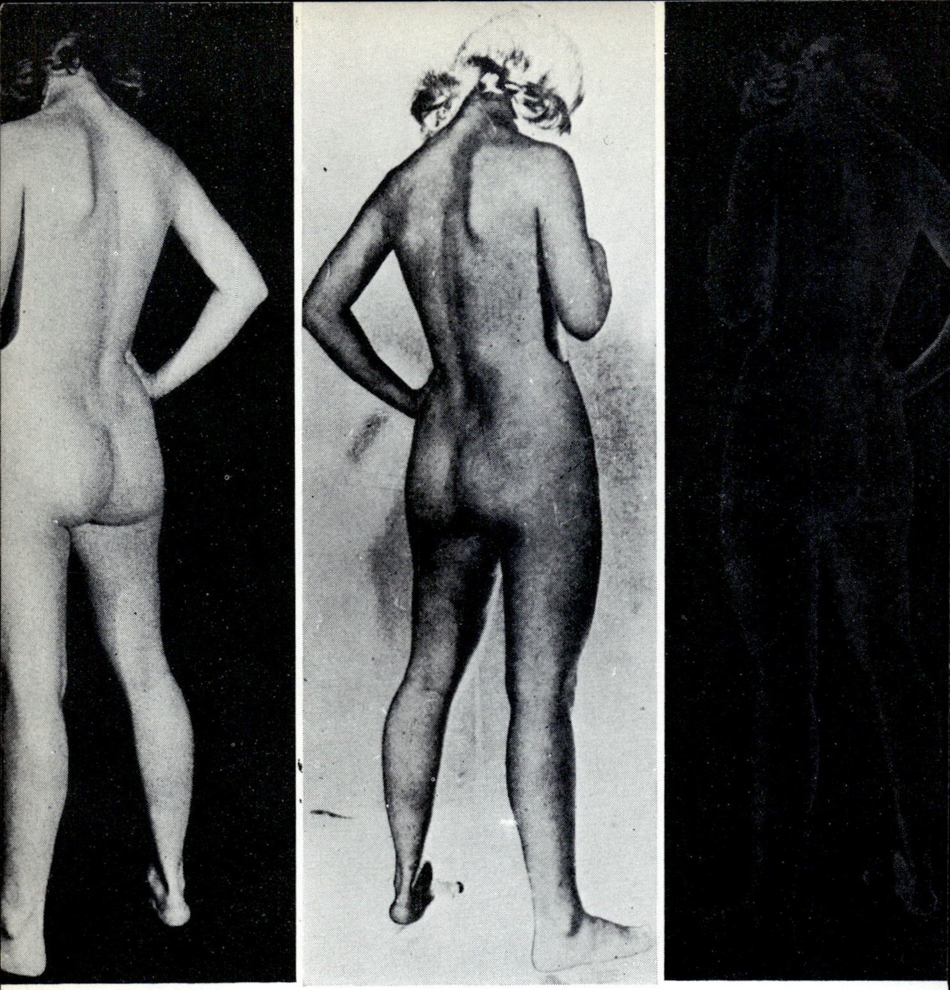

Nude series, *left to right:* 1, Normal print from negative. 2, print using 1 as a paper negative. 3, direct print of 2 flashed during development. 4 and 5 further negative variations derived from paper solarization and 6 a coarse grained positive made from a paper negative which itself originated from a paper positive.—*Heinrich Charusa.*

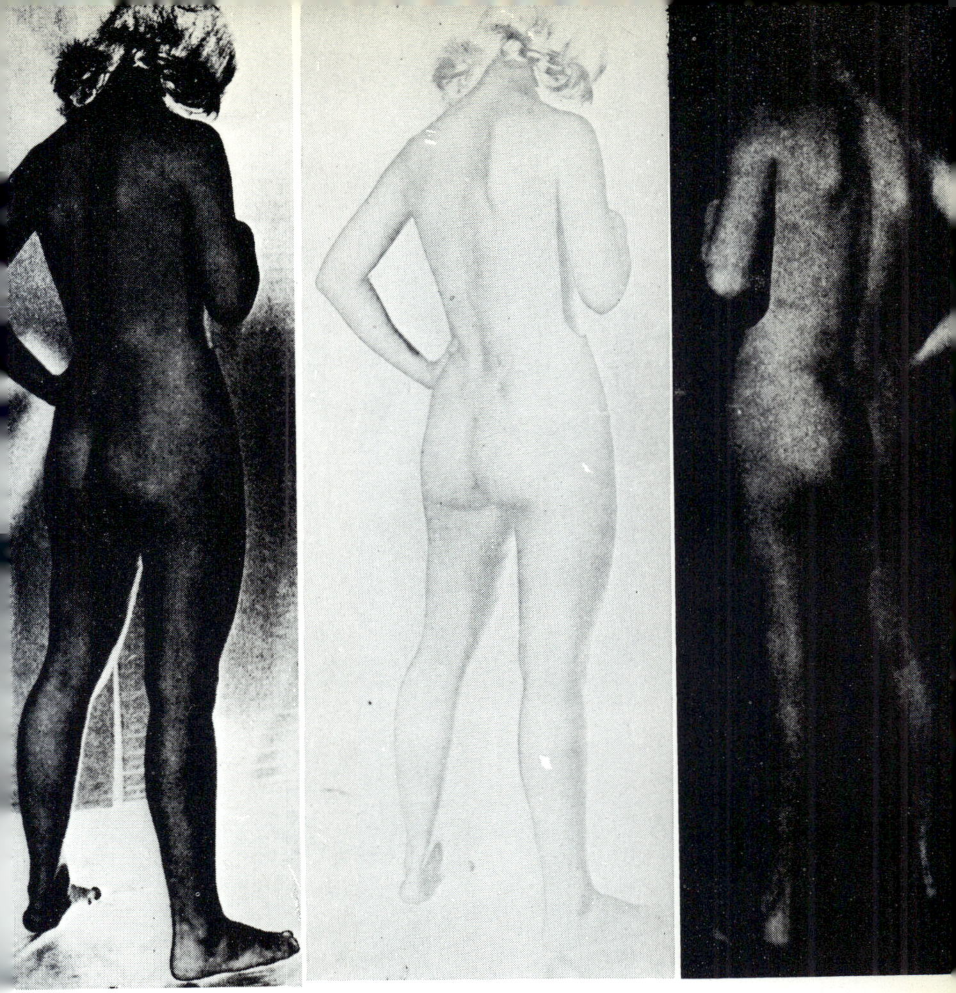

Page 176: Solarisation of the print, on *left*, gives a characteristic general dark tone, with a white or light grey line bordering the principal areas of tone. Complicated shadows, which are normally well avoided, add to the fantasy. Solarisation of negative, on *right* gives a characteristic general light tone, with the principal tone areas outlined in black. Original subject a white-glazed china animal lit with few shadows on a dead black background.—*Marcel Bovis, G. Markham.*
Bottom: Simple three-tone posterisation with its characteristic solid tone areas made by printing from separate contrast negatives printed in registration.—*Unknown photographer.*

Page 177: Print made from solarised duplicate negative of temple ruins. The effect can be strengthened by further printing on contrast material or by using contrast film for the solarised intermediate.—*Heinrich Charusa.*

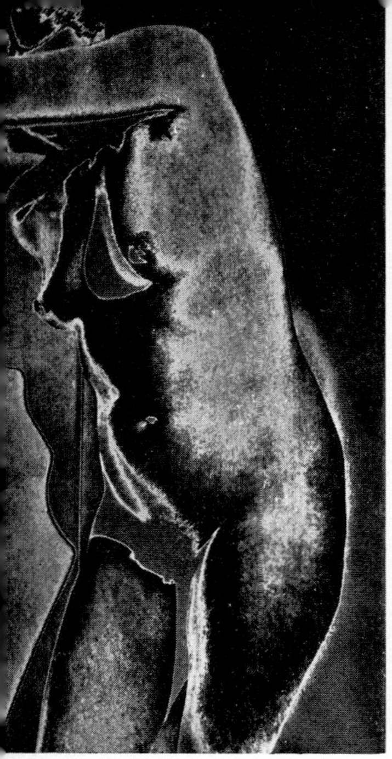

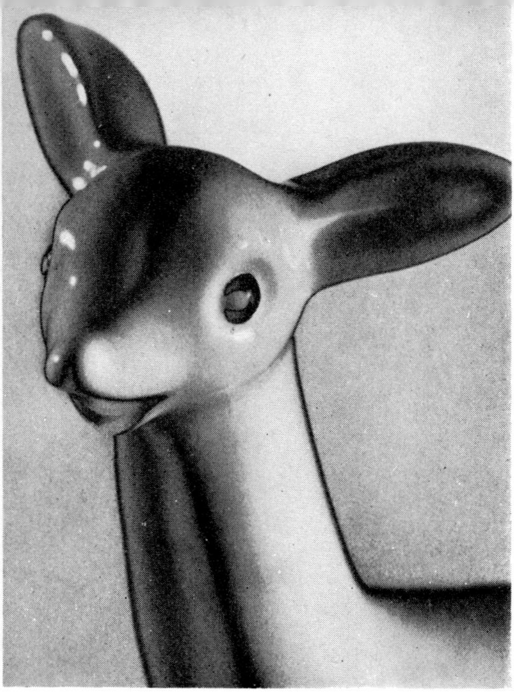

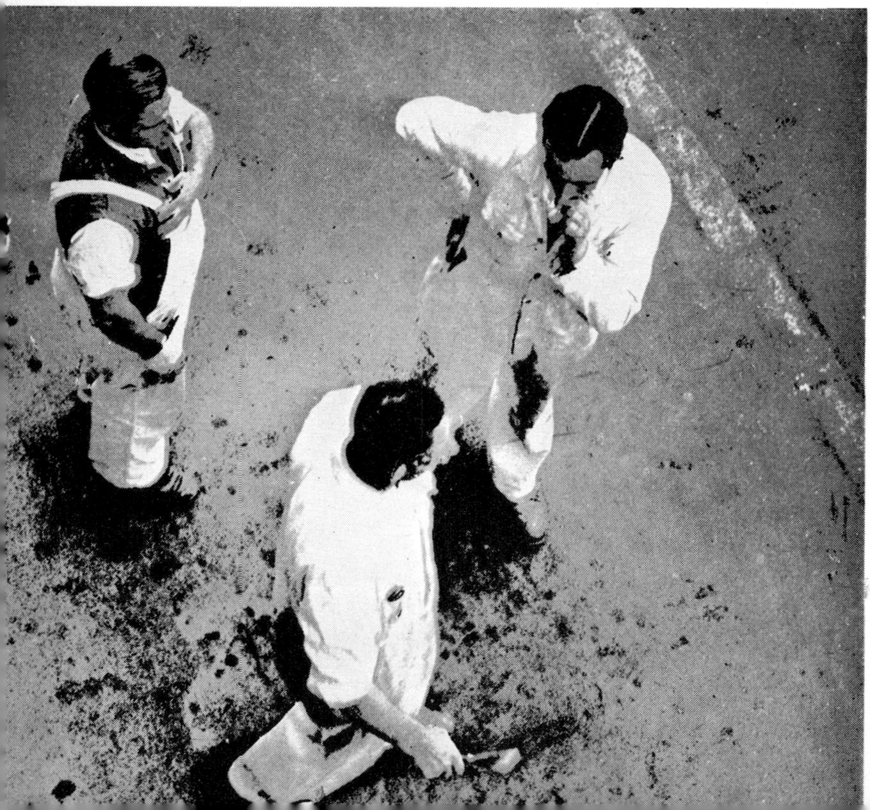

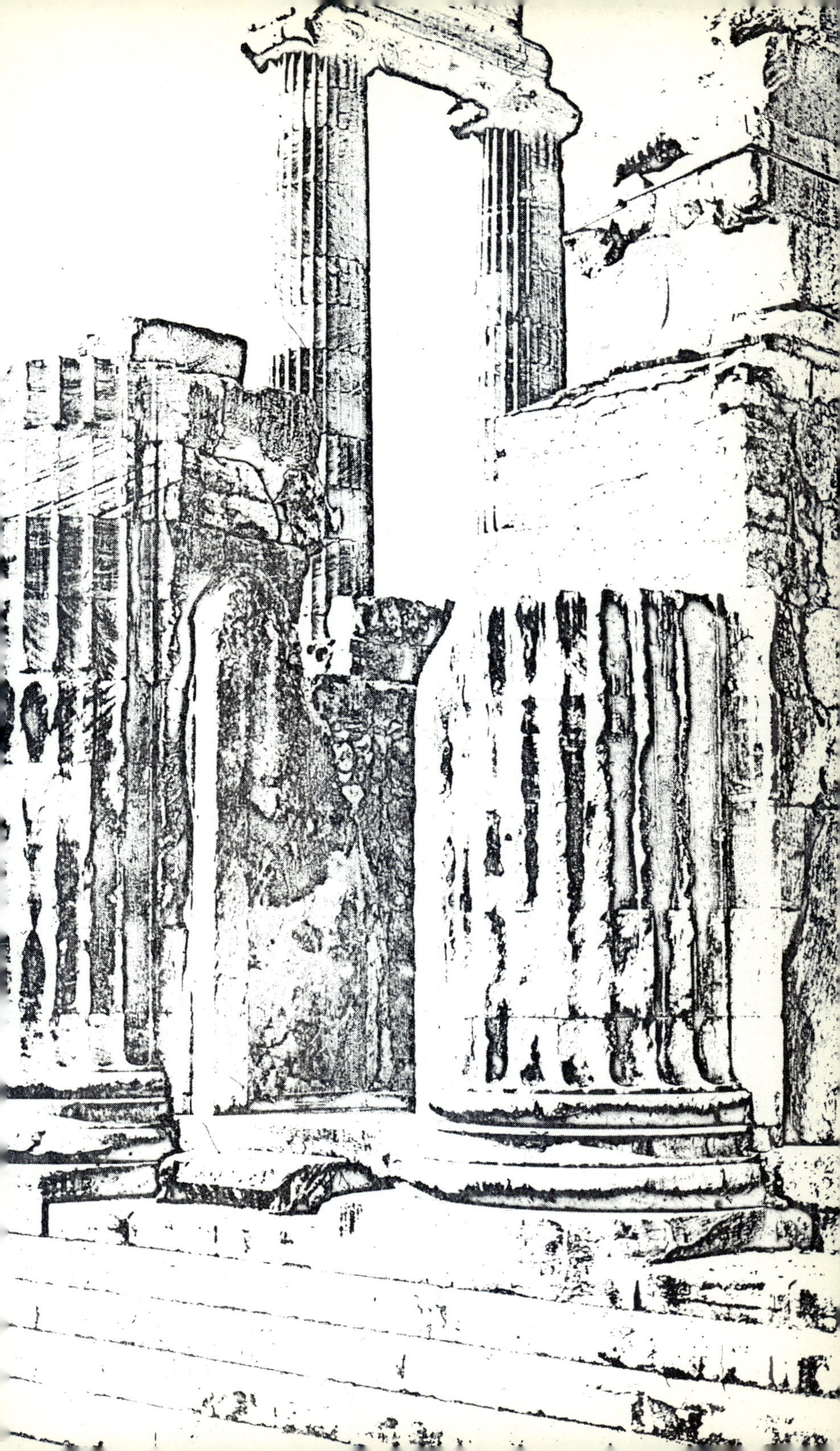

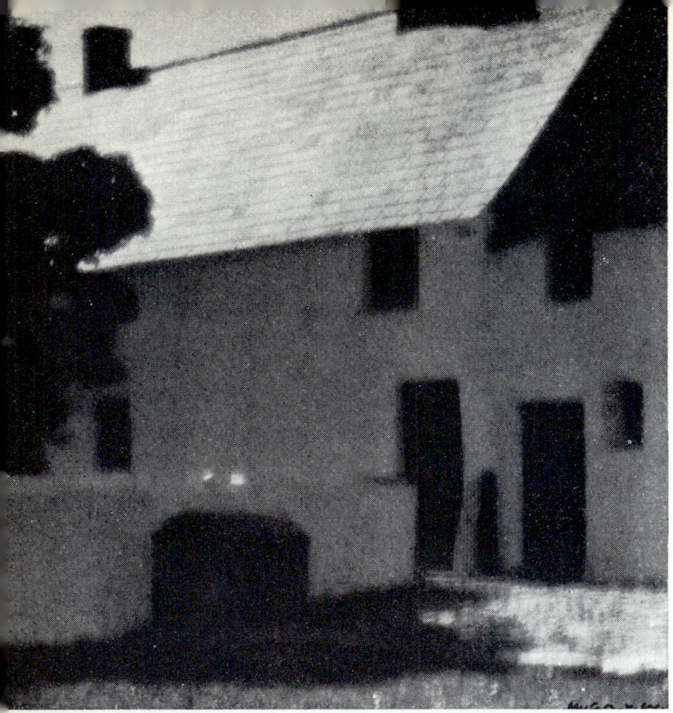

Taken in strong, contrasting sunlight, through a diffusing disc, this picture shows the characteristic softening of contrast and spreading of the highlights into the shadow areas.—*Hugo van Wadenoyen.*

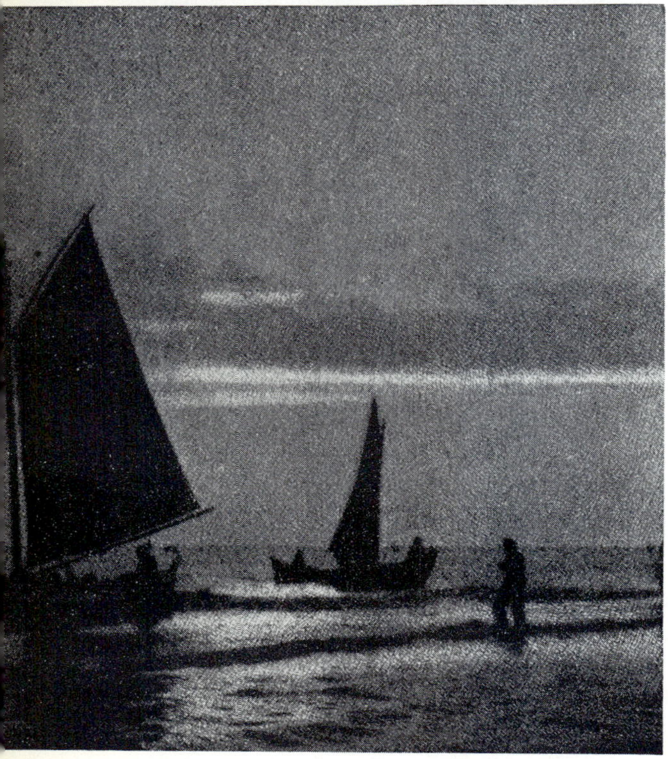

Artificial texture applied through a "Haille" screen used in contact with paper during printing, to give the crumbled stone texture of a lithograph.—*Unknown photographer.*

Opposite: Grain texture effect obtained by sandwiching the negative with a grain texture screen, which can be made by enlarging a small even area of image on to a sheet of copy film.—*Michael Barrington-Martin.*

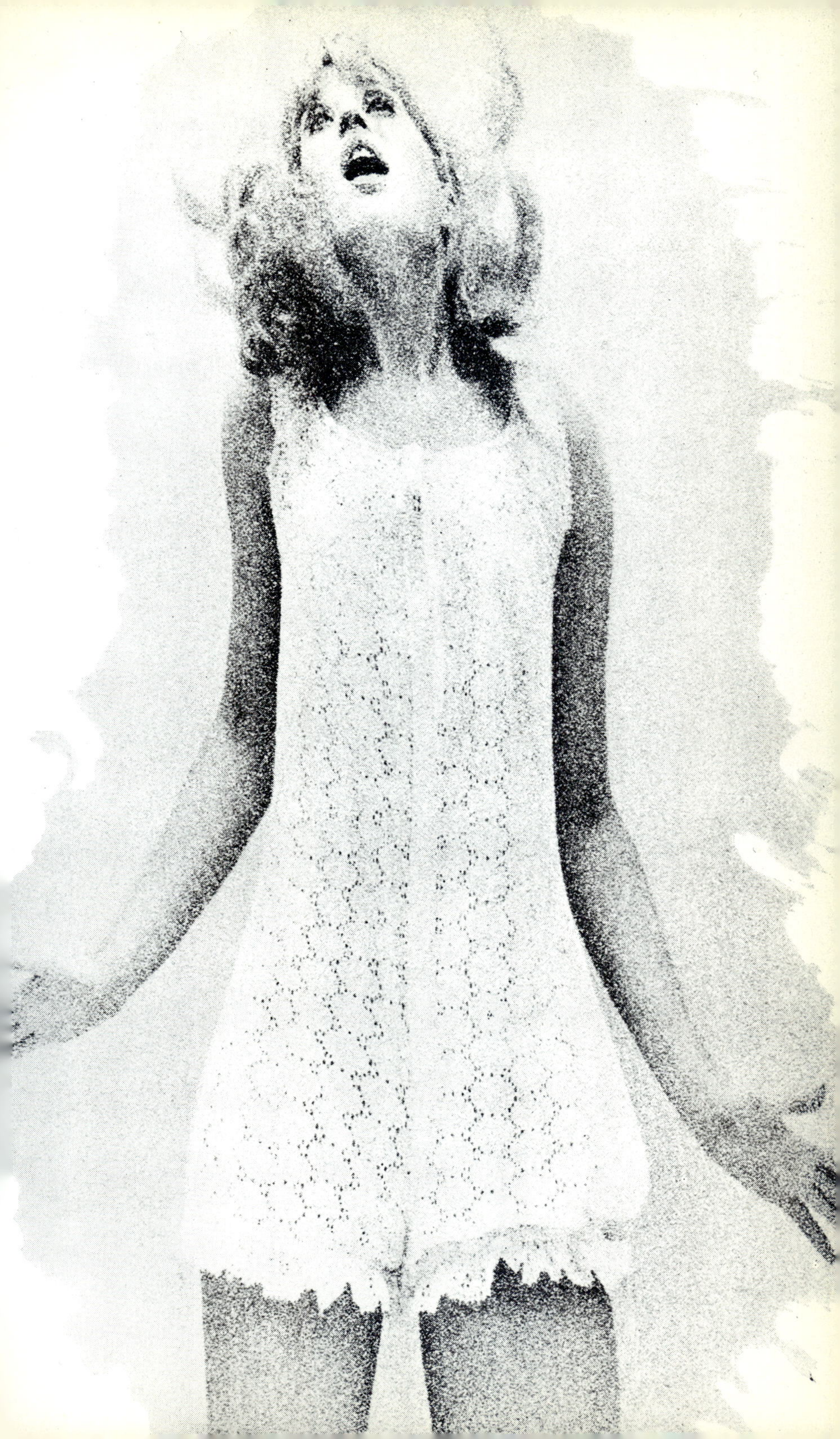

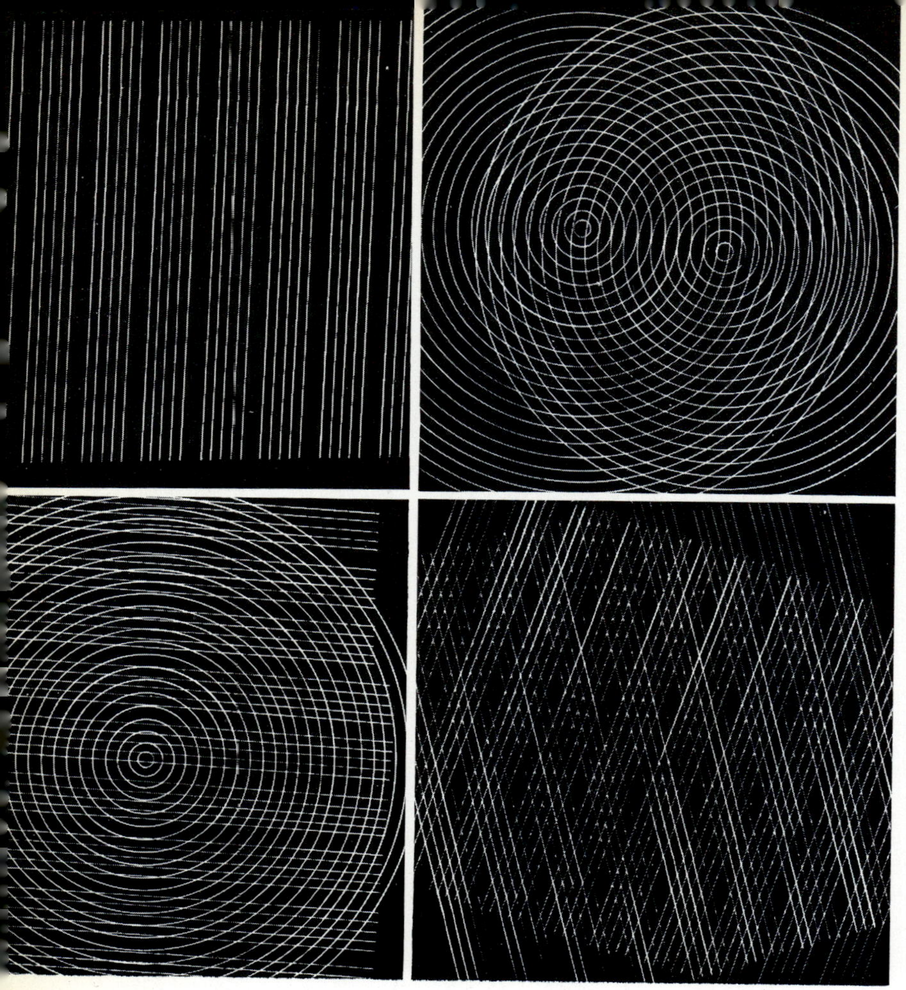

Four line-patterns without the camera, produced from clear celluloid screens covered with parallel lines in circular and straight formations. *Top left:* the second straight line screen has been moved during exposure to produce a third, half tone. *Top right* was simply produced from two circular line screens used greatly out of register. *Bottom left* is a combination of circular and straight screens; *bottom right* is two straight line screens used at an angle of approximately 45 degrees to each other. The borders of the pattern, which would normally be trimmed away, have here been left to indicate the method of production.—*Edwin Smith.*

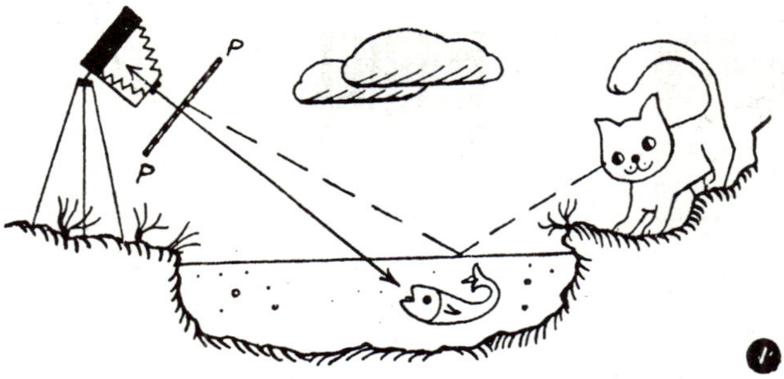

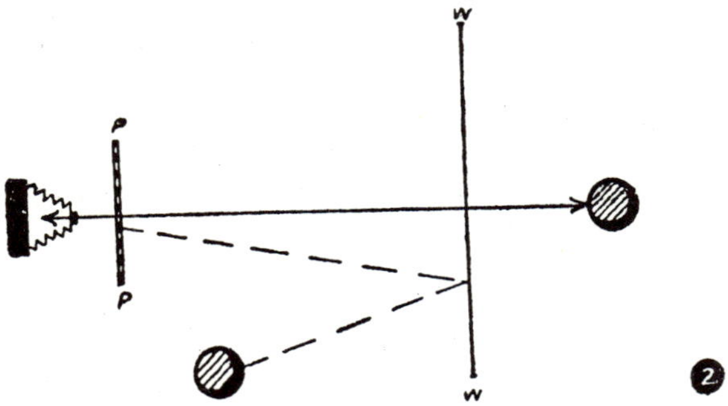

POLARISATION

The pola-screen or filter, *P—P,* passes all light rays vibrating in one plane only, and obstructs all those that seek passage from other directions.

In *1,* the image of the cat and glare from the sky, which would normally be reflected from the water's surface into the camera, is intercepted by the screen and the camera allowed a clear under-water view. In *2,* a clear image of an object behind a reflecting window, *W—W,* is recorded, and the reflection of an object adjacent to the camera avoided, by a similar use of a pola-filter.

Instead of using the pola-screen to polarise the light entering the camera, it can be used in larger sheets before any source of artificial light to polarise the light reaching the subject—the result is similar.

The uses of polarised light are concerned with reducing the reflections from any glazed surface occurring between the camera and the subject, such as, for instance, drawings and paintings under glass in museums, or similar sacrosanct situations, where the position of light and picture are not under control.

▷ *Goods and displays in shop windows, which are quite a troublesome problem under normal conditions, can be recorded through a pola-filter without the irrelevant reflections of vehicles and passers-by.*

▷ *Objects under water, which would normally involve the use of a viewing-box as described on page 248 for their clear recording, can be photographed directly with no other gadget beyond the appropriately adjusted pola.*

▷ *Just one pitfall to avoid. Only oblique reflections can be successfully side-tracked; those that are in the same direction as the rays of the subject can never be avoided. Thus, head-on views towards reflecting surfaces, with the camera back parallel to the reflector, will thwart the screen everytime.*

Exposure times must usually be increased by about two and a half times or according to manufacturers' directions.

Soft Focus

Soft focus, or diffusion, is a further means of controlling the manner in which the subject is recorded at the time of exposure. It concerns, quite clearly, the degree of definition and sharpness of the image, and less clearly, but no less definitely, the re-disposition of tone.

The use of a soft-focusing device, by softening contrast through the spread of areas of light into areas of shade, effects a considerable alteration to the tones of a picture, uniting small and fussy tone variations into larger simple masses in a manner considerably improving to many subjects. It is in this sense of tone distortion that diffusion finds its niche here.

The image obtained by soft focusing devices is only partially soft, and is not to be confused with the all-over woolliness associated with images that are just out of focus. The effect of *diffusion is made by a mixture of alternate sharpness and softness over the whole picture area,* so that the finished image is neither pin-sharp or feather-soft but a satisfying combination of both.

DIFFUSION DISCS. The most direct means of obtaining a soft image is to purchase a specially manufactured diffusion disc, which can be slipped on to the camera lens in the familiar manner of the supplementary lens.

Such discs are pieces of optically-worked glass on which a number of lines appear in the form of parallel rings, or other pattern, at regular intervals, the lines being either indented into the glass or raised up from its surface.

The plain glass portions of the diffusion disc pass a normal and unaffected light image. But the raised or indented lines scatter or diffuse the light that falls upon them, preventing it from reaching a focal point on the film surface and spreading this light into the adjacent areas of sharp focus.

Most diffusion discs do not affect the normal focusing arrangements of the camera or the focal length of the lens, and very few demand an increase of exposure time, some are made in two strengths for use with light of soft or strong contrast, but all are accompanied by instructions which render further comment here superfluous.

GREASE SMEARS. The effect of a glass diffusion disc can be conveniently imitated if a circular, or square, piece of glass is smeared by the finger with a little *petroleum jelly.* The fingerprint will leave a set of ridges similar in nature to the glass ridges or indentations of the manufactured article, and similar in effect--refracting any light that attempts to pass through them.

The all-over diffusion of the glass disc is simulated by making these ridges in circular formation, but interesting *variations can be contrived by forming the ridges in one direction only,* so that diffusion and tone distortion occurs in that single direction.

A glass disc or square so treated and arranged before the camera so that the ridges run horizontally, will give a diffused, or semi-sharp, image of all truly vertical objects, but a hopelessly confused, and nowhere sharp, image of horizontals. Arranging the diffuser so that the petroleum jelly ridges run vertically will produce the opposite effect—normally diffused horizontals, hopelessly confused verticals.

If one half of the disc is smeared with straight lines in one direction, and the other half with lines at right-angles—one half horizontal, the other vertical—the verticals and horizontals will be alternately sharp and confused on opposite sides. The effect is only half as hazy as it sounds and well worth trying on various subjects.

Discs that cause slightly less diffusion are easily made by *scoring thin lines in a disc of stout plastic sheet or gelatine, or drawing them with a geometrical-instrument pen charged with white poster paint or ink.* Such lines can be drawn in circular formation with a compass, or in parallel straight lines, in both cases the lines being approximately one-eighth of an inch apart—wider if less diffusion is required, nearer if more.

The white painted lines will have greater distorting effect on tones than those scored in the gelatine surface by a needle or sharp compass point, the white paint reflecting more light.

These home-made diffusion devices involve no increase in exposure times, in fact those produced with white drawn lines actually increase the amount of light entering the camera and so reduce the exposure time by as much as 15 per cent.

GAUZE. Other diffusion devices that can be simply extemporised at home include the use of such net-like fabrics as *gauze, tulle, and georgette crepe* stretched on small frames and held before the camera lens.

Like the bung-hole with a barrel round it, all are made up of holes of varying sizes connected to each other with threads of varying thickness and colour. *The smaller the hole, the lighter and thicker the threads, the greater the diffusing and tone distorting effect.* The larger the hole, the darker and thinner the threads, the less the diffusion.

A gauze of thin white net whose meshes are approximately one-tenth of an inch across, has what might be called a "moderate" softening effect when held an inch or two in front of the lens, pleasantly massing the tones without softening the definition of detail to the point of woolliness.

Smaller meshes are not advisable unless their excessive flattening of the picture contrasts is consciously desired, if so, these smaller holes can be simply obtained by using several thicknesses of net so that the threads overlap in another direction.

Coarse white muslin with a fine regular mesh makes an excellent diffusing screen. The effects are rather extreme but this can be minimised by cutting a small circular opening in the middle—about one-quarter of an inch if the lens is three-quarters in diameter—so that the central portion of the picture image records more sharply than the edges.

Since they reflect, diffusing screens of white material will

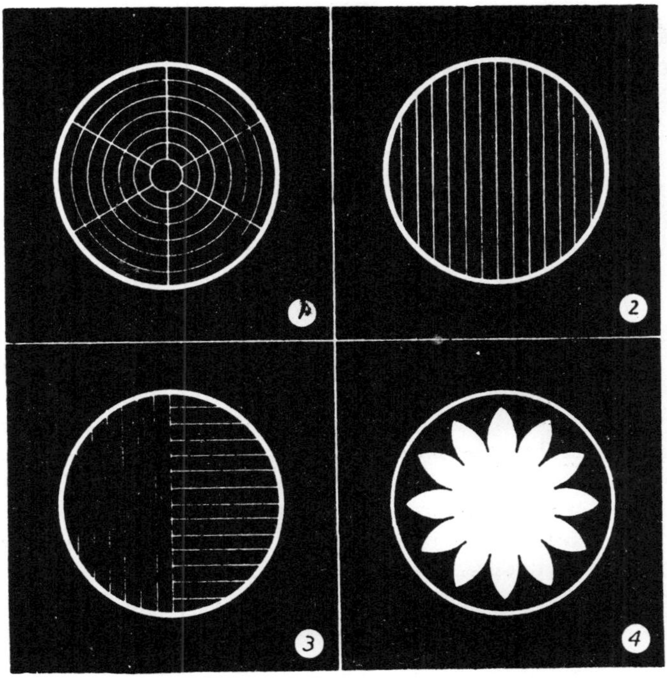

DIFFUSION

Drawings *1, 2* and *3* show various dispositions of diffusing lines on clear glass or gelatine discs. Such lines can be made in grease smears by the finger, drawn in white paint on the gelatine surface, and the straight one could be formed from thin white threads. *1* gives an all over diffusion, *2* gives diffused verticals or horizontals only—according to the direction of the lines, *3* gives a mixture of both on opposite sides of the picture.

Drawing *4* is a rosette stop suitable for use as a diaphragm with the spectacle lens. The diameter of the effective aperture would be approximately mid-way between the inner and outer extremes of the points.

increase the amount of light falling on the surface of the film up to a maximum of about 15 per cent, and exposure times can be reduced by this amount. Since they absorb, screens of dark or black material decrease the amount of light entering the camera to a similar maximum the other way, and exposure times should consequently be lengthened.

As the holes are usually square, or sometimes hexagonal, the diffusing effect of any gauze is uniform in all directions. One-way diffusion, of the kind produced by the straight jelly smears, can be easily obtained if white or black cotton threads are stretched in a single direction across an opening cut in a piece of card, at, say, one-eighth or one-tenth of an inch intervals.

SPECTACLE LENSES. Soft-focus pictures without the use of any supplementary diffusion device can be obtained by substituting a spectacle lens of the meniscus type for the normal lens of the camera. These lenses are uncorrected for optical aberration and produce an image in which the contours, though clearly marked, are surrounded by a soft light-halo.

Such lenses can be obtained from an optician and are commonly about one and a half inches (3.75 cm.) in diameter, their focal length being defined in terms of dioptres instead of the more usual inches or centimetres. If this dioptre number be divided into 100 the focal length in centimetres is obtained, so that a meniscus of +2 dioptres has a focal length of 50 centimetres or approximately 20 inches. A lens of this focal length would be suitable for use in a large format camera.

Due to spherical aberration, the marginal rays of the spectacle lens do not come to focus at the same point as the central ones, it may therefore be advisable to exclude them, either by *using the central portion of the image only, or by using a lens of longer focal length than normal*—as long as the camera extension will allow. Thus, for a quarter-plate camera whose normal lens has a focal length of about 6 inches or 15 centimetres, the diopter equivalent would be +5 or +6, but it is better, if the bellows permit, to employ one with an equivalent of 20 to 25 centimetres, 8 to 10 inches, or approximately +4 diopters.

The spectacle lens can be secured to the camera by fitting it into a filter holder of suitable size, or by arranging it in a short cardboard tube. *The concave, or hollow, side of the lens will face the subject; the convex, or bulging, side faces the camera.*

Diaphragms, or stops, are arranged in front of the lens and can consist of circular holes of different size cut into circular pieces of card, though some prefer stops cut in the form of a rosette, or many-pointed star, to the plain circle.

The value of any aperture can be simply obtained if the focal length of the lens is divided by the diameter of the stop proposed. Thus, with a lens whose diopter number is +4, or 25 centimetres (10 inches), a diaphragm whose diameter is 4 centimetres (1½ inches) has an approximate value of *f*6.3. This aperture, it has been recorded, is the advisable maximum at which to employ any spectacle lens for a tolerably sharp result. Larger than this, optical defects become unpleasantly pronounced, and much smaller, *beyond f8 or so, the image becomes sharper and sharper until all softness of focus disappears.*

In practice the spectacle lens will be found to pass a little more light than a normal anastigmat lens working at the same aperture, so that the *f*6.3 aperture recommended has an exposure value much nearer *f*4.5, and allowance should be made for this.

To further pronounce the softness of the image *two glasses* could be used in the form of a compound lens—*the greater the difference in dioptre numbers between the two lenses, the softer the resulting image.*

The dioptre numbers are added together and divided into 100 to find the focal length of the combination, so that two lenses of x2 and x4 combine to give a lens of +6 dioptre focal length, suitable for a quarter-plate camera.

The lens of the largest number is placed nearest the negative, convex side facing it; the one whose number is least is placed nearer the subject, convex side facing that way. Thus the two will have their concave sides facing each other with a diaphragm of the desired size between them.

Focusing with spectacle lenses must obviously be carried out on a ground-glass screen. Unlike focusing with an anastigmat *no attempt should be made to focus the image at maximum sharpness*. The effect to be aimed at is a sharp central image surrounded by misty diffusion. To practise until you feel confident that you understand the principle, it is advisable to focus, say, on two thick black cords or similar dark lines set against an intense white background or the sky seen through a window. Their image should be focused, by racking the lens panel to and fro, until the cords are edged each side with a dark misty halo that appears to make them broader. Moving the lens further out of focus in either direction will increase the area of halo until the objects lose all semblance to photographic images, the point to be judged is where the combination of softness and sharpness is just right.

Should the particular lens or lenses you acquire yield a result too woolly to be satisfactory, their *image can be improved if focusing and exposure is made through a yellow filter.* This roughly corrects the lens for chromatic aberration, holding back the blue rays which come to focus in a different plane to the yellow.

ENLARGING DIFFUSION. Soft focus can be introduced into any picture after the original negative has been made, by using one of the above-mentioned devices at the time of enlargement—placing a glass diffusion disc over the enlarging lens, smearing the lens with grease, intercepting the light rays with a gauze or white net, or substituting a soft focus or spectacle lens for the normal lens of the enlarger.

However, since, as we have previously noted, the enlarger is like a back-to-front camera, its effects of diffusion and tone distortion are reversed. The light it transmits darkens the paper to varying degrees and any *diffusion of this light spreads darkness into the lighter areas, contrariwise to the spreading of light within the camera.*

Thus, though the characteristic tone of a picture diffused within the camera is light and sunny, the appearance of a print diffused during enlargement, though soft, is drabber and darker than the original, and rarely satisfying.

Apart from all these devices to diffuse the sharp image given by a corrected lens, it is, of course, quite possible to use a lens specially constructed for the purpose—one known as a soft-focus lens.

These are still occasionally used by for 'society' and other breeds of portrait photograph. They consist either of optically uncorrected lenses, or corrected *anastigmats whose separate components can be adjusted* in relation to each other to decrease the sharpness of definition. In other cases *the use of certain apertures* gives the soft effect, the uses of others giving a normally sharp rendering.

Unless your lens is intended for such treatment, it is not advisable to attempt diffusion effects by interfering with the relation of its various components, much better to use one of the extraneous devices.

Diffusion is a little stuck in the syrup of sentimentality, but firm intent will pull it free. Basically, its power is one of destroying detail, and its use to smudge the character from ageing or rugged countenances, or to set a sticky halo round otherwise attractive children, has brought it into deserved disrepute. If examined sensibly and objectively, however, it will be found to bear use for better ends.

The microscopic detail of the perfectly corrected anastigmat lens is unique to the photographic vision and, to many, the camera's principal justification. But its disinterested insistence on the minute structure and texture of every seemingly plain surface is, perhaps, not suitable for all subjects.

Exaggerated concern with detail draws attention from the picture as a total composition and directs it towards personalities and peculiarities, away from Man and towards a male biped with a crumpled suit and a spot on the end of his nose. Whereas the simplified tonal structure of a diffused picture concerns itself more with the effect and intention of the picture as a whole than with the irrelevant details of which it is composed. More with the act and less with the actor.

Any picture, therefore, whose intention is a generality rather than a particularity, will be suitable; subjects where it is intended to convey the idea, say, of running, fishing or smoking, rather than the personal idiosyncrasies of a particular runner, fisher or smoker.

▷ *An important conspirator in the effect of diffusion is the relative contrast of light and shade in the subject. A characteristic of soft focus is the spreading of light into the shadowed areas of the picture with a consequent loss of contrast but gain of shadow detail. Unless the contrasts of the subject are strong, therefore, the results are apt to be excessively grey and flat.*

Strong summer sunshine, or a single powerful source of artificial light, where the shadows would normally be too coarse, are excellent material for diffusion, as are all brilliant against-the-light effects.

▷ *With most diffusion devices exposure times must be exceedingly accurate. Any suspicion of over-exposure is fatal to the already flattened tones, and destructive of the softly diffused contours. Generally speaking, unless otherwise advised by a manufacturer's instructions, give a bare exposure and slight over-development to increase contrast.*

▷ *The degree of tone distortion depends much on the size of the negative and the area of the print made from it. The coarser methods and effects are not suitable for miniature negatives, or those much below quarter-plate (9 cm. x 12 cm.). These acquire a certain amount of diffusion by enlargement and anything in the nature of a heavy diffusing screen intensifies the effect to an absurd degree.*

Solarisation

Solarisation, Sabatier effect, or just plain partial reversal, as this same process is termed, with different degrees of enthusiasm, by its devotees or the photographic text-book, is an excellent example of the ultimate value of occasional carelessness, and an implicit trust in the infinite.

How sick with yourself, how angry with an innocent aunt, if you inadvertently turned on the light, or she opened the dark-room door to see how you were "getting on," during open dish development of a film or paper.

But how unjust so churlishly to resent the help and intrusion of a force seeking to help the ungrateful photographer by fogging his film and overheating his hypo. Reassure yourself, say "Nicely, thank you" to aunt, continue development of the film or paper and, if your subject has been suitable and the accident a truly happy one, the infinite will reward a truly kindred spirit.

If you were developing a paper you may now have a solarised paper print. If it was a piece of cut film that, too, may be solarised, if, again, you did not immediately throw it away in disgust. But, assuming you are of a higher level of photographic education, fix, wash, dry and pull a print from it just as if the whole business was firm intention.

With film, the result of such an accident, or design, is to produce the effect of partial reversal of the negative image, high-lights remain clear and unaffected, but middle tones are fogged and areas that were black in the subject are reversed to white.

The characteristic of the printed result is a strong black outline around the main contours of the picture, sharper on the side towards the subject and softening out to the white of the background—the effect in fact of a pencil line sensitively drawn around the subject, without the hardness that actual handwork would involve.

Negative Solarisation

Apart from accidents, the effect of the black line of solarisation is obtained in the following manner.

The exposed negative is normally *developed for half the customary time,* removed from the developer, *rinsed* thoroughly but rapidly, and any excess liquid *wiped off* with a soft chamois leather or viscose sponge.

The film is then briefly *exposed to a fogging light*—the red, or orange-yellow, printed safelight of the darkroom if the emulsion is the usual panchromatic type or the normal white light if it is ortho, and returned to the developer for the *second half of the developing time.*

The significance of rinsing and wiping the emulsion surface after the first half-development, and before fogging, is to make sure that *streaks, spots, or bubbles of developer,* that would react differently to the fogging light and leave after evidence of their existence, are completely removed.

For the fogging, the film should be held by the edges at top or bottom so that the palm of the hand, or any other light reflecting surface, is not immediately behind the back of the negative. Such a precaution defeats the *tendency to halation* that a back-reflected light would give, and ensures an even distribution of one accident to one negative.

The process is uncertain, by no means fool-proof, and rarely consistent, appearing to work differently for each person, film developer and darkroom. The only real foundation for consistent results is personal experiment, on the above lines, with your favourtie materials and formulae, in your own darkroom.

Some technicians advise two-thirds development before fogging, one-third afterwards; some suggest the other way round. Again, it is claimed that the effect can only be successfully produced if the negative is left dormant for two or three minutes after fogging and before the second development, suggesting that it is during this period of rest that the characteristic black line appears.

The period of fogging is another element that appears to differ in each darkroom, it being impossible to ensure that conditions of light are universally similar. Time will depend on the strength of the light, its distance from the plate or film, and the speed of the film's emulsion. A fogging exposure of half a second to the 60 watt bulb suspended from the ceiling of a darkroom, or approximately ten seconds to the orange-yellow light of the bromide paper safelight, when the film is held about two feet away, are two times and conditions that have produced satisfactory results.

Your own darkroom will doubtless say different, but it can be induced to say the same thing every time if the strength of light, its distance from the plate, and the time, when ascertained, are kept consistent.

The rough chemical basis of the process is thus. Those parts of the negative that contain high-lights and other strong light tones are rapidly de-sensitised by the first period of development, so that when the film is fogged, these areas, being no longer sensitive, remain unaffected.

Those parts of the negative, however, that contained the dark shadows and middle tones of the subject retain, according to depth some degree of their original light sensitivity. When exposed to the fogging light, therefore, their densities are affected by it to different degrees, the black and completely sensitive areas reversing to an absolute density—or white, the middle tones being fogged in proportion to the depth of their original density.

Theoretically, these middle tones of darkness should be reversed to correspondingly different degrees of lightness, but in actuality they are bunched together in a single tone of rather foggy grey.

Here, then, is the partial reversal—the highlights of the subject remain unaffected, and the black and deeper shadow parts are completely reversed. But what about that black line?

Well, there it is, dividing the highlights from that which once was black and now is white, but its cause is not so clear as its presence. The line appears in every place where the tone contrasts of the original subject were violent—an intense light next to a dim shadow, a white object against a black background, and the appearance seems to indicate that the reversal of black to white stopped just short of the subject all round.

A method of instant solarisation is provided by a special equidensity material such as Agfa Contour. This is a sheet film designed for use under the enlarger, like printing paper. The film responds only to a narrow range of densities from the original printed down onto it. Full instructions for its use are made available by the maufacturer.

▷ *Subjects for solarisation must be chosen with care and, from the start, considered with a view to their finished effect.*

The distribution of light and shade, and its various intensities, must receive careful attention, in the attempt to anticipate how the parts will be affected by the fogging exposure. Remember that fogging leaves relatively unaffected the brightly-lit parts of the subject, turns the middle tones to a flat grey, and reverses intense blacks to brilliant whites.

▷ *White subjects against black backgrounds are the basic requirement, and are particularly suitable if the subject is flatly lit so that only highlights and light half-tones, and no deep shadows, are recorded.*

So the light expanse of say a white flower, a face, or a nude figure, should be lit with a diffused light from almost behind the camera, so that its negative image is a consistently strong density that resists fogging action, having few blacks to reverse, and printing normally except for the dark surrounding line of solarisation.

▷ *A contrasty light that throws deep shadows on the face, inevitably produces a partial reversal of these shadow areas and dark lines will ring the face in the least attractive manner.*

Therefore, in those instances where only the black-line effect of solarisation is sought, and the subject is otherwise to be seen as a normal image, this subject should display no dark tones and should receive an exposure long enough to ensure that its negative image is fully developed, and thus desensitised, by the first half or two-thirds development, and before the fogging exposure.

▷ *Contrasty emulsions will, for this reason, be particularly favourable for solarisation, and it is a good plan to make duplicate negatives, on contrasty film, from prints of chosen subjects. The loss of quality that this may involve is of no importance since the details and tone values of a solarised image are always considerably affected.*

▷ *Orthochromatic emulsions, if you can obtain them, are quite as suitable for solarisation as any other, and they bring with them the considerable advantage that the effects can be watched taking place in the red light of the darkroom safelight. But they must, of course, be fogged by white light, and not the orange-yellow to which they are much less sensitive.*

Positive Solarisation

The solarisation of a positive image, after contact printing or enlarging and partial development, is a simple matter and one that risks no more than a single sheet of printing paper, instead, perhaps, of a strip of film or an evening's work.

A print, by contact or enlargement, is made from a negative on a *contrasty,* not a normal or soft, grade of *thin printing paper.* Full exposure is given and the print *developed until the dark parts of the image show a full printing tone,* when the print is taken out and all *surplus developer removed* with a rubber squeegee.

The fogging *exposure* can be made by turning on the top *white light* of the darkroom or shining a bulb of low intensity a few feet away. A twenty-five-watt bulb, at a distance of three or four feet, should take no more than one to two seconds to produce the reversal of the whites required.

The print is left *until the light parts of the image have begun to darken.* A short *second development* is then made in *weak developer* to improve their tone, and the print normally fixed, washed, and dried.

Such a print will have the reverse appearance of a print from a solarised negative, being actually similar to the direct appearance of the partially-reversed negative itself. If the subject was generally white against a dark ground, the print will be a rich black and dull grey with the subject picked out in a rather dirty white line.

This print is used as a paper negative and prints can be made from it by lying it face down upon a sheet of contrasty printing paper and projecting light through the back. Prints are obtained which exhibit the characteristic effect of the print from solarised film.

Greater transparency is obtained if the negative print is oiled, or made on 'document' type paper, or even on special opalescent film.

▷ *Like negative solarisation, fogging of the positive is suitable only for subjects that show a juxtaposition of extreme contrasts. Owing to the action of the second fogging exposure in producing densities on all the previously unexposed areas, the finished effect of such pictures is a uniform white, or light foggy grey, with a very few darker half-tones, grouped together, and a strongly-marked black line around the principal contours or boundaries of tone.*

Partial Reduction

As a means of bringing the fierce contrasts of an over-exposed or over-developed negative within the more restricted range of normal printing paper, reduction is quite common practice. But since, apart from the super-proportional reducer, the orthodox technique reduces every density a proportional amount, no noticeable interference with the general disposition of tone results. If, however, parts of the negative are protected during the reduction process, the tones of the treated negative will be distorted in relation to each other, losing the balance of nature and gaining a balance purely photographic.

The protecting medium must, of course, be *proof against water and the action of the reducer,* and these conditions are satisfied by most negative varnishes, by asphaltum varnish, and a varnish-like fluid known as etching ground.

Any chosen varnish is applied carefully with a brush, following the outline of the areas to be protected, and left for a while to dry. Normal reduction of the unprotected area can then be proceeded with to any degree required.

When the negative has been reduced, washed, and dried, the protecting varnish is dissolved in any normal spirit solvent such as benzene, turpentine, or petrol, and, after a further washing, is ready for contact printing or enlarging.

Theoretically, clear cellulose varnishes are transparent and should not interfere with the printing quality of the negative, and therefore should not need subsequent removal. It will depend on the size of the negative and the area of the print to be made from it, but it seems rarely possible to apply a varnish so perfectly that no streak or blemish is projected when printing.

If, instead of the darkening effect of reduction, the lightening effect of intensification is required, the varnished negative may be intensified in the normal manner. However, the same effect can be, to a degree, simulated by dipping the negative into a solution of *neococcin,* or very diluted red ink. By staining the image and rendering it less transparent, these make it yield a printed image of relatively lighter tone than the untreated areas.

This technique is useful in adjusting and distorting particular tones of a picture, of any area and to any degree. It is particularly suitable to those occasions where an object must be made to stand clearly away from a fussy and over-emphatic background, where such a background is essential to the character and mood of the picture, but whose tones can never be sufficiently subdued by lighting control or other normal photographic methods.

▷ *Reduction of backgrounds, since it darkens their tones, is most appropriate when the general tone of the subject is light, and its contrasts weak.*

▷ *Intensification, or staining, since it has a lightening effect, is better where tones are full and contrasts strong.*

▷ *Aviod a tendency to excessive reduction or intensification, the slightest variation of background and subject tone will be sufficient to differentiate one from the other. Extreme differences will separate them so much that any interested spectator will wonder if they were ever even remotely connected.*

Tone Separation

The perpetual problem of the photographer is to capture on *paper* the brilliance of *light*, and when it is realised that the very whitest paper base reflects only a proportion of the light it receives, and, further, that the range of brightness possible to any print—namely the tonal range between the paper base and the deepest black—is rarely more than 40-1 as against a range of more than 100-1 in nature, one quite understands why there are so many muddy prints in the world and what a miracle it is that a photograph is even able to *suggest* the brightness of the day it was taken.

A brilliantly-lit scene makes its pictorial point principally by the rich contrast of deep shadow and sparkling highlight, both of which are seen in full detail by the automatic adjustment of the iris of the eye. The iris, or diaphragm, of the camera, however, does not automatically (however automatic the camera) adjust itself during the one exposure, neither does the method of compensating development help to record detail at both ends of an extreme range from brilliant light to deep shade. But, even where it captured on a negative, no printing paper obtainable could yield a print of its full range.

The best that a carefully exposed film and paper can give is a compromise—a correct rendering of the middle tones, and, despite considerable tonal loss at each end of the scale, give just enough shadow and highlight detail to carry the day and forestall complaints. Attempts to be fairer to the shadows gives a negative in which the highlights are as featureless as a white-washed wall, and better attention to the highlight detail produces an image in which the shadows are less inviting than coal-cellars. We are left with two negatives, each of which is perfect at its own end of the tonal scale, but only one sheet of printing paper on which to make the print. Either we must content ourselves with the original compromise or print our two perfections on a single surface.

The use of *two negatives, one of which supplies the detail of the shadows, the other the details of the highlights, to make a single print,* is the basis of what is known sometimes as the tone

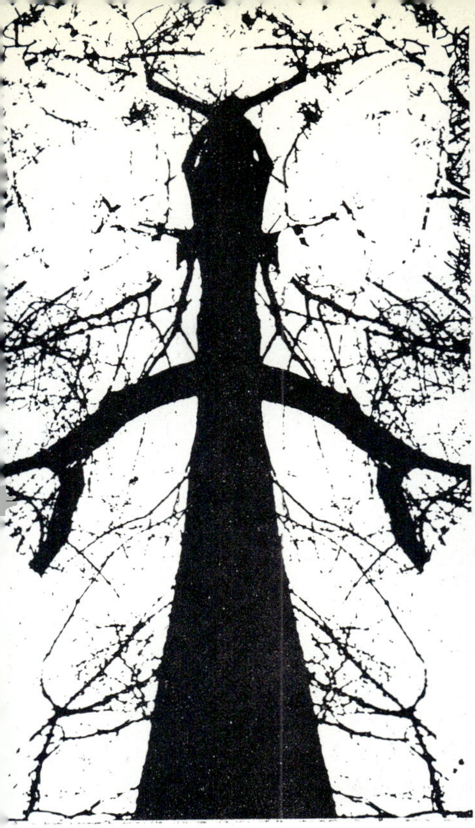
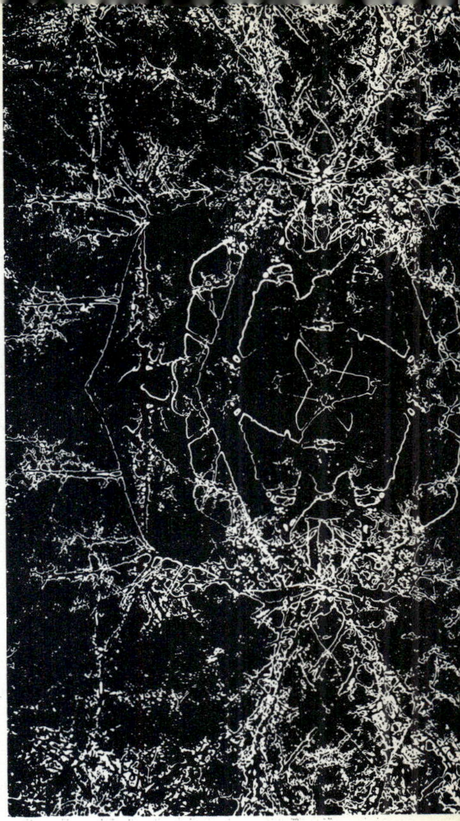

DARKROOM FILM TRICKS

Left: Join by symmetrical printing of a lith duplicate negative of tree branches. One half of the paper was exposed first with the other half masked. The second half was then printed with the negative reversed. *Right:* Solarised tree branches symmetrically printed.—*K. W. M. Stegers*

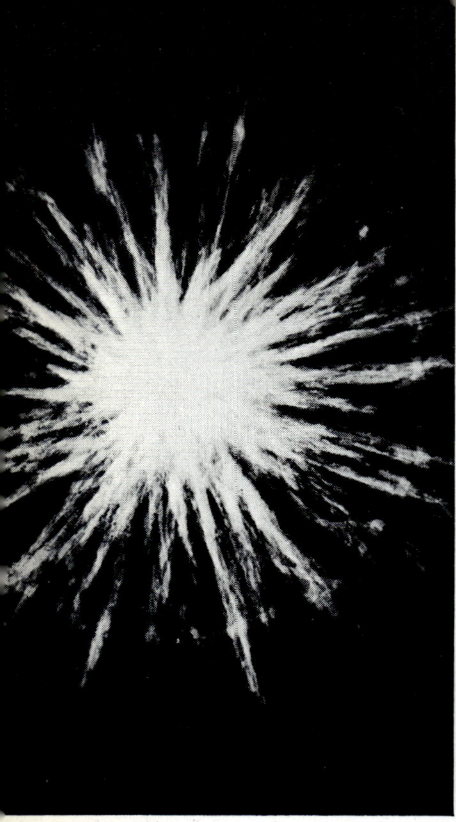

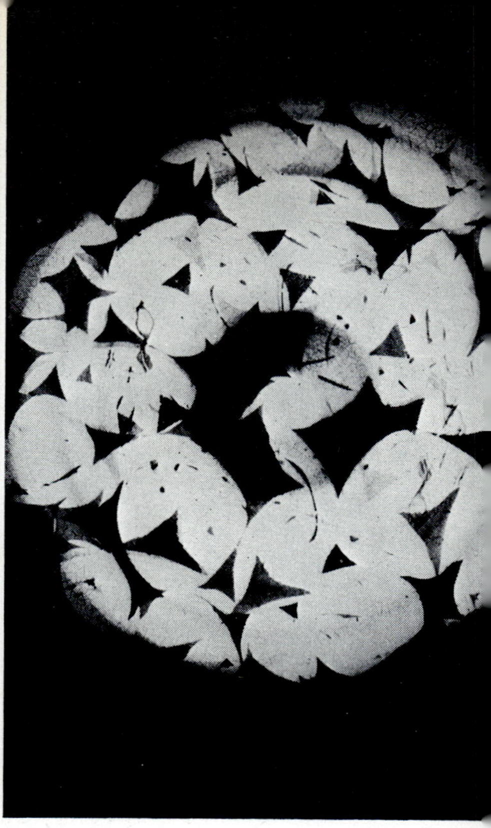

Pattern making by repeat printing. These can also be assembled by combining specially prepared pattern negatives whose shapes interfere with one another and create a new effect. Varied exposure introduces new tones in repeat printing, but beyond a certain point elaboration is less effective—in other words, more is less.—*Wolfgang Schreier.*

Pages 200 and 201: Designs made up from separate prints of a single subject, enlarged to the same ratio. For two prints the negative was inverted. The examples on these pages were printed on lith materials: in the first case all the images are positive. In the second, one each of the inverted and normal images has been put through an extra stage of printing to yield a negative image. The four images were then joined up and the result re-copied.—*Rainer Kiedrowski.*

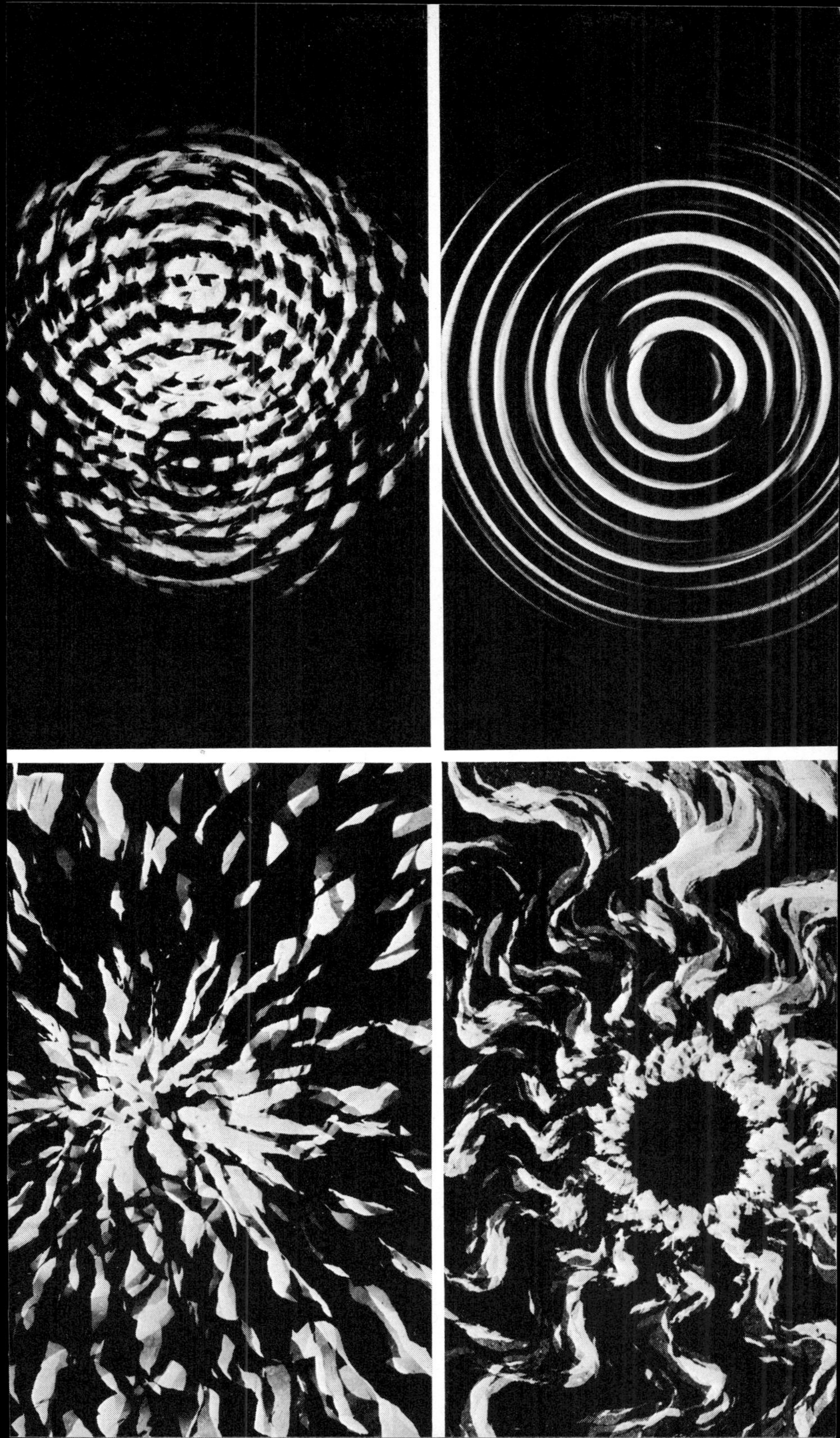

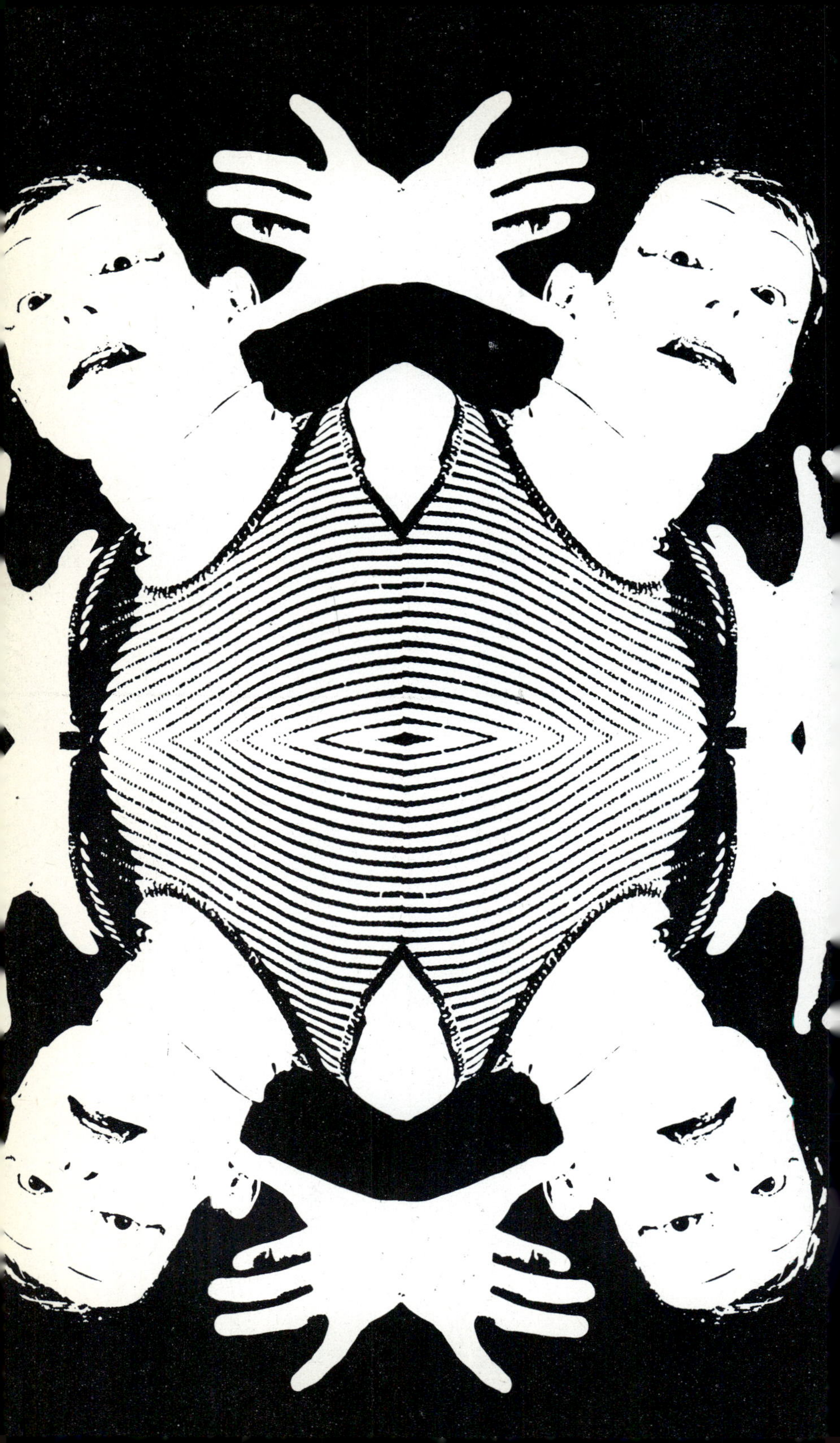

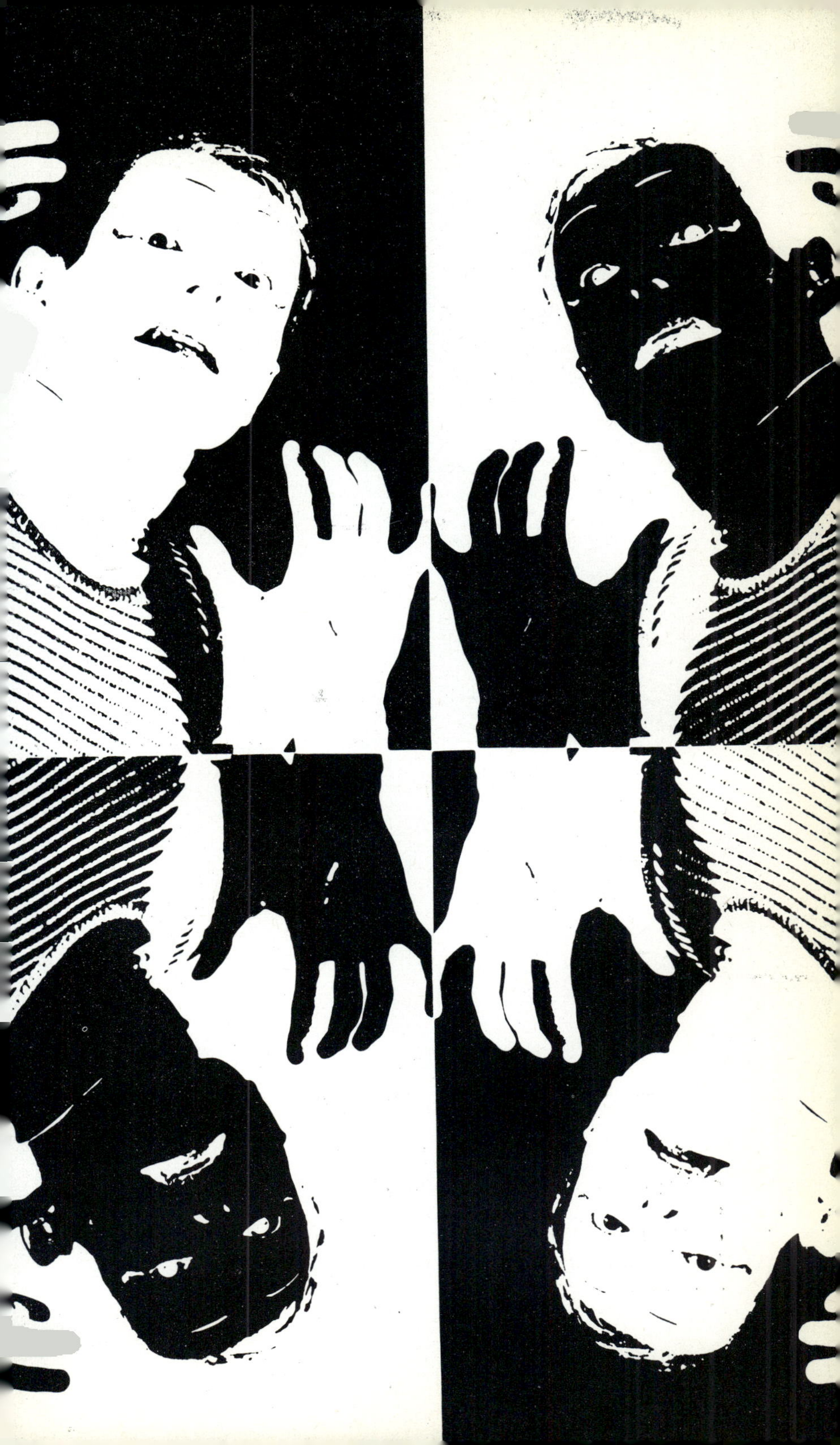

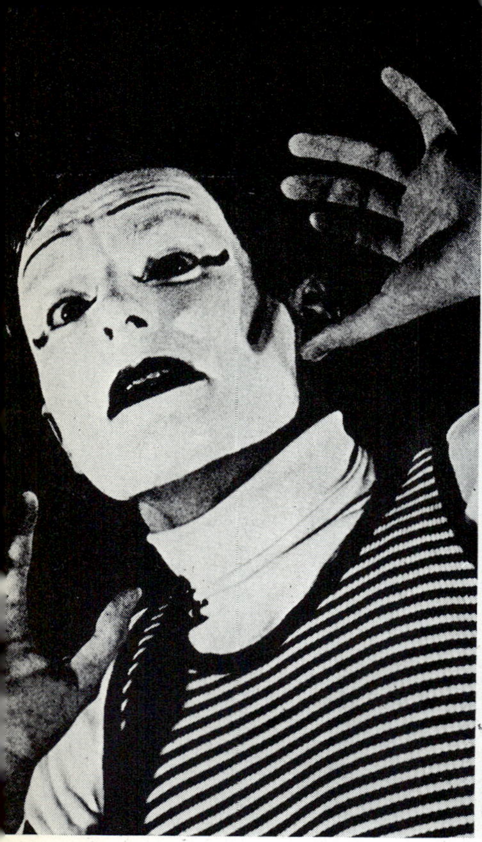

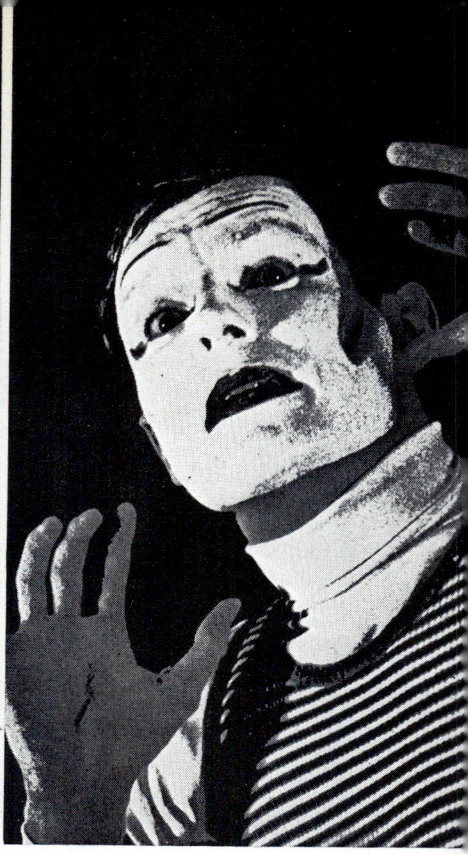

Straight photograph *above left* and darkroom derivatives: *above right* posterised print. *Opposite, top left:* negative and positive of posterised example combined and printed out of register. *Top right:* solarised negative image, *bottom left:* solarised positive and *bottom right* total solarisation —*Rainer Kiedrowski.*

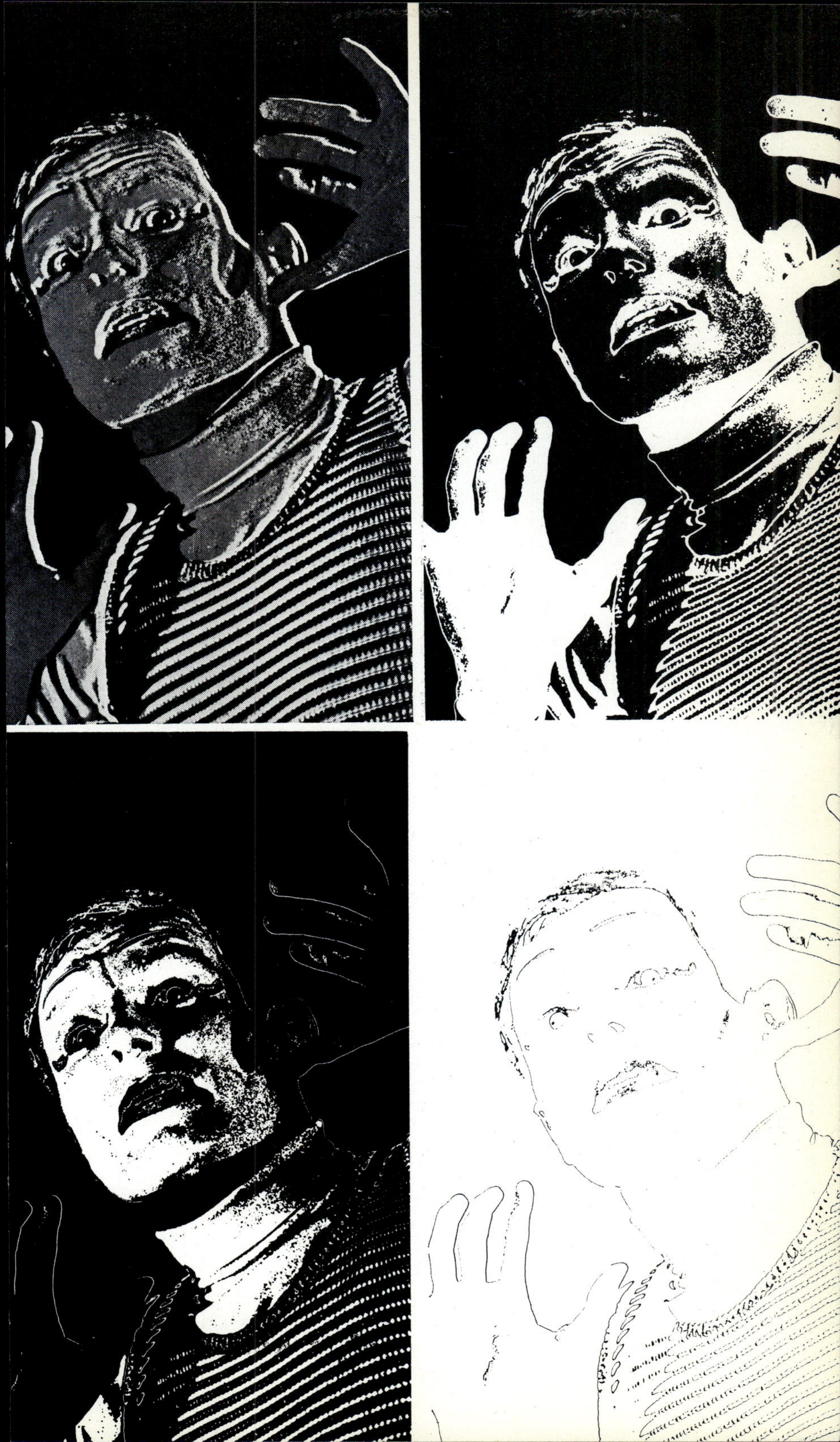

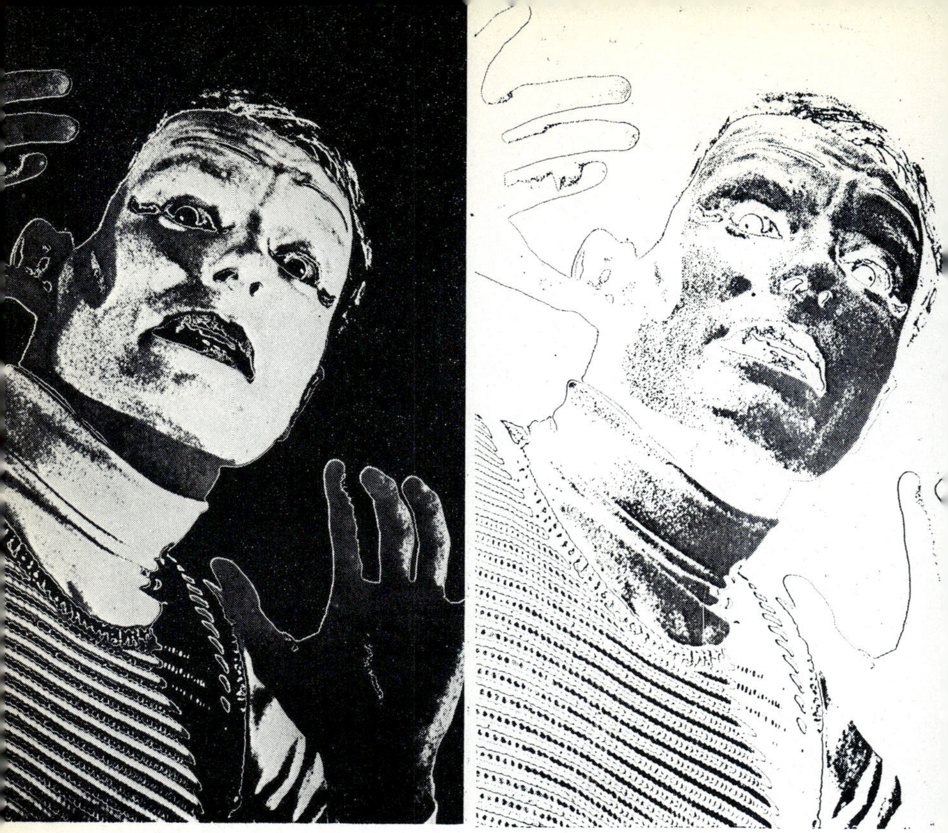

Left: Solarised print of original solarised initially at the negative stage on contrast materials and *right* full solarisation combined with highlight negative —*Rainer Kiedrowski.*

separation process. The negative that supplies the *shadow detail* is made with as much *contrast* as possible so that the highlight areas are completely blocked and quite opaque, whereas that which provides the *highlight* detail is made as *thinly* as possible so that the shadows and lower middle tones are without density and nearly transparent.

However, since modern film emulsions have considerable latitude, and are usually processed in a developer which does little for the contrast, it is rarely possible to make two successful exposures that contain respectively no shadow detail, and thoroughly dense highlights. If, of course, the exposures are made on "process" or extra contrasty material, the matter is simpler. But, since such films are not thoroughly colour sensitive and insist upon snowy-white skies and black daffodils, a superior alternative is to make two copy negatives by way of contrasty transparencies from a single original exposure.

The *single original,* made on any film material, in any photographic manner, must be *brilliant in tone with good hard contrasts, and, though dense in the highlight end of the scale, show full shadow detail.* Such a negative is obtained by slight over-exposure in sunny conditions and a fairly prolonged development.

From this negative *two diapositives* or transparencies are made—in the normal manner described in the chapter beginning on page 218.

The first transparency is obtained, by long exposure, on a fairly high contrast film to pick up all the *high-light detail.*

The second is obtained, by short exposure, on a similar film to retain all *shadow detail*.

From these developed, fixed, washed and dried transparencies, two new negatives are made, preferably on process material, the first of which will show fine detail and good gradation in the highlights, but clear gelatine in the shadows, and the second of which shows strong detail in the shadow areas, but highlights that are hopelessly clogged and therefore opaque.

From these two negatives the final print is made, the negative for shadow detail being printed first and longest, the highlight negative being printed next and shortest, on the same sheet of printing paper, in perfect register. To recapitulate then, after so long a journey. We have:

1. The original negative—with hard contrast, shadow detail, and, consequently, rather dense highlights.

2. A transparency from *1.* in which, by long exposure, all highlight detail is recorded and shadows quite bunged up.

3. Another transparency made from *1.* in which, by short exposure, shadow detail is retained but highlight areas left quite transparent.

4. A new negative, on a brilliant working "process" film, made from *2.* in which the lower middle tones and shadows are glass clear, but the highlight detail much in evidence.

5. A new negative, on a similar film, made from *3.* in which the higher middle tones and highlights are absolutely clogged and opaque, but the shadow detail strong and clear.

6. An exposure made of *5.* by contact, or through the enlarger, on printing paper of vigorous or contrasty grade.

7. An exposure made of *4.* on the same sheet of printing paper, in perfect register, and the paper normally developed, fixed, washed and dried.

If the original negative is of sufficient density, with enough heavy tone in the highlight areas of the image, one transparency process can be obviated by using this negative in place of the specially prepared shadow one—No. 5. Or, if not already of sufficient density, it could be normally intensified until the highlights clog.

Printing times vary with each negative, as the first will be excessively dense and the second so thin that anything longer than a few seconds will fog the paper. To ascertain the approximate exposures, tests should be made, under actual working conditions, on two separate sheets of printing paper. Both are developed at the same time in the same dish—as would normally be the case when printed in combination.

The enlarging light should be adjusted, by reducing the aperture of the enlarging lens, so that the exposure time for the highlight negative is not less than two seconds, and not more than five, on a bromide paper of normal grade. Such an adjustment may involve an exposure of some three to four minutes for the shadow negative, at the same lens aperture.

With a little thought, or thought-free in practice, the necessity for so short an exposure of the highlight negative will be obvious, if you recollect that it consists mainly of absolutely transparent film or plate, except for occasional areas of highlight detail. Long exposure of such a negative would inevitably fog the shadow detail already existing as a latent image on the printing paper.

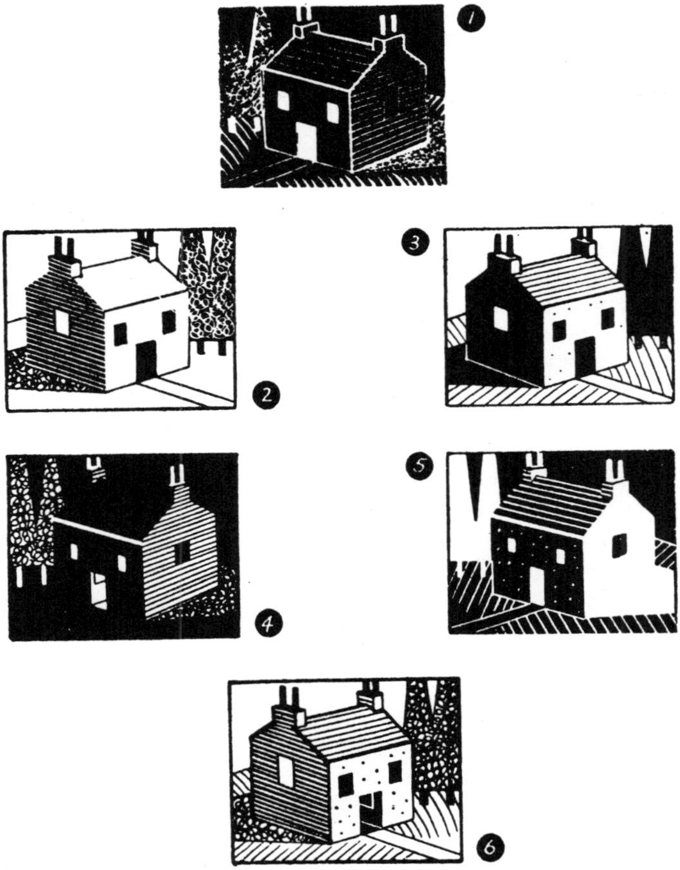

TONE SEPARATION

From a negative of brilliant contrast (*1*), is made a transparency (*2*), with good shadow detail but clear highlights, and another transparency (*3*) with highlight detail but blocked shadows. From *2* is made a negative (*4*) with strong shadow detail, but clogged highlights. From *3* is made another new negative (*5*) with highlight detail but transparent shadows. *4* and *5* are printed on a single sheet of paper to produce *6*.

Eventual success, apart from tone and exposure adjustment, must depend upon *perfection of register* of the two images on the single sheet of paper, and no pains should be spared to ensure absolute accuracy. Two short parallel lines, if drawn on the original negative at right-angles to the edges of the picture in the middle of each of the four sides, will be recorded on each transparency and duplicate negative subsequently made. The position of these four sets of lines will be marked on a key sheet of paper placed in the paper holder beneath the enlarged image of the first negative, and this same key sheet used to correctly align the second negative in relation to the first.

In the case of 35mm negatives, and, though it tells of unbelievable industry and patience, many successful tone separation pictures have been made from such negatives, the registration marks can be made on the small pieces of emulsion between the perforations each side of the image.

The intention of tone separation is to give a tonal interpretation of nature closer to human vision than a normal photograph. But in this it does itself injustice, for, like many mediums that seek a more "truthful" image of nature, it succeeds only in presenting pictures more peculiar than those of the process it hopes to improve.

By confining its attentions to the extreme ends of the tonal scale, the tone separation process tends to neglect the middle tones in which the normal photograph excels. Thus, from the "natural" point of view, though the straight print tends to be deficient in the shadows and highlights, the tone separated print is quite as deficient in half-tones.

The characteristic of prints made by this process, therefore, is a combination of rich and detailed shadows with sparkling highlights that could be obtained by no other photographic means. But, because each negative used to produce the print initially neglects them, and because the exposure of the highlight negative partially fogs them, the half-tones, even when detailed, are rendered rather flatly in a low tone of grey.

This combination of three main tones of deep black, neutral grey and clear white, gives to tone-separation pictures the conventional and simplified air of an old-fashioned handpainted poster, though they by no means imitate the effect of a painting, and one would rather say that the poster imitates the tone separation, than the other way round.

High Key

A great variety of tonal change can be wrung out of any negative, obtained in a normal manner and with no initial thought of tonal control, by the grade of contrast and the nature of the surface of the printing paper, or by "holding back" and "printing up" any chosen areas by the shading and spot-printing methods described on page 66.

The tone of any print is also influenced by exposure and development time, but though it is a matter of elementary technique to obtain a print of sometimes attractive and mysterious darkness, the opposite condition, of a print whose general tone is very high in key yet with fully-developed half-tones and shadows, is not at all so simple.

The obvious, and mostly accidental, way of producing a weak print is to under-expose and subsequently under-develop, but the image tone of such a print is far from pleasant, being flat, dull and grey.

The paradoxical process of production is actually to *prolong exposure and develop for a long period but in a dilute developer.*

The exposure-time necessary to produce a print of normal tone in standard print developer is found, and an exposure made, on a similar paper grade, for twice that period. This exposed print is then developed in a solution that contains only one-tenth the quantity of developing agent present in the normal developer. Such procedure involves, quite naturally, a considerably prolonged period of development, up to as long as half-an-hour, and unless precautions are taken to avoid chemical fog, by including in the developer some anti-fogging agent, such as *Johnson's 142,* a dirty and discoloured image will result.

The use of warm solutions must be avoided, which makes it very difficult to print high-key pictures in hot summer weather, or indeed at any temperature above 65°F. (18°C.). It is best to avoid an attempt at higher temperatures, but, should it be unavoidable, 2 ounces of crystalline Glauber salts or sodium sulphate in every 20 fluid ounces of developer will prevent excessive swelling of the gelatine emulsion. And 5 per cent of chrome alum added to the fixing bath will effectively harden the softened and delicate surface.

Developers which contain a solvent of silver salts, or include pyrocatechin, are unsuitable.

The characteristic effect of a picture printed in high key is an extreme softness of contrast, delicacy of gradation, and an absence of full dark shadows.

It is, therefore, not every subject that can be satisfactorily treated in this manner. Any negative containing a high proportion of deep shadows, or predominant effect of low tone, is obviously unsuitable, as are those that are fierce in contrast.

▷ *Since the direction of light has an influence on the disposition and area of shadows, pictures intended for high key printing are most successfully made with the sun, or other light source, nearly behind the camera—just over the left or right shoulder.*

Such a direction, though considerably flattening to the subject's modelling, will ensure the desirable absence of large areas of shadow.

SCREENS

Like the colour of your shirt or the pattern of your socks, the surface texture of your prints is matter for individual taste, and as with most personal preferences, a good deal of prejudice and guarded hostility towards those of the opposite camp is involved.

Thus the matt faction regards the frank brassy shine of a glazed print with a disgust only equalled by the contempt of the glossy cats for any sentimental softness.

However, whichever surface you prefer or whatever your attitude as a mere spectator, it cannot be denied that, apart from prints specifically intended for process reproduction the intended character or mood of a print is considerably helped along by the apt choice of a suitably surfaced paper.

Though there has been a tendency in recent years for some firms to reduce the range of papers available the variety offered for sale is still bewildering. Even so, the range of surface effect is comparatively restricted to simple variations of three or four basic types.

The printing screen is a simple means of bestowing upon any photographic paper of ordinary surface the apparent texture of a figured or granular material or surface. Such a screen can either be incorporated permanently with the picture image, by a double exposure on the same film or separately for each print—by contact with the paper or projection through the enlarger.

On the Negative

To include the texture of any particular surface or material permanently over a negative image of any subject, a *second exposure* is given of the chosen surface before developing the film though there is no technical reason why it should not be the *first exposure* if this is more convenient.

The surface can be of any kind that exhibits a texture

considered suitable to the subject, or is considered to make an improvement on the pictorial qualities of the print, and there is a very wide choice:

Papers may be of very rough and grained surfaces—linen paper, rag paper, parchment. Materials of distinct surface, silk, coarse linen, canvas, tweed or towelling; substances such as leather, materials like wood, stippled and figured glass, stippled paint, sand, cement stucco or any surface of granular or figured texture that occurs to you will serve the purpose.

The *lighting* for such surfaces should be of *low power* and arranged at a *glancing angle* so that it strongly emphasises the peaks, and leaves in dark shadow the valleys, of the particular formations. Surfaces of shallow texture might be improved for screen purposes by rubbing the surface lightly with a hard ball of folded cloth on which has been dusted a little graphite powder from a pencil. This has the opposite effect of light, in that it darkens the hills and leaves white the valleys of the texture, but this is of absolutely no importance in the rendering of its effect.

Exposures must be short so that the screen image does not fog the subject image of the previous exposure. The result required is one of small specks or pimples of light that strongly suggest the material whilst leaving the rest of the negative relatively untouched.

The comparative scale of the two images is a point of vital importance, and must be adjusted so that they are quite congruous. A screen of large texture taken in close-up, for example, would be unsuitable for a previous exposure showing a landscape of small scale and fine detail.

Unless the texture is minute, it will generally be wisest to *avoid extreme close-up focusing* for the screen exposure, using an area of the chosen material not less than two or three feet in its longest dimension. Exceptions, of course, can be left to taste and judgment.

Through the Enlarger

If the screen exposure is made on a *blank negative* in the normal manner, instead of over a previously exposed one, the resulting screen negative can be combined with any other negative and the two projected simultaneously through the enlarger.

The screen negative is made as before, lighting the surface to obtain maximum contrast of texture, and either *under-exposing or developing weakly* to get a *thin* negative image.

The effects obtainable are identical with those of the previous method, the real advantage being that the subject negative is not permanently wedded to one screen, or the screen with any one negative.

A collection of thin negatives, exhibiting variations of all the textures you can think of or obtain, could be a very useful addition to your printing equipment, and an eccentric obsession to collect and record.

By enlargement there is also the advantage that *any screen can be employed in different degrees of definition,* and a screen that is tiresomely insistent, and over-emphatic, when placed face to face with the emulsion of the subject negative, can be subdued if separated by the glass pressure plates of a glass-type negative carrier, or placed back to back so that the emulsions are slightly separated.

Naturally sharp focusing is carried out on the subject image, the screening negative being appropriately softly defined.

Only in so far as the second negative will increase the density of the subject image will exposures need to be prolonged.

By Contact

Yet a third method of applying an artificial effect of texture to a photograph is to use a screen of photographic negative, paper, or material, in *actual contact with the printing paper* during an enlargement exposure.

This, the simplest method of screening, is the prototype of the technique; and screens such as these come onto the market from time to time. They offer a number of variations to give the effect of an etching, a photogravure, or silk surface.

As before, any pronounced texture can be *copied on to a negative* large enough to cover the biggest print you are likely to make. However unless you have a very large format view camera the negative might have to be enlarged on to a piece of sheet film of the required size. The film is substituted for the printing paper beneath the projected image and developed and finished in the manner normal to a film negative.

The screen can also be *enlarged on to very thin printing paper,* which after developing, fixing, and washing is made *thoroughly transparent* by soaking in a mixture of petrol and refined paraffin in equal volumes.

Paper screens of this kind have a characteristic *softening effect* on the whole subject image. The grain of the paper is added to that of the screen, which in any case registers less strongly than the same texture used on a more transparent screen of film.

The *texture of any desired paper surface* can be transferred to tracing paper by rolling printer's ink, or oil colour, over its rough surface so that the hills are darkened and the valleys left untouched. The ink or colour should first be rolled out thinly and evenly on a glass plate and transferred to the paper by means of the rubber roller. This wet paper is then placed face down on the thin tracing paper and the pair pressed together through an old domestic mangle with rubber rollers or anything that will do the same job. The resulting figured tracing paper can then be used in the normal screen manner by placing it in contact with the printing paper and making the exposure through it. The effect is coarse, but very attractive for subjects of simple tone and little detail.

Screens can also be made by the *reflex method* to be described on page 237, the thin printing paper being laid emulsion side down over the required surface and light allowed to shine on the back of the paper for a short time. Such light will be reflected back on to the paper emulsion by the white parts of the texture and thus create its image for use as a screen. All white surfaces should first be treated with the cloth ball and graphite process recently mentioned, or the printing paper will merely be fogged all over. The paper screen so obtained must naturally be rendered transparent, after developing and finishing in the usual manner, by immersion in the petrol and paraffin solution previously mentioned.

All transparent, or translucent, materials can be used as screens by laying them in contact with the paper and printing through them. Bolting silk, satin, thin tracing and tissue paper, even a fine wire sieve or zinc mesh—all give a characteristic pattern over the picture's surface, though the latter is coarse and extreme.

Unlike the first two methods, the screen in contact with the paper reduces the intensity of the printing light and involves an increase of exposure—the denser the screen, the greater the extra time.

▷ *These three screening techniques are a convenient means of imparting the appearance of texture to the surface of any smooth printing paper, obviating the necessity of stocking supplies of various surfaces, and obtaining a variety far outside the range of those normally available to the purchaser.*

The use of any particular screen, and the manner in which it is employed, is a matter of personal taste, but after the excitement of discovery and experiment, the effects should be used with great care and critical restraint. Carried to great lengths, imitation is a tedious thing.

No rules can be laid down as to which texture is best used with what picture. Apart from the suitability of scale of both images the combinations are a matter for your own choice. They may be made subjectively so that, for instance, a wooden or leathery subject is screened with a leather or wood texture, or objectively by fitting a specific screen to a particular picture because in your opinion it enhances the pictorial effect, and ignoring any subjective implication that the texture has.

▷ *The first two methods leave the definition of the subject unimpaired, the two separate or combined images being sharply defined on the same plane, giving the effect of a rough surface without any of the disadvantages that such printing papers have of cutting up the detail of the subject.*

Naturally, the smaller the chosen texture the greater the effect on the picture image, fine grains of sand, for instance, breaking up detail and flat tone in the same manner as the grain of a coarse emulsion.

The third method, where the screen is used in contact with the printing paper, has the maximum diffusing and disturbing effect on the subject image, the screen being recorded with absolute sharpness even when the enlarged image is soft and diffused.

Negatives for this kind of screening must be chosen with care. Those with much detail and little variation in tone, or planes of the subject, being quite unsuitable to this method. The effects of a picture screened by contact are not made by detail but by broad masses of flat contrasted tone that indicate the various planes of the picture in the manner of a hilly landscape seen through mist—the coarser the screen the more pronounced this mist or fog effect.

▷ *With contact screens the grade of printing paper has a marked influence on the strength of the screening effect, the unexposed areas or dots left by the screen seeming harder or white according to the contrast powers of the paper. It is advisable, therefore, to use only those negatives whose range of contrast can be successfully rendered on papers of soft or normal grade. Grades of fiercer contrast render the screen so prominently, and so out of proportion to the strength of subject image, as to be quite grotesque.*

▷ *The whole method of screening is, of course, a clear echo of the double exposure method mentioned in the photomontage chapter on page 119. Just as the printing of, say, an image of newsprint over a portrait is as much screening as photomontage, so, basically, the printing of a texture, particularly when it is bold, and unusual, over another picture is as much photomontage as screening.*

Patterning Screens

Combining two or more special screens as ends in themselves rather than as a means of giving texture to another picture, is a method that can be simply used to produce all-over patterns of a rich and pleasing nature.

Effective patterns can be produced if the screens used show a number of close parallel lines over the whole surface. The lines can take various forms as long as they are close and parallel. They can run straight—in one direction or the other, in the form of many concentric circles of ever-increasing diameter, of a wavy or zig-zag formation, or any manner that can be conveniently drawn in parallel form.

The screens can take two forms: *stout cellulose or plastic sheets* used in contact with the printing paper under the enlarger, or in the form of negatives combined in the enlarger and projected to the desired size.

In the first case the lines should be drawn, with a geometrical instrument ruling pen, over the whole surface of a sheet large enough to cover, at any angle, the sheet of printing paper to be patterned. On a sheet, say, twelve by ten inches (30 cm. x 25 cm.) the lines would be drawn about one-sixteenth to one-eighth of an inch (1.5 mm. to 3 mm.) apart.

Two or three of these sheets will be necessary for the production of any one pattern, and, needless to say, the lines must be drawn accurately with a tee-square, or a compass if circular, and with either a jet-black paint or Indian ink.

If the pattern is to be made by enlargement, the lines are drawn in *black on white paper,* or in *white on black paper,* and recorded by the camera on *contrasty or process film,* not on a plate.

The method has the advantage that only one set of lines has to be drawn, the extra one or two screens being easily produced by making as many separate exposures and negatives. Development should be arranged for *maximum contrast* so that the black lines are clear gelatine and the white ground an absolute density.

▷ *To make the patterns, the two or more screens are laid over each other, at different angles, to produce effects of intersecting lines. Thus, if two straight-line screens are placed so that the lines of one run at right-angles to the other, a simple pattern of black squares or crossing white lines is obtained. By changing the angle between the two, from a near right-angle to near parallel, effects from wire netting to shot silk are variously obtained.*

▷ *Patterns with circular figures screens are made by placing them so that the circles of each screen are either much or little out of register with each other, and any other disposition of parallel lines can be treated the same.*

▷ *If, in the original drawing, every fourth or fifth line, or similar interval is missed out on each sheet, the lines will group themselves in units that effectively cuts up the pattern into repeating compartments, adding a note of complication and, perhaps, of extra interest.*

▷ *The effects can be extended by using a single screen, and interrupting the exposure to shift the screen to a second position over the paper. Then, besides the plain black and white, a third tone of middle grey is introduced to give extra colour to the pattern.*

Those parts of the paper protected, in both exposures, by parts of the black lines remain white, those that are protected during one exposure only print grey, and those that were under the clear gelatine for both exposures print a full black.

▷ *The method might still further be extended by copying the simple pattern of a bold wallpaper, or other patterned surface, on to two or more negatives and projecting these simultaneously through the enlarger in varying degrees of register.*

TRANSPARENCIES

Besides having an interest, and several uses, on its own account, the positive transparency, or print made on film, makes possible a range of effects based on combination printing with a negative of the same subject.

The technique of producing a transparency presents no more difficulty than the making of a contact print or enlargement of the same negative, the process in each case being identical. Special transparency or diapositive films may be purchased, or the ordinary film normally employed for making negatives can be conveniently used. For preference, the emulsion should be such that *good contrast* is ensured, and the convenience of working with a darkroom safelight indicates either an orthochromatic or an ordinary (blue sensitive) film.

Contact transparencies are simply made by placing the subject negative in contact with the film, *face to face,* under a sheet of heavy glass or preferably in a printing frame, and exposing under the enlarger or any other white light source.

The edges of the printing frame protect the edges of the film from being fogged by light seeping in at the sides, and the backing plate prevents any light being reflected from the back to form halation despite the presence of an anti-halation backing on modern film materials. Therefore, if no printing frame is used, some precaution against these two conditions must be taken by using a *mask* and a *dark matt paper base* to lay the film upon.

Enlarged transparencies are made by projecting the negative image on to sheet film, laid on *dark matt paper* beneath the enlarger, *emulsion side uppermost.*

The average *density* of the transparency will depend entirely on the *length of exposure* given, which again depends of course, on the density of the original negative. It will need to be greater or less according to the purpose for which the transparency is to be subsequently used.

Development is carried out in the normal manner. As in the negative process, the contrast of the positive image will depend on the *length of development, contrast increasing as development is prolonged.*

Unless they represent a source of direct light, or reflection, the *whites* of the subject should *never be recorded as clear glass* or gelatine on the transparency, but should have a perceptible tone.

If the transparency is not required for a further printing process, but is to be used for projection or normal viewing, it may be suitably *toned* to any colour by any of the techniques used for toning prints. But, since most toning processes act as intensifiers, it will be advisable to *develop such transparencies more thinly,* and *give exposure a longer time* to compensate for the slight loss of detail in the lighter tones.

The transparency produced for printing purposes, is of course, not to be compared with reversal monochrome transparencies for projection, which have a much higher contrast and are rather hard for printing.

Metallic Backgrounds

A rich and fascinating appearance, slightly reminiscent of the metallic shimmer of the Daguerreotype, is obtained if an enlarged or contact-printed transparency is attached to an *opaque support* consisting of highly polished metal-foil paper.

For such mounting purposes the transparency should be of *thin density and soft contrast*, so that the image is very clear and no shadow is quite opaque. It should be made for preference on a *glass plate* so that when it is placed in contact with the mount the effect will be of a glass framed image.

If the picture is small, and subsequently to be framed, the backing of the frame will keep the foil and transparency in close contact, which is essential for the complete success of the effect.

Otherwise both the emulsion side of the plate, and the foil paper it is to be mounted on, should be *coated with linseed oil, or canada balsam diluted with xylol,* and pressed into contact, under light pressure, so that wrinkles and air bells are not formed.

Silver, and the cool-coloured, foil papers are most suited to transparencies of black tone. The gold and warmer tones are better suited to those that have been toned sepia, or brown, by the toning process.

Other papers and materials, including white and light coloured silks can be substituted for the foil paper with appropriate and characteristic effects.

To frustrate chemical deterioration and fading of the transparent image it is advisable, after mounting and framing, to coat the back of the foil paper and edges of the glass with a *good copal varnish* to prevent penetration of air from the back.

Luminous Backgrounds

If paper treated with luminous paint is mounted behind the transparency, in place of the foil paper suggested in the previous method, the picture will glow like a ghost in the dark, the more transparent areas there are in the picture, the lighter the effect.

Glows of greater intensity are made by spreading *luminous powder on to a sheet of fixed, washed, but undried, printing paper* that has had the surplus moisture removed with a squeegee and still remains *tacky*.

Like a back to front printing paper, this surface, when dry, will be rendered light and luminous by the rays of the sun. If placed under the transparency as if making a contact print, before exposing it to the sun, a luminous image of the picture will be formed. Such an image is only transient as the whole paper will begin to glow as soon as the light reaches the previously covered areas.

However, by mounting the paper permanently beneath the transparency the effect can be held, and the picture adds a new excitement or terror to the nocturnal hours.

As the constituent chemicals of most of the luminous powders that can be purchased contain elements unfriendly to photographic emulsions, the transparency should be isolated by coating it on its film side with a clear *cellulose varnish.*

Unregistered Combination (Bas relief)

Effects of slight relief, in which a subject appears to stand slightly away from its background in the manner of say, the head on a medallion or coin, the image on a plaque, or the figures on a panel sculptured in very low relief, can be obtained by the simultaneous projection through the enlarger of a *normal negative, and a transparent positive,* placed slightly out of register one with the other.

The negative to be so employed should be of *good contrast, but thin density*, and the transparency produced by contact from it should be relatively the same—thin but definite.

The two films are placed in contact, *face to face,* and moved one over the other so that the two images just fail to coincide in absolute register, but slightly overlap so that a faint halo of transparency appears in outlines around two adjacent sides.

The amount of such separation depends on the character of the subject and the coarseness of the relief effect desired, but it will rarely exceed the smallest fraction of an inch (a few millimetres) with a negative that is below quarter-plate (9 cm. x 12 cm.) in size, since the amount is increased by enlargement.

Besides the amount of displacement of the images, the nature of the effect and degree of relief will depend upon the relative densities of the negative and positive, and the grade of printing paper used.

A dense transparency tends to produce, in the final print, the appearance of a negative, a thin transparency produces more the normal effect of positive. The effect of relief is more marked on a paper of soft contrast then on a harder one.

▷ *The best subjects for bas relief treatment are those of a severe simplicity of detail, outline, tone, and surface texture. Pictures whose effect depends upon the simple lighting of plain unbroken surfaces, and where the subject is seen in more or less clean silhouette, are most suitable.*

▷ *As expected, the combination of two transparent surfaces, whose tones are the exact opposite of each other and which consequently tend to cancel the tone effect of each other, reduces the tones of the picture to an almost uniform series of grey, and the only contrast is afforded by the light which manages to escape through the small cracks of bad register and form a black tone.*

The surface texture of the subject is completely falsified, and detail is destroyed. Surfaces take on the grey and flat appearance of petrified stone or marble and the whole effect is strongly reminiscent of what we usually call a bas-relief and hence the name of the process.

Pictures with much detail and complicated tones will just look like nothing so much as a severe case of camera movement, and you can call them what you will.

Registered Combination

A method that echoes the last, with the slight variation permitted to an echo, involves the combination projection of a negative and positive image, but this time in correct register.

The vital variation that gives a characteristic increase of modelling and depth of perspective consists of *making two negatives of the original subject, but with lighting from opposite sides in each case, and combining one negative with a transparency made from the other in exact register.*

Set the subject up solidly, and, without moving either camera or subject between whiles, make two exposures, arranging the light for the first diagonally from the right, and the light for the second diagonally from the left. The two positions of the light in relation to the subject and camera should be, as near as possible, diametrically opposite. It is as well to use two lights of identical power, setting them up each side of the subject, equi-distant from it and the camera, so that each is used in turn without movement between exposures.

Exposure and development of each negative must be precisely the same, and, when dry, the negative whose direction of lighting looked least attractive to the subject, is placed in contact with another film or plate and a *transparency of soft contrast and thin density* made.

Printing is performed by combining this transparency *face to face in accurate register* with the negative showing opposite lighting, and projecting the pair through the enlarger in the normal single negative manner.

The effect of the picture is more simply seen than described. The highlights of the second exposure occur on the ridges and surfaces where the shadows of the first fell, but, since these second highlights are printed from a positive, they print as dead blacks and add lines and ridges of emphasis to the printed shadows of the first exposure. Similarly, the shadows of the second exposure fall where the highlights of the first occurred, but, being again printed from a positive, register as reversed, or white, areas that broaden the effect in a curious manner.

Verbally, the effect can only be described as stereoscopic. Detail, even in the shadows, is very clear and modelling is first-rate, but the surface texture is completely falsified.

▷ *No particular purpose can be suggested for this odd technique which is just a photographic curiosity capable of giving interest perhaps to a commonplace still-life subject that sadly lacks it.*

The condition, encountered previously, of giving two separate exposures to the same subject, without moving either it or the camera, make it difficult to treat any but subjects of a very quiet or inanimate nature.

Small dark objects, with hollows that are difficult to light and detail that is difficult to see are rendered particularly well, with excellent modelling, and detail that is a possible compensation for false surface texture. Presented with the print from a straight exposure, to display this lacking texture, information might be conveyed that would be difficult to give in any other photographic way.

▷ *If the object so treated is on a plain background that registers shadow, the shadow of the transparency being a density will print white so black shadows will appear on one side of the object and white ones on the other. This is quite an effect within its own right, but, if objected to, can be obviated by placing the object on a glass sheet that holds no background shadows of any kind.*

▷ *When, as often happens, the pictorial effect of the negative is superior to a print taken from it, this attractive negative appearance can be perpetuated on paper by projecting the transparency, made from the negative, through the enlarger on to a sheet of bromide paper, or by contact printing it in the normal manner.*

SPECIAL SURFACES

If your thirst for surface texture cannot be quenched by the range of the manufacturer, or by your own collection of screen negatives, and particularly if you have a taste for the bizarre or the perversely inappropriate, almost any odd material or surface can be printed upon if it is impregnated with a light sensitive emulsion, and if you have the facilities necessary for its preparation and application.

Any surface whose tone or colour is changed by the action of light is a potential printing surface for a photographic image. Fruit, whose colour gradually changes colour by the sun's rays, is a homely, if odd, example.

Here is a method by which you may print your own portrait on every apple in the orchard.

Printing on Apples

Choosing a big apple, with a good smooth surface, that grows upon a sunny bough, and retard its ripening by tying it up for *three or four weeks,* just before harvest time, in a *black bag* of opaque material or paper.

Immediately after removing the bag apply a *contrasty negative* to the apple's surface, securing it with *adhesive* made from the white of an egg, and taking good care that *absolute contact* is made.

If the apple is left on the tree so that it ripens in the sun to a good rich colour, the parts obscured by the densities of the negative will remain green in the shapes and tones of the picture. After the ripening, the negative is soaked off in water to reveal the picture on the apple with say green highlights and red shadows.

Unless the apple is a monster, with a good flat surface, it will only be possible to use small negatives or cut-out parts of large ones. The chosen negative should naturally be as bold and *simple as possible,* the nearer it is to sheer silhouette the better, for nothing in the way of complicated detail can be effectively recorded.

In fact it may be as well to relinquish the use of a figured negative and cut simple shapes, profiles or letters, out of thin black paper.

A similar photo joke can be played upon a tomato, in precisely the same manner, except that here the exposing and ripening process can simply take place on the ledge of sunny window or greenhouse.

Of course, if anyone has the heart, the apple or tomato may be eaten with safety, if not with relish after so long a labour.

Printing on an Egg

Continuing these odd printing pranks, the surface of an egg may be printed upon if it is immersed several times in a solution of *one part salt and fifty parts water,* sponging the surface so that it is completely impregnated and afterwards dried.

It can then be rendered sensitive to light, in the darkroom, by immersion and sponging in a solution of *twelve grains silver nitrate to one ounce of water,* taking care, by wearing rubber gloves, to protect the hands from the blackening action of the silver salts.

A small negative is placed in contact with the egg's surface, held in position by black passe-partout tape, and the rest of the egg obscured from the light. The egg may now be brought into the light and *exposed* in the obsolete mode of printing-out paper, in which the image appears direct, without development, and is afterwards *fixed* and *toned.*

After exposure and processing, the egg is dried and exhibited as a farmyard curiosity, but is not eaten.

Printing in a Bottle

Without descending from the plane of elevated phantasy on which we began, and to add another oddity to your shelf of photographic curiosities, you can print whatever you may consider is an appropriate negative on the inside of a bottle.

An essential to the success of the trick is a bottle, or other glass vessel, made of good, thin, clear glass without too many waves or blemishes. *Clean* it well and pour into it a solution made from the filtered mixture of the *whites of two eggs, thirty grains of ammonium chloride dissolved in a drachm of spirits of wine, and half an ounce of water,* all *beaten* together into a frothy state.

Twist and turn the bottle so that an even film is formed on the inside surface, pour out the residue, allow the film left in the bottle to *dry*, and *repeat* the process a second time.

To render this base sensitive to the action of light, a solution of *forty grains silver nitrate to an ounce of water* is poured into the bottle which is once more turned about to form an even coating inside. When dry, this emulsion is *impregnated* by holding the neck of the bottle for a few seconds over another bottle containing *ammonia,* after which it is ready for exposure.

The chosen negatives are applied to the *external surface* of the bottle and *fixed* with strips of black passe partout, or a similar substitute. All parts of the bottle not so obscured are covered with opaque material, or paper, so that no light passes through it.

The *exposure* is made in the printing-out manner, by bringing the magic bottle into the light and rotating it so that the exposing time and intensities of light are consistent all round. Development of the exposed emulsion is in the approved printing-out manner, the tones forming directly, without development, then density being observed by carefully detaching a corner of the negative. *Fixing and toning* solutions are poured into the bottle for the required periods.

After washing, the prints may be given a plain, instead of an otherwise transparent, background by swilling the bottle round with thick white, or any suitably coloured, *enamel paint.*

Printing on Silk

If a suitable subject is chosen, a print on the surface of silk or other fine similar material can please both the eye and the sense of surprise. Any good quality material may be used, but it is suggested that Chinese silk gives the best results. Formulae for sensitising the surface of the material are numerous and complicated to the extent of inducing fatigue and fear of failure; the following are among the simplest.

PROCESS A. The silk is well *washed* in warm soapy water, thoroughly *rinsed* in hot water which is *cooled,* by gradual addition of cold water, until it is itself quite cold.

When dry, the silk is floated on to a solution of dye in ordinary *washing starch, dried* in total darkness, and painted with a *6 per cent solution of potassium bichromate,* so that it is evenly and thoroughly impregnated. It is sensible to treat similarly one or two small pieces, to be used as guides for the duration of the subsequent exposure, which can be made under the enlarger or in contact with the actual negative, after the silk is thoroughly dry.

Development is simply accomplished by washing the exposed material in clean water, as it comes from the tap. The unexposed parts of the image, or those that have received no impression of light, wash out and leave the exposed areas as insoluble tones of varying depth on the surface of the silk.

Such development is slow, but no attempt should be made to hasten it by interfering with the surface of the silk or the image itself will be removed.

PROCESS B. After thorough washing the silk is bathed, in darkness, for three minutes in a solution of 150 *grains of ferric oxalate and 62 grains of silver nitrate,* dissolved in that order in *2 fluid ounces of distilled water,* or greater quantity in proportion.

When absolutely dry, printing may be done by enlargement or contact, in the manner of a print-out paper, the image darkening directly by the action of light and not by subsequent development.

After so printing, the silk should be *washed* for about fifteen minutes in running water, and fixed for a similar time in a solution of approximately *5 per cent hypo, washed* again and *dried*.

Since the image continues to darken in tone during the first washing process, *printing is best stopped when the image tone is about half the density* ultimately required.

Silk treated by this process can be cleaned by any method suitable for the plain material itself, and, if the silk resists a desire for it to lay flat, it may be pressed down with a warm iron without any damage to the image.

▷ *Negatives suitable for silk printing should make their pictorial points by rich tone rather than by fine detail. The range of tones should be on the dark side. Pure white areas should be small, enclosed incidentals surrounded by darker areas and not running out to the edge of the picture.*

▷ *The effect being inevitably reminiscent of Oriental silk painting, the most successful subjects have been those that have been so treated by the Chinese or others. Landscapes of dark and simple tone, flower subjects showing white blooms against a dark grey ground with leaves of a rich black, and subjects of a similar simplified nature.*

▷ *Portraits, unless in the form of a severely silhouetted profile, are rarely satisfactory since the subtle gradation of half tones involved is not adequately rendered by the process. Tones must be bold and simple.*

▷ *Depending naturally on the area of material covered, the print may be made for subsequent mounting and framing, or could be repeated at regular intervals over the surface to form one unit of a repeat pattern.*

For the latter purpose, the separate images can be printed with large white margins. These look particularly effective, or they could be repeated in adjacent conjunction to give an all-over pattern. This last, of course, calls for considerable skill in joining unless the background consists of an even tone round all the margins of the picture.

▷ *If the print is a single one and large enough, it may be mounted over papers and cards of various tone and colour. These being half-seen through it, affect the colour of the printed image. Metal-foil papers, with their range of rich colour, are particularly good as mounting bases of this kind.*

The silk is stretched across the mount, turned over the back, and fixed into position, working alternatively from opposite sides so that a flat and unwrinkled surface is obtained.

THE TABLE TOP

The top of the table is a convenient location for all indoor photography involving a small inanimate subject. Rather selfishly, the specific title "table-top" has been appropriated for that specie of photographic inanity consisting usually of some poor little novelty shop figure wallowing in a salt or cotton wool snow-storm, or a rickety construction of oddments doing their best to look like something else, often without too much success.

Here, an attempt is made to storm the dull fortress, reclaim the phrase and collect beneath its banner some methods and effects that can be achieved within a small compass, embracing little more, and often much less, than a square foot or two.

To begin with the table, let it be *solid and firm, free standing* so that it is possible to walk all round it and place lights or backgrounds in any position. Ideally, it should be of less than normal table height, no more than eighteen to twenty inches (40 cm. to 50 cm.) high, so that *viewpoints from above* can be made without perching the camera on an impossibly high tripod extension.

Extending the Focal Length

The point about close work that most interests the camera is the commonly short distance between it and the subject—the intimacy involved. To the *camera offering long extension* whose tubes or bellows can extend to twice the focal length of its lens, this close-range work presents no difficulties. It can, if necessary, copy objects size for size without reduction of scale.

But, for the camera whose extension is limited, and whose minimum focusing distance is somewhere in the region of three feet or one metre, many effects of the table-top inevitably involve the use of a *supplementary lens,* or other means of altering the focal length of the lens to permit the sharp focusing of very near objects. The supplementary lens in the form of the close-up *'"portrait" attachment* is well known, and perhaps already a part of your everyday equipment. Slipping on to the mount of the lens it gives a new, nearer, distance for each of the distances on the focusing scale, permitting in many cases the sharp recording of objects a few inches away.

Less orthodox means, however, should not be neglected and with many seemingly fixed extension cameras, a little care and ingenuity can often find a way of increasing the distance between the lens and film beyond the last marked distance on the focusing scale. Ways and means, of course, depend entirely upon the construction of the camera, and it is not suggested that you tamper with the mechanism of an expensive and finely-adjusted miniature camera.

Cameras with interchangeable lenses, of course, allow the standard lens to be removed and mounted on special extension rings of various depths to increase the lens to film distance, or better still, adaptable bellows which are more versatile. Failing these it is sometimes possible to make up a cardboard tube, box or some similar arrangement which can be mounted on the camera and the lens attached to the front.

If you are using an old bellows or large format view camera, the bellows can often be extended further than usual by *temporarily unscrewing any small barrier that prevents the lens panel sliding* indefinitely along its track. This will do no damage to its correct and accurate working.

Without interference with the normal extension of your camera, its powers of magnification can be greatly increased by the lens of a *magnifying glass,* the front component of an *opera or field glass,* or a *spectacle lens* suited for a person with long sight.

These lenses are known as "positive," and can be used before the lens of the camera in the manner of a supplementary lens. All will give a real image on a piece of ground glass placed at their focus; the "negative" lens does not give a real, but what is known as a "virtual" image, its rays cannot be brought to a focus and it will not give an enlarged image when combined with the lens of the camera.

The two types can be simply distinguished since distant objects seen by the eye through a "positive" lens are blurred and not distinct, whilst those seen through a "negative" lens are sharply defined but considerably reduced in scale.

A positive lens, therefore, when positioned before the camera will give images considerably enlarged in scale. The shorter the focal length of the positive lens the greater its magnification. Spectacle lenses should be of the plano-convex type—one side flat, the other curved—used flat side to the camera, and not the meniscus with no flat side.

If the orthodox portrait attachment is slipped on to the lens, in addition to using a magnifying glass or other positive lens, the combination will be shorter in focal length than either used alone, and the image is enlarged accordingly.

It should be realised, that the size of image given by these optically outcast methods is a result of the nearer camera viewpoint that their use makes possible. They do not enlarge the image from a standard viewpoint, as the orthodox telephoto lens or standard lens with a 2x or 3x tele-converter attachment.

Though it is not strictly germane to the present purpose it is worth noting that opera glasses, field glasses and telescopes can all be used *in the manner of a telephoto lens* to give enlarged images of distant objects. The optical quality of the results are naturally not equal to those obtained by a telephoto lens of first-rate photographic quality, since no attempt was made by the optician to bring to the same focus both the visible and invisible rays of light. If, however, only the centre of the image is used the results are surprisingly good. A further method available with some equipment is to use the standard or some other lens as a supplementary close-up attachment, normally by reversing it and screwing it on to the front of the lens already on the camera. Special mounting rings are sold for this purpose, but the method is generally only used for ultra close up work, because the camera lens is in effect an exceptionally powerful close up lens.

The size of the image obtained depends upon the extension of the camera. A *short extension gives a small image in which the edges of the picture are noticeably less sharp than the middle; a long extension enlarges the image, but reduces its sharp centre definition* to an all-over diffusion. The definition at any extension is *improved by stopping down* the aperture of the camera lens.

Focusing and Exposure

To return once again to our main subject, it will be obvious, of course, that all jugglery with the focal length of your camera in the form of increasing extension, or supplementary lenses of any kind imply a means of focusing the camera so that the sharpness or otherwise of the picture can be actually observed.

Cameras that lack this facility can sometimes be focused by removing the camera back and substituting for a while a piece of *ground glass* held in position by rubber bands. If the tripod bush is on the base of the camera and not attached to the back, the film can easily be inserted and the back replaced when the image has been focused, without shifting the position of the camera. Single lens relex and view cameras are ideally suited to work where a visible image must be focused, and, of course, need no special techniques for it.

Once you begin to play tricks by adding to or subtracting from the lens of the camera, its nice convenient arrangement of apertures of consistent value is no longer reliable for estimating the amount of light entering the camera. *Relative values of the lens aperture are upset* and exposures cannot be determined by them.

With any particular combination, experimental exposures must be given to determine just how much the effective aperture has been reduced by the addition of the odd lens. Having once ascertained it, the figure will be constant for that combination.

The normal portrait attachment, when used alone, does not materially alter the necessary exposure times, which remain the same as if the camera was being used alone and unaided.

Lighting

Very little apparatus is needed for lighting subjects of small scale on the table-top. Bulbs of the normal domestic wattage are adequate, but if a brighter light is felt to be necessary it can easily be provided by the small *over-run type of bulb* known as photofloods.

The bulb should be used in a *portable fitting* that can be placed as desired, and that concentrates all the available light on to the subject without wasting it on the ceiling and the four walls of the room. The normal top light of the room is useful when setting up your subject material and if a general light is needed during exposure, but some portable and concentrated light is always necessary.

To get the utmost power and concentration from any particular bulb the shade should be opaque, painted white on the inside, or lined with white or silver foil paper. The *polished metal* reflectors bulb that are sold to accommodate the photoflood lamp are ideal.

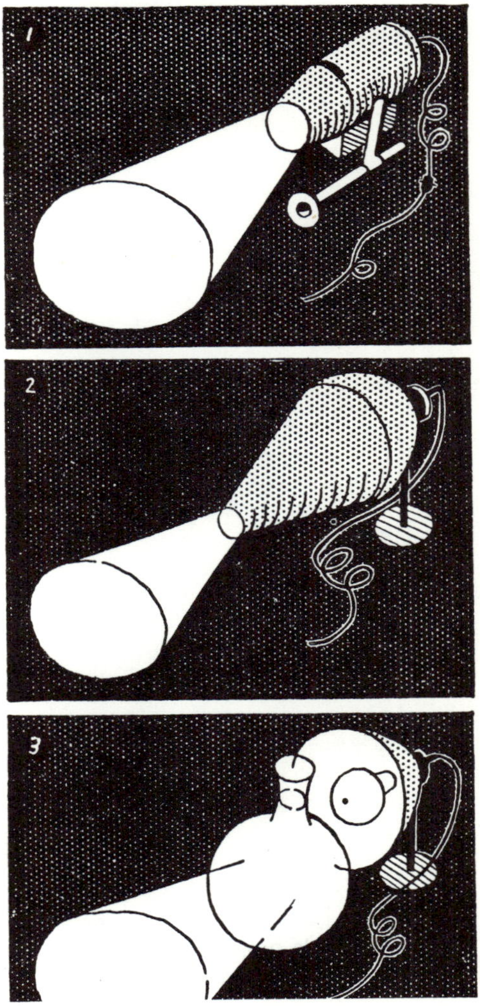

SPOTLIGHTS

1 shows an enlarger, minus lens and lens panel. *2* shows a normal photographic lamp with a cone of silver-foil paper, silver inside. *3* shows a flask of water used, with a normal photographic lamp, to cast a concentrated spot.

Placing the bulb in a white-glazed pudding bowl gives a light of powerful concentration, but, since this is neither very portable, or convenient to place in the downward direction that is most often required, it is best either to fit a silver-foil paper cone inside a normal domestic desk lamp or use a special reflector that can be hung or stood in any position.

Length of exposure usually being of no importance with the still subjects of table work, it will not be necessary to flood the subject with light. The effect of light in the camera is accumulative, the film adding up each small gleam until it builds up a dense tone on the negative, the finished effect being much brighter than was visible by the eye at any one time.

Therefore, when the subject appears attractive under a weak and low-powered light source, providing exposure is adequately prolonged, the effect can be successfully recorded. In particular the effects of *candle-light* on small subjects is most attractive, having a softness and diffusion that particularly suits objects with many reflecting surfaces, such as jewellery and small metal subjects.

With its characteristic concentration of light into a small powerful circle, its long sharp shadows undiluted by diffusion, and its general effect of harsh contrast, the *spotlight* or its simulated effect is indispensable for many table-top subjects. The weakest point in the lighting equipment of most amateurs is the absence of a spotlight, because professional or semi-professional models are relatively bulky, expensive, and consume more current than can safely be taken from the domestic circuit. A relatively inexpensive and safe alternative is the small domestic spotlight.

The spotlight's concentrated power is derived from a condenser lens and this is not exclusive to itself, a condenser being an integral part of many modern enlargers, and, in a more modest form, some pocket-lamps or torches. If the lens of a condenser enlarger or slide projector is removed, together, if possible, with the panel or component into which the lens is screwed, the powers of its beam of light are greatly increased, and can be used as a spotlight for subjects within an area of one or two feet. By substituting a photoflood lamp for the normal one, the power is still further enhanced, but care must be taken not to leave such a lamp burning too long or its great heat will scorch the lamp-house, and possibly crack the condenser. Use such a combination during the short time of exposure only.

Bulbs that have the maker's names and voltage value, etc.,

engraved on their bottom are not entirely suitable for use with a condenser, since such lettering will be projected as an image on to the subject. This is not important in a complicated subject that has much detail in many planes, but can be very obvious in one with any plain and empty surfaces.

A *pocket or portable torch* with a small condenser lens makes a perfect miniature spotlight for the very small table-top subjects, its brilliance and power, of course, depending on the power of the bulb and the nature of the torch. Don't let comparative dimness discourage you; a long exposure will set this right.

Less polished spotlight effects, but quite good enough for the small occasion, can be achieved by *fitting a truncated cone of silver-foil paper over the bowl of a normal photographic reflector*. The cone is rolled out of a largish sheet of the paper and arranged so that one end fits over the reflector—held in place with small clip clothes-pegs, paper clips or a strong rubber band—the other presents a small hole towards the subject some four inches in diameter. The longer the cone, and the smaller the hole at the subject end, the more concentrated and contrasty the lighting will be. If it can be managed, the effect is much improved by fitting a condenser lens of a suitable diameter inside the cone, but this is a refinement and not an absolute necessity.

Another idea for concentrating light into a spot formation is borrowed from the antique work-room of the wood engraver, who was accustomed before the era of artificial illumination to concentrate the available light to a small area through a *spherical glass flask filled with water*. The flask is placed between the source of light and the subject, the light being provided, at convenience, by a window or any artificial light source from a candle to a photoflood in a relector. The nearer the flask to the subject, and the nearer the lamp to the flask, the more powerful the concentrated spot of light. The further each is from the other, the weaker the light and the larger the spot.

Suitable *diffusion* can be introduced if the liquid in the flask is clouded with a tiny quantity of milk. This scatters and diffuses the light in a manner more attractive to certain subjects than the sharp harshness of clear liquid. If the water is tinted by dyes a colour filter effect is obtained. The subject being lit by a coloured light is exactly equivalent to using a filter of that colour before the lens of the camera, without the possible disadvantage of affecting the optical quality of the lens.

When the light source is artificial, the bulb should be of the "*pearl*" variety, or diffused through silk or thin paper, otherwise an image of the filament of the lamp may be cast on the subject.

Besides the means of condensing and increasing the contrast of light, some means of diffusing and reducing its contrasts should be always near at hand. This can simply take the form of small squares of *white silk or satin, or light-coloured net curtaining* of very fine mesh, stretched, either over the reflector bowl, or on a small wooden frame held before the light. The lighter the colour and the smaller the mesh the greater the diffusing effect, the light being broken up and scattered so that shadows lack sharp definition. A *wire or zinc mesh* held before the light makes a good diffuser, particularly if the wire is highly polished or of chromium plate; a good mesh would be between one-half and one-quarter of an inch.

Scenes in Miniature

The title "table-top," as pointed out earlier, has been exclusively claimed for any small scene so composed in miniature that its finished effect conveys the idea, if not of reality, of a parallel so apt that it makes one smile, either in agreeable surprise, or with easy patronage upon a soul so simple, while there are chairs to sleep in or cats to caress, thus to waste his time.

Fundamentally this is not a photographic activity, the skill required being devoted almost entirely to ingenuity of construction and imitation, and the choosing of objects and materials whose actual size and origin are not immediately apparent in the final photograph. The part of the camera is rather incidental, being confined to the mere mechanical recording of the finished tableau or scene. Thus, anyone with the ability to make an indoor photograph of an ordinary still-life subject, can photograph a miniature scene, if, first of all, he has the kind of fantasy necessary to conceive it and the type of non-photographic skill to execute it.

One has no right to expect horticultural hints in a work on flower photography—one presupposes the existence of the flower, just as, here, it is hoped, one is permitted to anticipate the existence, either actual or potential, of the particular miniature scene.

Apart altogether from the scornful, two approaches are possible to the building of any scene—the serious and the comic. For success in either it is essential that the underlying purpose of the scene be made clear and more or less obvious in the final print.

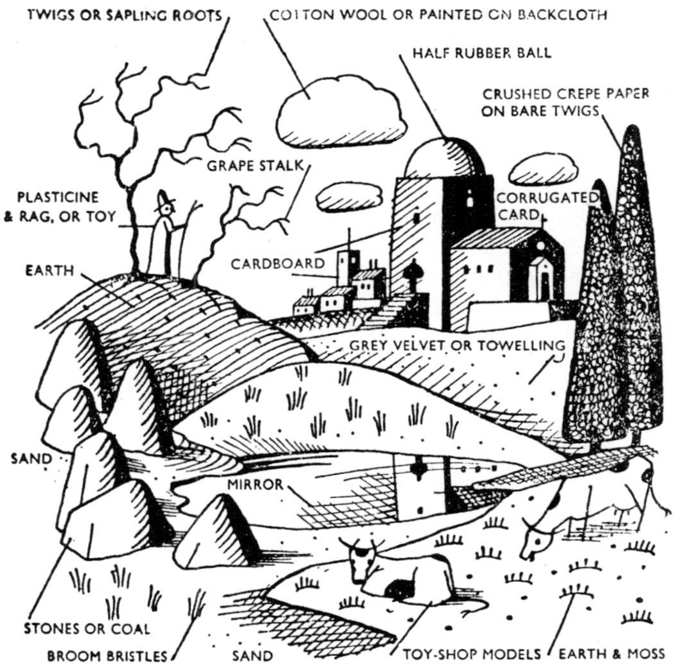

TABLE-TOP

This scene, so carelessly mixing its architectural and topographical metaphors, attempts to indicate *What's What* in the realm of table-top materials. No further explanation needed, none offered.

The aim, if not definitely to create a picture that tells a story, is at least to create one that suggests an easily grasped idea or comic thought. Scenes on the table-top are essentially a means of producing genre or narrative pictures, and a clear conception of the narrative or idea you intend to portray should be in your possession before you begin.

Taking the skill and taste in combining and grouping the separate elements for granted, the basis of effect in these pictures is the apt and happy choice of materials or miniature objects, and their treatment to suggest or caricature the grown-up world.

It is the encouraging of improbable oddments to simulate something other than themselves that constitutes the principal opportunity to display originality and ingenuity. The following is a brief catalogue of natural elements, and the materials that have at some time been used to imitate their pictorial effect.

EARTH is the foundation of most out-door scenes and can most successfully be mimicked by the real thing. If the soil chosen is of fine texture without large lumps or stones its scale is suitable to any but the tiniest scenes, and for these can be used building or fine bird sand.

Small pieces of grit, tiny stones and pebbles of various shapes are valuable to give local incident to the earth, and to break up any suspiciously bare patches.

The effect of ploughed land can be matched by running a fork through fine earth, or, on a larger scale, by sprinkling earth on corrugated cardboard.

GRASS is well simulated by rough turkish towelling of a subdued colour, helped out, here and there by well-placed pieces of moss. Long grass could be simulated by suitably-cut pieces of fur, and isolated patches of sparse weed or grass can be made from the bristles of a short and well-worn broom planted at intervals in the sand or earth.

Distant grassy slopes, or nearer smooth lawns are made from velvet of a subdued middle tone of grey or a colour that photographs in that range.

Small flowers from miniature Japanese and other rock gardens will give rich effects of flower-strewn meadows, if placed immediately prior to exposure, to thwart their rapid tendency to wilt.

TREES and twigs are all of the same family, the smaller offshoots look surprisingly like winter versions of their hoary parents. Suitable collections of twigs from woods and hedgerows, with a little imaginative pruning, can produce the effect of almost any tree formation.

The weak feature of the twig, from the tree-imitating point of view, is the absence of small branches near the top to give the effect of branches becoming smaller and more numerous on the fringes of the tree. An excellent dodge for defeating this drawback is to gently pull up a very small seedling tree from the woods, and use it upside down in the scene so that its fine and numerous roots become branches.

Grape stalks from which, obviously, all the fruit has been removed make excellent bare trees, their small and complicated joints and contours seeming just right in scale for the small bare tree.

Foliage for bare twigs can be fitted to bare twigs by cutting it in the form of a fringe from a piece of folded crepe paper. When opened out and crushed together several times, this network can be draped on to the branches in the manner of leafy clusters. It sounds odd but looks alright.

Sea lavender is an excellent substitute for small saplings with a spring-like effect of bursting buds. Many other small shrubs, conifers and evergreens, when trimmed and fitted with wire trunks can make good leafy trees.

Whitewash splashed thickly onto bare black twigs can give the effect of snow patches, if dropped adroitly on the joints and other places where it collects in Nature. It can also give the effect of rich spring blossom when dropped on the tips of certain small shrubs.

Trees, more fantastic than realistic, can be created from suitably-bent wire, bound round and round with crepe paper, leaves—natural and artificial—being attached with wire, adhesive, or plasticine.

ROCKS are best imitated by the real thing in small lumps, chosen so that scale and subsidiary detail is suitable to the scene depicted. Granites and marbles have a characteristic texture and scale that makes it difficult to successfully employ them, but others, particularly limestone, with its pronounced strata formation, can be used to great advantage to form cliffs and similar groups.

Coal can produce magnificently jagged and forbidding rock shapes if its dark tones and bright highlights can be reconciled with the rest of the picture, otherwise they could be suitably dusted to reduce light reflection.

WATER is, of course, a reflecting element and can be reproduced by any other reflector. Failing the possibility of using the real wet stuff in shallow dishes, and tins, let into the base of the scene, pieces of mirror glass on which are sprinkled earth or sand and edged with moss to form a bank, are suitable for still, reflecting, pools.

Other water surfaces can be suggested by a variety of material placed beneath plain glass. Grease-proof paper that has been wrinkled like corrugated cardboard, for instance, will suggest the ripple of gently-moving water when placed beneath glass; and white or grey paper can, when used in the same way, be used to advantage when the effect of a light surface, without deep reflection, is required.

Cellophane is good for obtaining the impression of waves, ripples and the general liquid shimmer of broken water surfaces. It can be used over a number of different materials and coloured papers to suggest clear or muddy water, or the darkness of great depth.

Waves are made by pulling and stretching the Cellophane into rippling shapes. It can be made thoroughly pliable by steaming for a few moments over a boiling kettle, and is fixed, while still wet, to the baseboard so that it dries as crinkly and unevenly as possible.

For some scenes the particular effect will be well suited by a black ferrotype glazing plate, which gives a very dark and ominous reflection contrasting well with light-toned subject matter.

Water of small scale, as seen from a great height or distance, can be successfully matched by dry-mounting tissue laid on black paper. The minute reticulations, when lit from the proper angle, give a realistic suggestion of light shimmering on the tops of small waves. Actual waves or ripples can also be made by drawing the dry mounting iron across the tissue in one or two places so that it cockles in the appropriate manner.

SNOW is just too easy, and this is doubtless why we get so many tedious snow scenes in table-top work. Anything white and powdery that happens to be handy will serve: salt, flour, castor sugar, or isinglass from the domestic stores, powdered alum, chalk and sodium phosphate rubbed through a sieve, from the dark-room chemical cupboard, can all be suitably employed.

To economise in whatever substance you use, hills and other irregularities of the scene are best formed in stiff brown paper, over which is laid some white cotton sheeting or similar light-coloured material.

For arctic scenes, icebergs can be made from large lumps of washing soda or Cellophane folded into block form, ur used as it comes off the cigarette or sweet carton. Icy-looking rocks can be stones wrapped in Cellophane, immersed in water, and sprinkled with coarse salt whilst still wet.

ARCHITECTURE, being a man-made affair, of simple geometrical shapes, is reasonably easy to fake on a small scale. Buildings can be constructed from cardboard and, since they are seen from a single viewpoint, need not be made absolutely solid but built in the simple manner of stage scenery.

Windows and other openings are best cut out rather than painted on, to give greater depth of effect, window bars being made either from thick thread stretched across and fixed at the back, or from cut paper according to scale.

Circular towers or tall chimneys can be combined from cardboard tubes of suitable length and diameter, columns can be made from wood dowelling or from painted pencils if they suit the general scale. Domes can be simulated by any suitably shaped object. Electric light bulbs arranged so that the cap portion is obscured in the framework of the building made first-rate domes, as will half-concealed rubber balls or other circular objects. A tiled roof, if not too small in relative scale, can be made from corrugated cardboard arranged either so that the lines run down, or across, the roof to suggest pan or plain tiling, or from small strips of thin card gummed one over the other to leave evenly-spaced ridges.

All small building constructions should be given a coat of emulsion or poster paint, so that they present more accurately the textured effect of matt stonework. Apply the colour thickly so that it has body and texture, and streak a little darker colour into it to suggest the various tones and weatherings of age.

FIGURES are usually the vital point of the picture, and the point at which most table-top pictures break down, bringing, as you must confess they do, the rather silly small and precious quaintness of the novelty shop, and other bazaars on the borders of pleasant taste.

If you have no aversion to these oddments or can successfully overcome it, they should be treated with glycerine or thin varnish and dusted with face powder to remove their unnatural gloss and highlights, and substitute the texture of flesh.

A better solution to the problem of the figure, if you can summon up the necessary patience, is to construct them of a suitable size from lengths of stout wire. This skeleton is then padded with modelling clay or cotton wool to give the necessary body, and clothed with oddments of fabric roughly shaped and stitched into position.

The business of clothing is actually not so tedious as it sounds, as the appearance is only desired from a single point of view—that of the camera, the other sides being left as rough.

The heads, hands, or other exposed flesh of such figures is modelled in modelling clay and dusted with face powder of an appropriate flesh shade.

BACKGROUNDS. Excepting those cases where a high viewpoint permits the base of the scene to run out the top of the picture, a background of some kind must be arranged—to stop the eye and to picture the objects against.

The effect of the back of the scene running out of the picture can be obtained, with lower viewpoints, if fore and background are made continuous without any definite joint. This can be achieved, when the base of the picture is a plain surface, by using paper or other material long enough to be gradually rolled up behind the scene so that it passes imperceptibly from the horizontal to the vertical plane.

In those cases where the nature of the foundation does not permit such tactics, and where the viewpoint necessitates an actual backcloth, this can be arranged at any distance behind the scene.

In many examples, all that is required in the way of background will be a plain even tone of a certain depth, and this can be obtained from atmospheric space left behind your construction, or from actual card or paper of a suitable colour or tone.

Papers with various types of surface should be collected for their background possibilities; grease-proof or other shiny surfaces, for instance, when crumpled up and roughly smoothed out, catch the light in odd patches and made an effective mass when seen in soft focus. The broken tones suggest clouds or dim mountainous shapes according to position and lighting.

If the backcloth is made from some thin translucent material, thin drawing paper, or a sheet of heavy tracing paper stretched on a light wooden frame, background shadows of a suitable nature can be cast upon it by placing objects, or cut-out shapes, at the back—between the cloth and the source of light.

Sheets of celluloid, of which the back surface has been matted by rubbing with sandpaper, make excellent misty backgrounds for the back projection of these shadow shapes, as, of course, do sheets of ground or opaque glass if they are available.

When making use of a shadowed backcloth, the general lighting of the front scene must be arranged from the side and towards the back, so that the depth of shadow is not washed out by too much front light.

If the subject is one that you hope will be funny, or frankly miniature with no intended illusion of reality, shadowed backgrounds can be made by casting the shadows of the actual picture objects on to the background, by a low concentrated light from the front.

Pictorial background effects, to suggest distant landscapes, seascapes or merely clouds, can be achieved by painting sheets of cardboard in the appropriate manner. The skill required is reassuringly negligible, the oddest smudge, providing it has the basically correct outline, will adequately suggest distant and out-of-focus objects.

The straight lines of horizon or evenly sloping ranges of hills, seen as flat receding tones, can be made from pieces of material, stretched so that they cut across in the desired planes, and are seen only dimly and with soft definition.

Photographic backgrounds, as dealt with on page 160, can easily be used if the scene is sufficiently small or the enlargement of great enough area. Clouds, or other background material, might be printed in by photomontage in the enlarger or by double exposure in one of the previously described ways.

The background of the scene must be adequate in extent so that the camera can be adjusted without fear of moving outside its area. The scene, also, should be set up with a goodly margin on either side. The camera's angle of view is wedge-shaped, spreading out towards the background. So, if your material is set up on a rigid rectangle, you will either have to include less foreground, or give a satisfactory explanation of the two small triangles of plain table that appear in the top corners of the picture.

TECHNIQUE is a matter almost of elementary ability, focusing being the chief means of making the photographic effect seem tolerably natural to the eye.

Large apertures should be employed so that *focusing is selective*, there is little depth of focus, and sharp definition is confined to the principal plane. The subject matter of your scene cramps into a few inches, at most a foot or two, what would in reality extend for several hundred yards; the suggestion of this space must therefore depend on a certain softness of the distance and a quick falling-off in definition from foreground to background.

Objects should be considered with the eye of the camera, in different degrees of focus, rather than with the sharp and critical gaze of the eye. It is the photographic, rather then the actual, appearance that is of principal interest, and choice of possible materials should be made by watching their effect on the focusing screen or through half-closed eyes.

Lighting must be arranged simply and in a direction that minimises any crudity or roughness common to the small objects portrayed. Texture should only be emphasised if it is in scale with the rest of the scene, and the glare from shiny surfaces, if not removed by a smear of putty or a dusting with powder, should be studiously avoided.

Tilted Glass

If the camera back is kept parallel to the background, or at right angles the general directional line of the subject, whatever the angle of the original exposure the print will always tend to be read as if the subject stands in the vertical plane.

A similar phenomenon was observed on page 102, where objects and persons actually laid on the floor and photographed from above, were made to assume impossible feats of acrobatics. The method is here extended, by the use of glass sheets, to include work on the table, or, on a smaller scale, on the floor.

This method consists of arranging the subject matter on a sheet of clear glass, supported only at the extreme edges, laid either completely flat in the horizontal plane or tilted at an angle. The camera is arranged so that it points down to the subject, its back parallel to the glass plate; the floor, or any other flat or tilted plane behind the glass, becomes the background.

The advantages of the method lie in the fact that objects can be shown in a position, apparently in the vertical plane, that they could not otherwise achieve unsupported, and that would be impossibly difficult to support invisibly, and objects can be shown without any connection with background or floor, seemingly floating in the middle of the picture space.

Backgrounds can be mere space stretching out behind the glass, or cards of different tone and texture placed at an

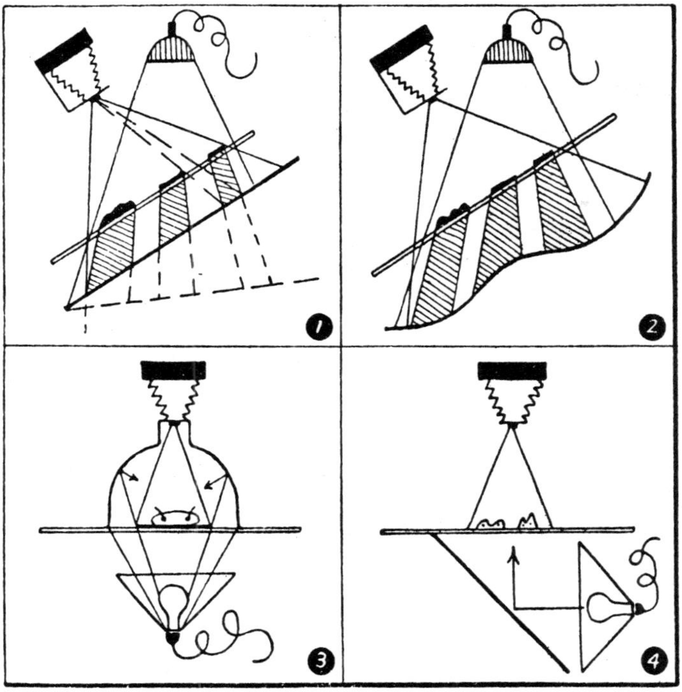

DISTORTED SHADOWS

In drawings *1* and *2* flat objects are laid upon a tilted glass sheet arranged parallel to the camera back. The light shines from above at an angle to the glass and throws the shadows of the objects on to a background sheet below.

In drawing *1* the background is flat, in one case parallel to the glass—but with a dotted alternative. In drawing *2* the distorting effect of an oddly-curved background is shown, the shadows going alternatively thick and thin and waving alarmingly in the final result.

Drawings *3* and *4* are alternative methods of obtaining shadowless backgrounds on a sheet of glass. In *3* by shining the light up into the inverted bowl of a lamp reflector, objects arranged on a small opaque background. In *4* by directing light at right angles to a sheet of white card, which reflects it upwards to the objects arranged directly on the glass or the transparent background.

appropriate distance behind it. Pictorial and patterned backgrounds could also be used if the need arose.

Very dark, or perfectly black backgrounds, may often convert the glass into a shiny reflecting surface in which is mirrored a second image of the subject, and the camera, or any bright surrounding objects. Unless this can be defeated it is as well to avoid them.

Lighting must be arranged *not to flare on the surface of the glass* or reflect an image, bulbs are best used in reflectors that concentrate their light upon the subject and leave the rest of the room in comparative darkness.

In many cases fascinating effects of depth and stereoscopy can be obtained by introducing *light between the glass and the background,* so that it shines strongly upon the latter and provides a strong back light for the subject material. Combined with a low-powered front light, or a white or silverfoil paper reflector, to send the light back, such an arrangement of light throws the subject into very high relief.

Most backgrounds, particularly the plain variety, are best kept out of focus. The effect of tone variation and lines of light, to enhance the direction of a particular composition, can be made by an out-of-focus spot-light, wavy silver-foil paper, Cellophane, or grease-proof paper lit in an appropriate manner.

The method, of course, need not be confined to a single sheet of glass, and the effect of several overlapping planes can be effectively obtained by the use of two or three glasses on which can be arranged isolated objects, or cut-out shapes, to suggest the receding planes of mountain ranges and the like.

Special attention must obviously to paid to the cleanliness of the glass, and grease, finger-marks, or any dirty blemish must be removed by polishing with French chalk and methylated spirit. Any glass is suitable, if reasonably free from waves or internal blemishes, but polished plate is naturally the ideal.

▷ *In particular, the method is suitable to simulate situations that could rarely, except by super-human skill or good fortune, be obtained in the normal vertical plane. The most effective uses of the method exploit this aspect.*

Figures, and objects may be shown suspended in mid-air. Small transparent glass witch balls or glass beads of various sizes could be used as floating soap bubbles, or air bubbles from the mouths of toy fishes or miniature under-water figures of that kind.

▷ *More mystifying and arresting still are similar effects produced, not in the miniature table-top tradition, but from real objects of suitable size.*

Falling cards, flying crockery, scattering skittles and similar conceits are among the odd effects that can be brought into being by adroit arrangement of the objects, on glass sheets, in the various required planes, disposing them so that the apparent movement seems natural to the occasion.

▷ *When necessary, the artifice of the glass can be helped out by supporting some objects at a particularly difficult angle on small lengths of thread, similar in tone to the background shade.*

Lettering, and any other shapes, can be cut from paper and laid on the glass so that they are strangely suspended over the subject matter. The effect is still further enhanced if the lighting is arranged so obliquely that the shadows of the letters are thrown on the subject below as a separated image.

▷ *This trick of removing objects from their cast shadow is a useful one, and, by the necessary oblique direction of light, effective compositions of light and shade, and separated duplication, can be achieved.*

The further the background from the glass, the larger and less distinct the shadow, but for most effects the background board need not be moved more than a few inches away. The shape of the shadow can be amusingly distorted by inclining or curving the sheet of paper or other material that forms the background.

▷ *Still-life objects may be made to overlap each other in a manner not possible in the vertical plane, and, illusion apart, jewellery, and similar brilliant metal objects, look well when pictured upon a glass sheet. Sparkling double reflections and the highlights so obtained, over a dark background, look particularly well.*

Shadowless Backgrounds

Backgrounds without shadow, in which the objects are seen cleanly isolated against a luminous background, are often a necessity to the successful photography of tiny objects, and they can be contrived by arranging them on glass above a brilliantly-lit surface.

This surface can consist of a white sheet of paper used in the manner of the backgrounds of the previous examples. It could be placed at an angle of 45° and the lighting arranged so that it is directed at right-angles to the glass and evenly illuminates the paper.

By this means indirect light is reflected up on to the undersurface of the glass, and the object-shadows, which would normally be cast on to the background sheet by the lights for the subject, are not formed.

Another ingenious method of producing a similar result on an opaque background, and with the added advantage that no sharp reflections will be formed on any shiny surfaces that the subject might possess, is to place the objects on a small circle of opaque card, or other material, on the surface of the glass.

A bowl-shaped reflector that would normally be used to increase the light from a photo bulb, but from which all such impedimenta has been removed, is lowered on to the subject so that it completely covers it, the camera looking through the small lamp socket hole on the top.

The circular background must be just a little smaller than the internal diameter of the reflector bowl, so that a small ring of glass is left all round. Light from below enters the bowl through this ring and is reflected back from all sides of the reflector on to the subject. The objects are thus lit indirectly from all sides, no shadows are thrown and there are no disturbing reflections.

Under Water

Given a camera with the necessary extension for close work, or an arrangement of lenses to alter the focal length, any number of subjects may be treated on the table-top. The following collection have only a connection with water in common.

Aquaria of tropical fish, or other specie, are rich material for the camera if the problem of rapid movement and focusing can be solved.

The best solution is effected by obtaining a sheet of glass the same length as the tank, which can be lowered into it to *decrease its depth, from front to back,* to a matter of some three or four inches. This prevents rapid movement of the subject and leaves a narrow area needing a small depth of field to completely cover everything within it.

Rocks, weeds, and other natural background material in the further half of the tank, are clearly seen through the temporary glass plate and retain the genuine aquarium atmosphere. It is advisable, unless the weedy growth is thick, to ensure a neutral background of dark tone behind the whole tank, to properly display the silvery tones of fish scales.

Artificial lighting should be arranged with extreme care since

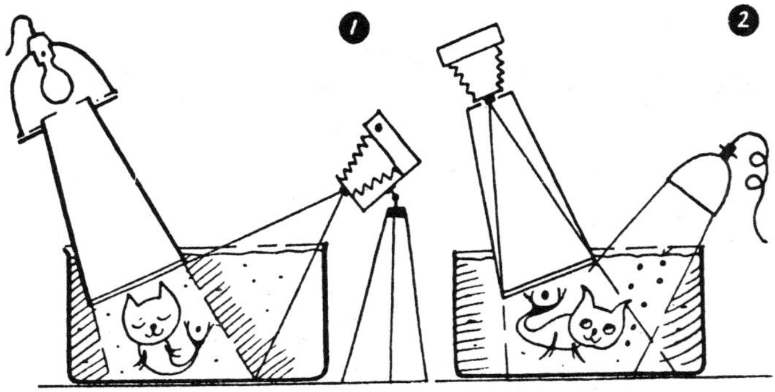

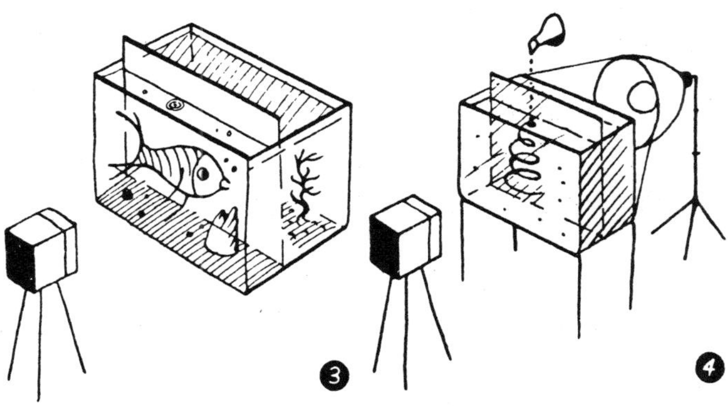

UNDER WATER

Drawings *1* and *2* are alternative methods of using an under-water viewing-box. *1* as a means of projecting light beneath the water's surface, and *2* to permit the camera to see clearly below the surface when the light source is normally outside. The room must be otherwise in darkness for success with method *1.*

A glass sheet is used as a false side to narrow an aquarium for photographic purposes in drawing *3,* and 4 shows the arrangement of camera and light for the best recording of ink and similar currents.

it tends to *concentrate heat* in a small area on one side of the tank, on the other side of which is relatively cold water. The results of such a condition could be unfortunate, and it is best to use any near lights during the brief period of exposure only, otherwise using a flash bulb.

Aquaria apart, the surface of the water is in itself a strong reflector of light, and the surface must either be very still, and without reflection, or a rectangular *viewing box* should be used. This is a very simple addition to your equipment, and consists of a rectangular tube, approximately equal in area to twice the size of the camera's picture space, and anything from one to a couple of feet long. One end is open for the camera, the other is closed by a piece of clear glass firmly attached to it.

The tube could be easily constructed from a sheet of zinc or other metal, painted a *dead matt black on the inside* to frustrate reflection, the joints between glass and metal being made absolutely water-tight with a sealing compound.

In use, the tube is arranged so that the glass-closed end is immersed for a few inches into the water, the camera looking down at the under-water subject through a small card screen that prevents any light, from outside, entering the top of the tube.

Lighting is arranged *from above the surface of the water,* at any required angle, and the view through the tube, with all surface reflection removed will be crystal clear.

If a *light source is substituted for the camera* at the open end of the tube and a beam of light projected into the water, providing the room is absolutely dark, and no stray beams escape from the top of the tube, under-water subjects can be simply photographed by pointing the camera down at the subject and making the exposure.

▷ *Light under water has an attractive quality of diffusion, strong shadows are not observed, and shiny surfaces do not display complicated reflections. Thus, small gleaming objects of metal or jewellery that are difficult to record adequately by any other means, can be reproduced by immersing them in water and photographing them through it.*

▷ *As a curiosity, the currents formed in water by ink and dyes, or by various liquids such as glycerine, methylated spirit and petrol, have considerable pictorial attraction and may be recorded in small glass tanks similar to those used for small aquariums or accumulators.*

If a narrow tank is not to be found, one can be narrowed by the temporary addition of a false side as recently described. The camera is set up and focused so that the depth held is adequate. It is helpful to use some construction like the effects box described on page 111, or some other screen, between camera and the side of the tank to keep unwanted light from the lens.

Lighting is arranged on the far side of the tank so that it shines through the water towards the camera, and it should be diffused, and so distributed evenly over the whole area, by placing tracing paper, tissue paper or a piece of ground glass on the side of the tank nearest the light.

When all is ready, the ink or other liquid is gently dropped into the water from above and the exposure made as the separate drops break up into strange flower shapes, or other formations, and diffuse into the water.

The formations will vary with the manner in which the liquid is sprayed, dropped, or poured, and according to its strength and concentration. If the effect is being photographed in monochrome for very pale and thin liquids it may be advisable to use a filter of complementary, or opposite, colour to the tint of the solution—a green filter for a red solution, a blue one for a yellow, an orange one for a purple, and so on.

WATER DROPS. Drips from glasses, bottles or tips of needles are quite a problem for fast shutters and rapid judgment. They can more easily be recorded if the drop is made from glycerine, a solution of gum tragacinth in water, or best of all a solution of gelatine in warm water.

The drop is prepared naturally in warm conditions and taken into a cool room, where it freezes or stiffens into a solid drop of gelatine, staying put for any length of exposure.

WITHOUT THE CAMERA

Photography does not necessarily demand the presence of a camera. The fundamental basis of the medium is essentially a conspiracy between light and a light sensitive emulsion, for which a means of controlling the light's action—a door-keeper for the darkness—is the only absolute necessity.

All techniques appropriately have their tools, which are both a convenient means of attaining a desired end and a stimulus and inspiration for its conception and completion. But, in a happy medium, the tool is rather the respected servant than the admired master. With photography frequently one has the feeling that the camera receives disproportionate respect. Is it not often the camera, or the means, that we are asked to admire, rather than the picture, or the proper end?

The biggest obstacle to a good photograph could be the camera receives disproportionate respect. Is it not often the self-respect of the photographer, the following methods suggest perfectly adequate means of making photographic prints without assistance from either camera or negative.

Direct Copying

When a copy is desired of the page of a book, a written document, an engraving, line drawing or any other black and white printed image, it may be simply obtained, without the intermediate help of the camera, if the surface to be copied is laid in contact with the sensitive surface of a sheet of thin printing paper of adequate size.

Light is allowed to fall, or is *projected through the enlarger,* for a short time, *on to the back of either the printing paper or the printed surface.* The result, when developed in the normal paper manner, is an image of the original in which the tones are reversed but is otherwise perfect and accurate in every respect.

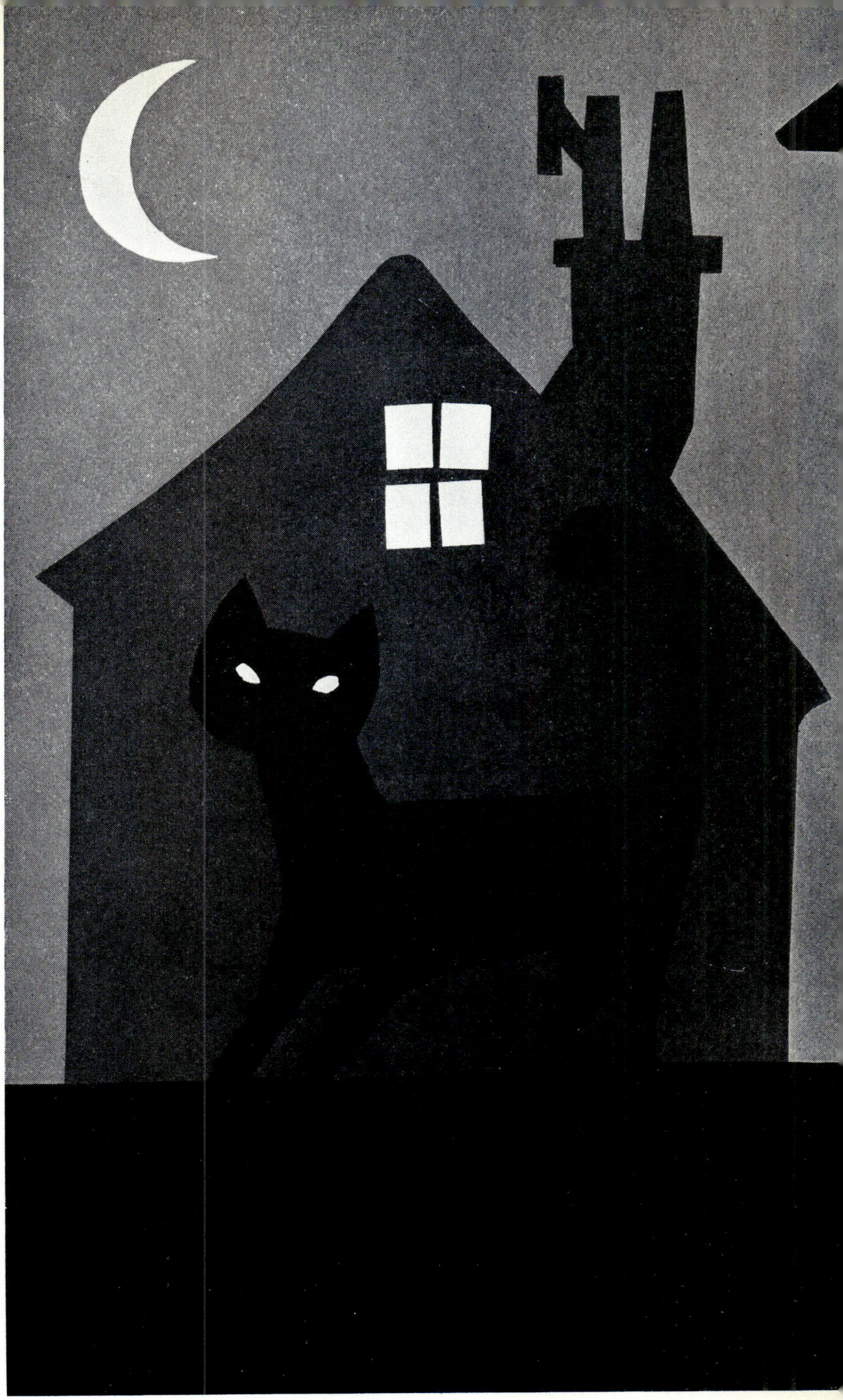

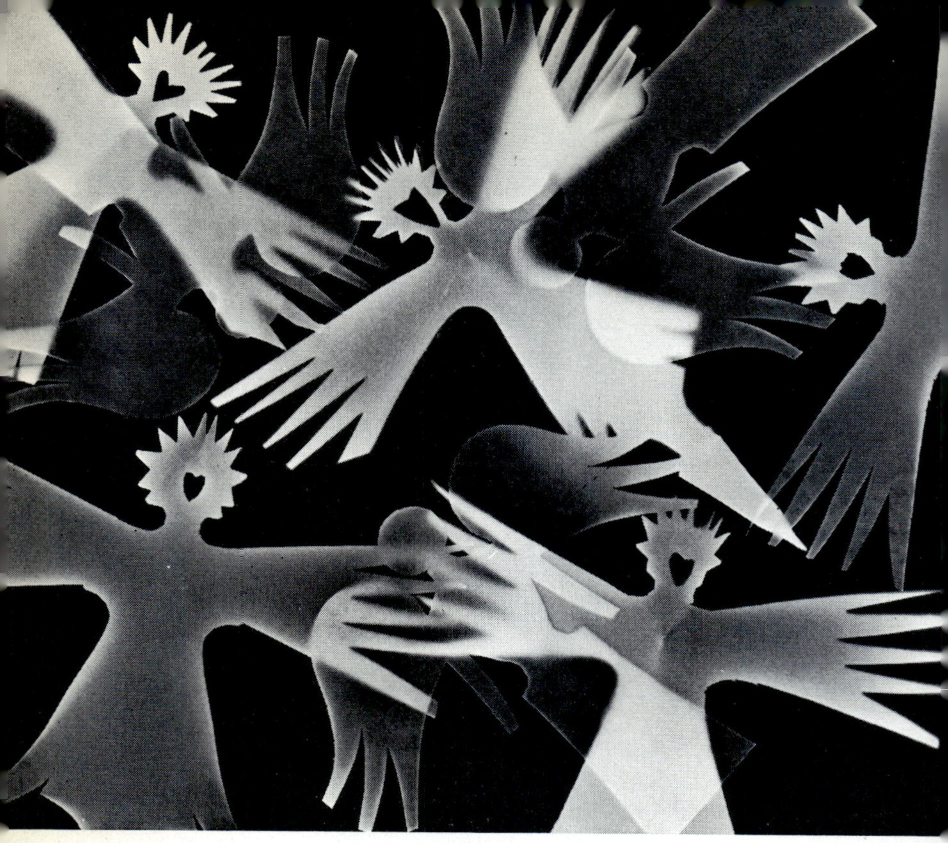

PHOTOGRAMS

Semi-photogram using translucent plastic sheeting. The figures were cut out and placed on the sheet of bromide paper. Where the sheeting curled up the density was greater and, consequently, the image lighter.—*Edwin Smith.*

Page 253: A photogram with cut paper masks. Cut-out showing cat and near building used to protect the paper for a four-second exposure and then removed. Cut-out showing background building placed in position for a 2 sec. exposure, then removed. Whole paper exposed for a further 2 sec. to produce sky tone, except for the cat's eyes, window pieces, and moon which remained in position throughout every exposure. The cat therefore had an 8 sec exposure, the background building 4, and the sky only 2 —*Edwin Smith.*

Opposite: Superimposition of leaves on a tree. Dried skeletons of leaves were laid on the paper and a conventional negative was projected through them.—*Edwin Smith.*

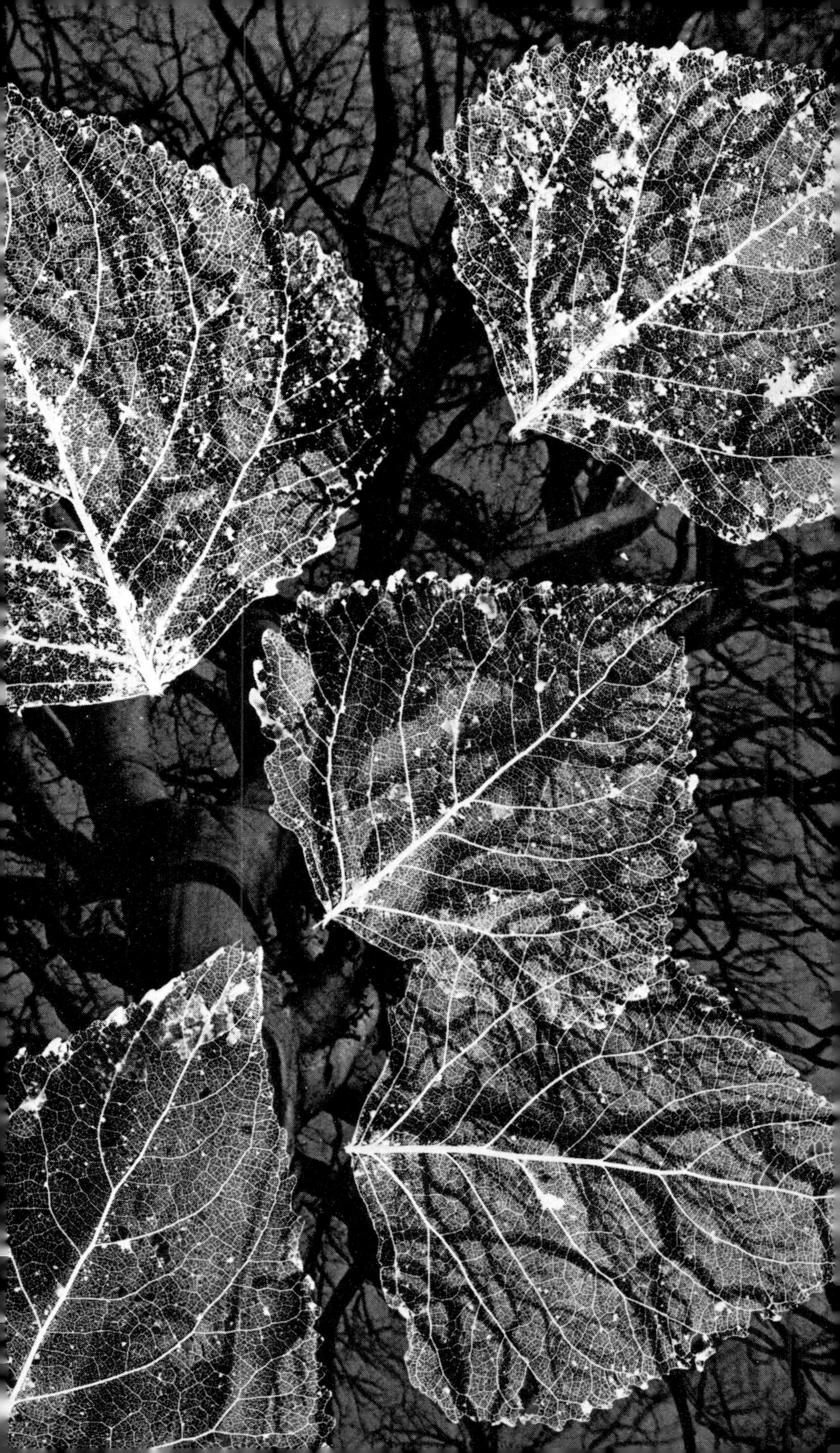

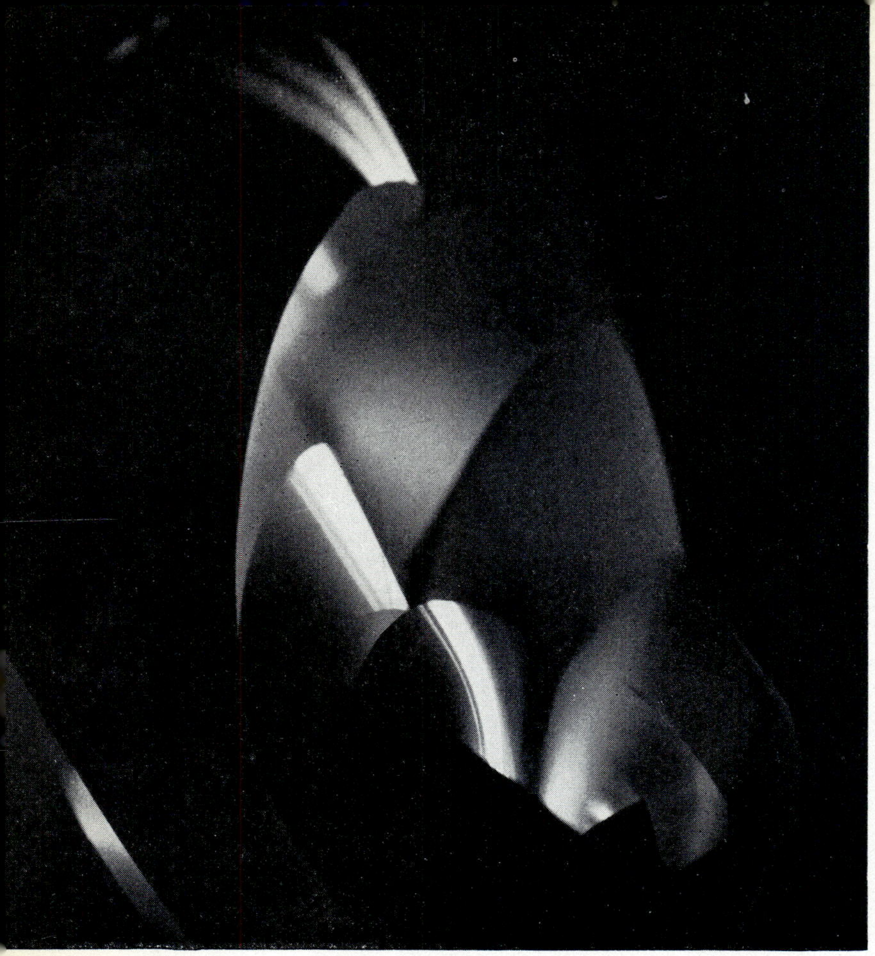

Light creates an abstract, rhythmic, pattern on shapes of cut paper. Strips cut from a single sheet, none being completely detached, bent and twisted to the desired forms, lit from behind and slightly to one side The effect of a puzzling photogram—achieved in the camera.—*F Brugiere.*

The particular sheet through which the light is shone depends on whether or not it has a second image or letter-press on the other side.

If the original is printed on one side of the paper only, it is placed face down on the printing paper and light projected through it, as if it were a paper negative. Such light easily penetrates the plain unprinted areas and exposes the emulsion below, but, being absorbed by the darker areas of print, leaves those areas of the paper untouched.

To avoid a double image from surfaces whose *both sides are printed,* it is best to project the light through the back of the printing paper, and place a *sheet of black absorbent paper beneath the surface being copied.*

Light, passing through the back of the printing paper, is reflected on to its sensitive emulsion by all the white parts of the original, the darker parts absorbing the light and reflecting nothing back. The dark backing paper helps to confine the reflection of the front surface and discourages light from the back of the paper being reflected through.

If the copy is merely required for record purposes it will be of no importance, as long as it is accurate, whether its form is negative or positive, but, if a positive is imperative, the copy obtained by either means can be used as a *paper negative*, placing it in contact with another sheet of printing paper and exposing through it as if it were a film or plate.

Absolute *contact* of the two surfaces is an essential condition for success, and it is advisable, after bedding the two on a perfectly flat board, to cover them with a *sheet of glass that is suitably weighted* to give pressure on the top sheet. Exposure is easily made through the transparent surface of the glass.

With both methods, but particularly where the light is directed through the printing paper, slight fogging and loss of contrast is inevitable, but this can easily be defeated if *development is contrasty*, say in *concentrated hydroquinone* used in cold solution.

Copies can be made in this simple manner by using a sheet of *luminous paper* as the source of light. It is placed behind the original, which must be printed on one side only, and the printing paper, backed by a sheet of black paper, placed over it. If left for a few moments, the printing paper will be exposed through the original by radiated light from the luminous paper, and can be developed and finished in the normal way.

Photograms

The emulsion of printing paper is exposed by the action of light, and any interception of the light, either by the varying densities of a negative, or the absolute density of objects and cut-out shapes, leaves a record of the intercepting shape as a white or grey image, according to the duration of interception.

Thus, any object whose characteristic shape is contained in the flat plane like a silhouette, can be recorded on the surface of the printing paper, without the use of an intermediate negative process, simply by *laying it on the paper and exposing a light above it*.

If such an object is allowed to remain for the *duration of the exposure,* and the exposure is long enough to produce a full printing tone, the shape is perfectly *white on a pure black ground.* But, if the object is *removed and the exposure is continued,* the previously protected paper receives a light that tones it to a *lighter or darker grey* according to duration. A full control of tonal range is possible by this means.

It is useful to make a simple *chart* of these tones, together with a note of the aperture, distance and exposure times that produced them, for future reference. The chart is made by placing a sheet of sensitive paper beneath the enlarger. Start by revealing a half-inch strip along one short edge, gradually uncovering the paper in regular half-inch steps, and at specific intervals of time, until the paper is completely uncovered. The first strip, receives all available light and prints jet black. The rest prints in an even gradation of tones—getting lighter and lighter until the last strip, which, receiving least light, prints lightest of all.

The time taken to expose each strip and uncover the whole will depend, on the power and distance of the exposing light, and this should be so arranged, by *altering the aperture* of the enlarging lens, so that the steps are uncovered at, say, something like two-second intervals.

Working backwards, from the lightest step that received the bare two seconds, it will be possible to *note against each strip the time needed to produce it* by adding two at each step. Such tones can then be reproduced by duplicating the exposure beneath an identical light source. With such a sheet as guide, it is possible to plan tone pictures from this range by arranging cut-out shapes of black masking paper to obscure the printing surface for the various times required.

▷ *The cut-outs can take natural or artificial forms, imitating the silhouette of natural shapes, or consisting merely of abstract shapes to form a pure pattern. Lettering for example as previously suggested in another chapter, can be printed by laying the cut-out letters on the printing paper and exposing to a light. Such letters will print white on a toned ground, but if a mask from which the shapes have been cut is placed over the paper, the letters will print as a dark tone on a white ground.*

▷ *Textured tones can be obtained by using sheets of tracing paper in the manner of screens, interspersed with the black cut-out shapes of the picture, single sheets or various combined thicknesses giving different tones and different texture.*

▷ *Objects that are flat and small enough, or cut-outs that are designed on a small enough scale, may be projected through the enlarger, the effect being more diffused with softer definition, or even out of focus.*

▷ *Any flat object, with a good silhouette shape, will produce effective photograms. Some appear merely as white shapes, others will show interior detail and texture according to their relative transparency.*

Lace, relying upon white mass for its pictorial effect, is a good subject, its shape and patterns recording with maximum brilliance. The delicate fronds of feathers also record with extremely faithful detail and little loss of pictorial effect; a small one, pressed between the glasses of the negative carrier, and projected through the enlarger yields good results.

Small patterned weeds of the sea, meadow grasses, ears of wheat and oats, have characteristic silhouettes suitable for this technique; household objects such as shaped knives and forks, the odd shape of opened scissors, and anything without too much upward body will also give good pictures.

Little skill is necessary for the creation of these pictures than that involved in making an attractive arragement of flat objects on the surface of the paper, and exposing a light above them, removing at specific intervals those that are to print a duller grey, leaving permanently those that are to print white.

▷ *Effects can be augmented by slightly shifting the position of an object during exposure, so that double images are formed. This treatment effectively varies the tones and object shapes and introduces a very necessary element of chance into a process which can become too obvious. The paper remains white in odd and unforeseen areas where it has been obscured in both posi-*

tions, greying to various tones where the movement has uncovered previously unexposed parts of the paper.

▷ *The technique of picture making with black paper cut-outs involves a little more creative and manual labour, since the whole picture, from conception to execution, including the production of subject material, must be undertaken.*

Any odd cut-out shape, without figurative pretensions, can produce intriguing shapes of light if moved about the paper in several overlapping positions, so that some parts of the paper are permanently obscured, others only partly, by its successive movements.

▷ *Given the necessary ability, pictures of a more or less naturalistic kind can be obtained by cutting the representational shapes, and using them as masks to obtain silhouettes in the depths of tone required.*

Thus, as an elementary example, the silhouetted picture of a cat sitting on a wall before a full moon would be produced by cutting the outline of cat and wall from the lower half of a mask large enough to cover the whole printing paper.

The part from which the cat has been cut, not *the cat shape, is used to obscure the upper half of the paper so that the lower half begins to expose to a dark tone in the required mask shape and position.*

When this exposure time has been long enough to produce a good deep grey (consult your tone sheet for this) the printing light is turned out and the mask removed. A circular mask, or any other moon shape, is then placed in position in the sky part of the picture and the printing light resumed long enough to produce the sky tone and with the addition of the previous exposure, to produce a rich black pussy on a pitch black wall.

On development, if no false moves have been made, the lower shape of the picture prints a full black against a medium toned grey sky, in which floats a fine white moon.

By such elementary means, pictures of any complication of shape and tone can be produced. One thinks more quickly in this medium by contriving to think consistently in the negative.

Remember that the black masking shapes protect the paper and leave a white image, the cut portions that show white printing paper reveal it to the light and thus create a tone, lighter or darker according to the length of exposure.

Crystallography

In photography the most improbable combination of elements can produce most unexpected images. Strange and fascinating pattern effects can be created without any hard work on your part, if transparent crystals of chemical solutions are allowed to form on one of the glass plates of the negative carrier and the image projected through the enlarger. Such hostile elements as oil and water, in the form, say, of glycerine and ink, produce exciting shapes of stunted trees and tropic undergrowth, which, when dry, may be projected and printed like a negative.

The glycerine is smeared on to a cleaned and slightly damp glass plate, then minute drops of Indian or other ink are dropped on and encouraged to run in the more or less desired shapes, twisting and turning to pattern the whole plate.

When dry the mixture has a varying tone and density very similar to a normal negative, in which manner it can be easily printed.

Shadowgrams

From flat objects laid or projected upon the paper's surface, and lit directly from above, we graduate to solid objects lit from various directions so that their shadows, cast upon the paper, and printing as a tone or density, form a definite part of the finished picture.

The method differs in no other way from the technique described, having the same basis of interrupting light directed towards the paper so that the shapes of the interrupting objects are left as white unexposed areas on the sensitive surface.

Here, though, one can add to the range of effect by including among the interposing objects things, however improbable, that extend in an upward direction, and *lighting them not from the top but from a side angle that throws their shadow,* on to the sensitive surface.

This shadow, being actually an absence of light, registers on the developed print not as a dark, but as a light or white tone. To prevent confusion between the shadows and the object shapes that cast them, it is sometimes advisable to use the *exposing light in a combined manner.* This is done by using a top light from the enlarger, beneath which the objects are conveniently arranged and letting it remain for the whole exposure, or for a short period only according to the effect desired. Combined lighting of this kind, light both from top and side, has the effect of weakening the whites of the cast shadows to a lighter or darker grey, according to the duration of the top light. This distinguishes them from the white shapes of the actual objects when such a separation is felt to be necessary.

Different effects are obtained if the side lighting is concentrated, in the manner of a spotlight or a pocket-torch with a condenser lens; or diffused in the fashion of a normal bulb in a common reflector—the edges of the shadows thrown by the first being more or less hard and definite, those cast by the second being soft and diffused.

Domestic utensils, such as hollow nutmeg or cheese graters, tea or coffee strainers, or similar shaped and fretted objects, yield fascinating light patterns if small lighted candles or a tiny pocket-torch is placed inside them. The light reaches the paper through the various openings, darkening it in small regular spots of varying size and intensity.

Yet another change can be rung by using the finished print, as a paper negative and making a *positive print* through it, in the manner of the *direct copying method* explained on page 252. This reverses the tones in the accustomed printing fashion and brightens an over dark picture.

A method of inhibiting accident and chance and of introducing a little more order and positive intention is achieved by placing the potential objects on a sheet of *translucent paper* on a sheet of glass. If you examine the shapes and shadows cast upon this sheet by peering up at it from below, you observe, as near as nothing, the pattern-making possibilities and the general effect of any particular combination. A similar arrangement, with a similar disposition of lighting, on the sensitive paper in the darkroom, will produce roughly the same effect—though in a negative form with white instead of black shadows, and on a dark instead of light ground.

▷ *Glass vessels of all kinds have attractive possibilities and those in the darkroom or the china cupboard are equally suitable.*

Spectacles, cotton-wool, electric light bulbs—clear and opaque, buttons, rings, sea shells, pine cones, acorns, hammers, chisels, saws and screws, hands and feet. A quite famous shadowgram by Maholy Nagy is entitled "Maholy Lays his Face on the Printing Paper."

▷ *Ideally, of course, and after the first pardonable sensation of amusement, the method is not a means of reproducing the haphazard appearance of a spectral junk shop, but a very perfect technique for creating abstract design and composition in pure terms of light—real light pictures, not just records of external reality.*

Here, the objects represent only themselves in an objective manner, without the psychological or subjective implication which is usually the case in the convention of representation.

▷ *Cultivation of this abstract, disinterested, interest in shape, texture, and tone, if one is not continually worried by what things "mean," gives very rich opportunities to think and work in terms of pure light forms.*

The lens of the camera can be removed and a small circle of paper, in which has been cut a small shape or design, temporarily substituted. If light from the weak source of a candle or pocket-torch is allowed to fall through this opening on to the sensitive surface of the film, lovely patterns, ghosts and spirits can be conjured up that are unique photographic manifestations, having known no concrete existence beyond the boundaries of the film.

The suggestive shapes of rippling light on the brilliant surface of a silver-foil paper, the varied tones and textures of light projected from the side, or behind, sheets of strangely cut paper, have proved rich material for pictorial expression. They are the real stuff of photography: pictures written directly in light, undiluted by subject material, or tedious recording of reality.

Patterns

Yet further pattern possibilities are revealed if the lens of the enlarger is replaced by a number of pinholes arranged in a regular geometric formation. Each pinhole, in the manner of a lens of minute aperture, projects a separate image of any object in the plane of the negative carrier: at choice a normal negative, a cut-out shape in black paper or an actual opaque or translucent flat object such as a leaf or a feather.

The number of images in the pattern corresponds to the number of pinholes, and according to the distance of the printing paper from the holes the images can be made to overlap in almost an infinity of ways. The several cones of light can be intercepted at any distance, near to they will be complete and separate, but each will overlap those adjacent the more distant the paper becomes.

The most convenient type of enlarger is one where the lens panel can be removed leaving a large opening, but it is often possible to unscrew the component into which the lens fixes, leaving a circular aperture two or three inches in diameter.

Metal foil, just thick enough to be rigid in small squares, is the best recipient for the pinholes but the thin seal of a coffee tin will often just fit into the circular ended sleeve from which the lens panel has been unscrewed. In order that the images should all have identical printing tone it is essential that the holes be absolutely regular in diameter. To this end the metal is placed on a thin sheet of card, in its turn placed above a sheet of glass to resist the thrust of the darning needle used to pierce the holes.

Any pattern relies upon an accurate disposition of the units. The holes are therefore best punched through a sheet of squared graph paper, pushed straight down at, say, every half-inch intersection of the lines until the point is stopped by the glass. Each row of holes can be disposed directly below or above the other or they may be staggered so that each alternate row is above the other. A circular arrangement also has possibilities.

The smaller the pinholes, the longer the exposure, the sharper the images and the greater the latitude for moving the paper further from the holes and obtaining maximum effects of overlapping. Since the image from any pinhole is inevitably diffused, any negative used as a pattern-motif should be bold and simple in outline and contrast, the nearer to silhouette the better. Print on a contrasty grade of paper for the same reason.

SPECIAL USES

The man who lives in his eyes is continually confronted with scenes and spectacles that compel his attention, or admiration, and demand an adequate reaction. To pass on without pause is impossible, and to continue after purely mental applause is unsatisfying. Some real tribute must be paid.

Photography, to many of its addicts, is a convenient and simple means of discharging these ever-recurring debts to the visual world.

To analyse the engendered emotion, track it to its source, and express it in a significant form is beyond the powers of most, and would frequently be a payment out of all proportion to the obligation. But, to present the camera and press the button is a climax easy for all to achieve, and permits one to pass on with an easy mind and a free conscience.

Whether this is the way *you* collect so many negatives or no, eventually all photographers seem to collect many more than they ever get around to printing, or many more odd prints than they know what to do with.

Fundamentally there should be no need for this chapter, the picture ideally should be its own justification, needing no other function than the pleasing of the eye, but not all our pictures can stand so proudly on their own legs. If they are not to rot forgotton in some dark drawer some must be given the prop of common purpose.

It is to be candidly confessed that most uses for photographic prints, other than the pictorial purpose for which we presume they were originally made, are connected with the laborious manufacture of articles of dubious use or decorative value, the admiration of which is very much a matter of personal taste.

However, if these things are not for you or me, there seems to be no reason why you should not unload your spare prints in these forms on one of the many willing victims.

DRAUGHT OR CHESS BOARDS may be made in which the various checkers are made up from prints of suitably small scale. These prints should be either light in subject matter or in general printing tone and will constitute what would normally be the white squares of the board, the black ones being formed from pieces of printing paper, exposed to a uniform rich black beneath the enlarger, and finished with a similar surface to the picture prints.

The squares are pasted up with rubber cement on a good white mounting board, arranged so that a small white margin of about one quarter or one half an inch is left all round each square checker to prevent confusion and give an added richness to the general effect.

To avoid confusing your opponent to a state of imbecility, and to prevent cricked necks, it is advisable to arrange the pictures of one half of the board all facing the same way—preferably towards the player, and those of the other half facing the opposite way. This suitably accommodates attention, and, you hope, encourages meditation.

To preserve your work it is best to mount it on a firm support of ply or similar board and cover the whole thing with glass, then you can forget about the game and just have your tea upon it.

PLAYING CARDS can be used as a motive for photographs, the effect of the court cards being simulated by two prints of a specially posed portrait. Such efforts can scarcely be used in the normal game, but they make a quite amusing use for a portrait, and, if mounted and framed would make, perhaps, suitable decoration for a card room or similarly used corner of a normal one.

To obtain the characteristic effect of reversal, one of the prints must be reversed left to right—by turning it over in the enlarger, or contact printing it wrong way up under a condensed light. The two prints are joined across the middle, by cut and paste, or one of the masking methods of montage, so that the effect is the same whichever way up the result is turned.

If the person occupies the whole of the available space, the pose must be made with an inclination in one direction or another so that room is left for the pip that indicates the card's suite and value. These symbols must either be added by hand or arranged to print through a mask of their cut out shape, laid on the paper before development of the portrait image.

The traditional costume of the kings and queens of the normal pack of cards, unless you have good costume facilities, can just be ignored, any modern dress of a decorative kind being quite as suitable, particularly if the pattern is confined to a panel in the centre so that it joins well across the middle of the card.

GREETING CARDS are an ever-recurring problem that might periodically be solved in a photographic manner.

The lettering involved can be simply done by writing on the blank side of the folder mount, or incorporated in the final print by any masking method during printing, or by writing with opaque paint or ink on the back surface of the negative.

MOUNTS are a matter outside the scope of this book, but a simple and cheap means of obtaining a plate sunk effect is reasonably relevant. Plate sunk mounts are those in which the picture is sunk into a shallow recess just a little larger in area than the print itself.

It is an effective means of definitely indicating the termination of the print and the beginning of the mount, and has the added advantage that the glass and the mount are not separated by the thickness of the print, but are permitted to touch in close contact.

Sunk mounts are easy to purchase, but it is difficult to find, among the range of standard sizes, the one that exactly fits the usually odd dimensions of the print.

Any mount that is not as thick as elephant hide can be simply ridged in the plate sunk manner if a sheet of stout card is cut a little larger in every direction, than the print itself, and placed in correct alignment on the mount. The mount and card are then turned over so that the card is below, and the mount pressed down over it with a blunt instrument such as the bone handle of a knife or the bowl of a large table spoon.

LAMP-SHADES can be made to display transparencies of your favourite negatives, in manners which are quite your own personal affair. The rigid, four-sided, variety can be used to take glass plates, if the framework is suitably made of wood or metal, and allowance made for the slight expansion of the glass by the heat involved.

Glare can be avoided, and a pleasant softness introduced, if the transparency plates are backed with pieces of ground glass of the same area.

Transparencies of film could be applied to shades of the cylindrical variety, if these are of transparent material such as parchment or vellum. The films could be gummed into position along their edges, and these suitably masked with coloured passe partout or other gummed paper strip. The diffusion of the shade is an excellent substitute for the ground glass suggested in the last sentence.

ETCHING EFFECT. The hard and relatively tough surface of a glossy and glazed print that has been soaked in a solution of formaline, or formaldehyde, of 5 parts to 100 parts of water, can be used as a substitute for the copper plate of the etching process, the printed image acting as a guide.

The lines of the subject are cut into the gelatine of the hardened print with an etching needle, or a substitute made from a gramophone needle that has been sharpened to a degree where it will cut cleanly with a single stroke, and without tearing the gelatine and causing it to flake away from the paper base.

Progress, or otherwise, can be easily watched by holding the print in an oblique light, so that the glaze of the surface shines white, showing the cuts as the dark lines they subsequently will be.

Printing is in the approved copper plate manner, printer's ink being rubbed into the lines with a rag of soft flannel material, and the excess wiped cleanly from the print's surface. A sheet of thin paper, or any paper that has been slightly damped either with water or turpentine, is now placed over the "plate" and the two run, between boards, through an etching press.

Failing the materialisation of a press, the image will appear, with patience, if the paper to be printed is soaked in petrol (no smoking) and the two placed in close contact in a printing frame. The petrol successfully coaxes the ink out of the grooves.

PEN DRAWING EFFECT. With a little more skill the effect of a pen drawing can be imitated by using a photographic print as a guiding base, and subsequently bleaching its image cunningly out of existence.

The subject should be printed in very light tone on the surface of a glossy or matt printing paper, your choice being determined by the fineness of the intended drawing.

Make the drawing over the printed image with a soft nib, as used for work on a lithographic stone, and a water-proof black ink, taking care not to tear or otherwise injure the delicate surface of the emulsion, or excessively swell it by using the ink in very wet patches.

As long as the vital lines are put firmly in, any areas of enclosed blackness are best added after the photograph has been bleached.

When the ink is thoroughly dry the print is placed in a normal Farmer's reducer, of Potassium ferricyanide and hypo, until the image bleaches to a consistent white tone. After a thorough washing, the large areas not previously treated may be blacked in and the drawing finished.

Slight differences of surface will be evident in certain directions of light, since the emulsion will absorb the ink to varying and unforseen degrees. For complete deception, therefore, the print should be copied on a contrasty plate through the camera, and subsequent prints made from this negative.

PENCIL DRAWING EFFECT. A vaguer, and rather nebulous, result that some, with charity, call a pencil drawing, is produced by placing a sheet of printing paper beneath the enlarger and projecting the desired image upon it.

You, or somebody, now proceed vigorously to darken with a soft pencil, crayon, or a stump of charcoal, all parts of the paper that are light in tone. These, naturally, would be the dark parts of any print made from that negative, and must so be blackened by your pencilling, following with reasonable care the main outlines of the image.

Areas not so light in tone are then treated to a pencil tone a little lighter than the first, and so on until the absolute densities, or white areas of the positive image, are reached and left untouched.

Since you are not working on the sensitive paper you may at any moment turn on the light to see how "things are going" and doubtless to assure yourself how much better the thing would look as a straight photographic print.

INDEX

All Enquiries relating to this book or to any photographic problem are readily answered by the Focal Press (31, Fitzroy Square, London, W.1) and its Circle of Photographers without charge, if a stamped addressed envelope is enclosed for reply.